AF557755

Reference and Information Services: An Introduction

Reference and Information Services: An Introduction

Piyush Ranjan

RANDOM PUBLICATIONS
NEW DELHI (INDIA)

Reference and Information Services: An Introduction

ISBN 978-93-5111-338-6

Published in 2014 in India by

RANDOM PUBLICATIONS

4376-A/4B, Gali Murari Lal, Ansari Road
New Delhi-110 002
Phone : +91-11-43580356, +91-11-23289044
e-mail: randomexports@gmail.com, sales@randompublications.com, info@randompublications.com

Type Setting by : Keystoneprintads, Delhi-110051
Printed at : Sanat Printers

Preface

The Reference and Information Services Section will address all aspects of reference work, in all types of libraries, in all regions of the world. Current interests encompass the new electronic environment and the resulting changes in reference work, the future role of reference work, and the quality of reference services. A variety of Reference and Information Services are provided at the Reference Desk which is located on the Main Floor of Library. Librarians at the Reference Desk will assist students in the use of the Library's Online Catalogue, remote catalogues, indexes and other reference sources whether in print or electronic format.

The librarians also give answers to specific questions, provide guidance in research work and conduct library orientation tours and subject specific library instruction sessions. The Library's E-Reference service allows you to ask brief factual questions using electronic mail.

This service is available to current students, faculty, staff and alumni of Lakehead University. Requests for factual information and questions requiring short, specific answers will be answered by a librarian. Responses will be sent by email within 24 hours (Monday to Friday). Requests received on weekends and holidays will be answered on the next working day.

I thank all members of my team who have helped in the preparation of the book. My special thanks go to "Random Publications" who have published the book.

—Piyush Ranjan

Contents

1

Basics of Information Technology for Librarians

INFORMATION SCIENCE

What is information science? The question, while seemingly simple, begs another, more complex one: *How is information science, or for that matter any field, to be defined?* This is a complex problem dealt with at length in philosophy and in other fields. Lexical definitions are necessary for providing a broad description and boundaries of the subjects covered by a field, but they cannot provide for a deeper understanding. Webster does not a field define. This is not to reject clear lexical definitions—not at all—just to establish their limitations.

In approaching the discussion of information science, I am taking the problem point of view as elaborated by Popper who argued that:

- [S]ubject matter or kind of things do not, I hold, constitute a basis for distinguishing disciplines. . . .*We are not students of some subject matter, but students of problems*. Any problem may cut right across the border of any subject matter or discipline.

Our emphasis is on problems addressed by information science. Although we provide definitions of information science and other fields in interdisciplinary relations with information science later in the chapter, we are doing this solely to advance the understanding of problems addressed by different fields and their relation to information science problems. Debates over the "proper" definition of information science, as of any field, are fruitless, and in expectations naive. Information science, as a science and as a profession, is defined by the problems it has addressed and the methods it has used for their solutions over time.

Any advances in information science depend on whether the field is indeed progressing in relation to problems addressed and methods used. Any "fixing," if in order, will have to be approached by redefining or refocusing either the problems addressed, or the methods for their solutions, or both. Information science has three general characteristics that are the leitmotif of its evolution and existence. These are shared with many modern fields. They can also be viewed as problem areas with which information science has to deal on a general level:

- First, information science is interdisciplinary in nature; however, the relations with various disciplines are changing. The interdisciplinary evolution is far from over.
- Second, information science is inexorably connected to information technology. A technological imperative is compelling and constraining the evolution of information science, as is the evolution of a number of other fields, and moreover, of the information society as a whole.
- Third, information science is, with many other fields, an active participant in the evolution of the information society. Information science has a strong social and human dimension, above and beyond technology.

A number of works that I freely consulted dealt with various historical aspects of information science.

Among those works are:

- Shera and Cleveland,
- Bourne,
- Herner,
- Salton,
- Cleverdon,
- Swanson,
- Lilley and Trice,
- Farkas-Conn,
- Buckland and Liu, and
- Rayward.

Still, a comprehensive history of information science is a project for a future historian of science. As yet only historical pieces and different perspectives of pieces exist. A history of any field is a history of a few powerful ideas. I suggest that information science has three such powerful ideas, so far. These ideas deal with processing of information in a radically different way than was done previously or elsewhere. The first and the original idea, emerging in 1950s, is *information retrieval,* providing for processing of information based on formal logic. The second, emerging shortly thereafter, is *relevance,* directly orienting and associating the process with human information needs and assessments.

The third, derived from elsewhere some two decades later, is *interaction,* enabling direct exchanges and feedback between systems and people engaged in IR processes. So far, no powerful ideas have emerged about *information,* as the underlying phenomenon, or *"literature"*, as the object of processing.

However, one can argue that the idea of mapping of "literature," that started with exploitation of citation indexes in 1960s, may also qualify as a powerful idea. In a non-historical sense this stage deals with these powerful ideas and with leitmotifs. They form a framework for understanding the past, present, and future of information science.

ORIGIN AND SOCIAL CONTEXT

Information science is a field that emerged in the aftermath of the Second World War (WW II), along with a number of new fields, with computer science being but one example. The rapid pace of scientific and technical advances that were accumulating since the start of the 20th century, produced by mid-century a scientific and technical revolution. A most visible manifestation of this revolution was the phenomenon of "information explosion," referring to the exponential and unabated growth of scientific and technical publications and information records of all kinds, so masterfully synthesized and illuminated by de Solla Price.

In a remarkable turn of events, the impetus for the development of information science, and even for its very origin and agenda, a respected MIT scientist and, even more importantly, the head of the U.S. scientific effort during WW II.

Bush did two things:

- He succinctly defined a critical and strategic problem that was on the minds of many, and
- Proposed a solution that was a "technological fix", and thus in tune with the spirit of the times.

Both had wide appeal and Bush was listened to because of his stature. He defined the problem in almost poetic terms as "the massive task of making more accessible a bewildering store of knowledge". In other words, Bush addressed the problem of information explosion. The problem is still with us. His solution was to use the emerging computing and other information technology to combat the problem. But he went even further. He proposed a machine named Memex, incorporating a capability for "association of ideas," and duplication of "mental processes artificially." A prescient anticipation of information science and artificial intelligence is evident.

Memex, needless to say, was never built, but to this day is an ideal, a wish list, an agenda, and, some think, a utopia. We are still challenged by the ever-worsening problem of the information explosion, now universal and in a variety of digital formats. We are still trying to fix things technologically. We are still aspiring to incorporate Memex's basic ideas in our solutions. A number of scientists and professionals in many fields around the globe listened and took up Bush's challenge.

Governments listened as well and provided funding. The reasoning went something like this: Because science and technology are strategically important for society, efforts that help them, information activities in particular, are also important and need support. In the U.S., the *National Science Foundation* (NSF) Act of 1950 established NSF and provided a number of mandates, among them "to foster the interchange of scientific information among scientists in the U.S. and foreign countries" and "to further the full dissemination of information of scientific value consistent with the national interest".

The 1958 National Defence Education Act enlarged the mandate:

> "The National Science Foundation shall..undertake programme to develop new or improved methods, including mechanized systems, for making scientific information available".

By those mandates, an NSF division, which after a number of name and direction changes is now called the Division of *Information and Intelligent Systems* (IIS), has supported research in these areas since the 1950s. Importantly, the field-defining studies that NSF supported included, among others, Cranfield IR evaluation studies in the 1950s and 1960s, large chunks of SMART studies from the 1960s to 1990s, and now the Digital Libraries Initiatives.

In the U.S., information science developed and began flourishing on its own in a large part due to government support by a host of agencies, as did many other fields. Historically, the support was a success—it was instrumental in creation of the whole enterprise of information science and even of the information online industry based on IR. But to the credit of information science it kept growing on its own even after government support slackened substantially. This cannot be said of a number of other fields or areas that floundered after government stopped being their main source and resource.

Social Context

It is a truism to state that information was always important for any society in any historical period. But the role of information and its degree of importance differed. With the evolution of the social order to a "post-industrial" society, or "post-capitalist" society or what we now commonly also call "information society," knowledge and information is assuming an increasing central role in every aspect of life. The classic study by Machlup, followed by a number of similar studies, documented the startling structural changes in the economy and society as driven by the growth of information and knowledge production and processing.

Popularly, they were summarized by Drucker:

> The change in the meaning of knowledge that began two hundred fifty years ago has transformed society and economy. Formal knowledge is seen as both the key personal and the key economic resource. . . [K]nowledge proves itself in action. What we now mean by knowledge is information effective in action, information focused on results.... The actual products of the pharmaceutical industry is knowledge; pill and prescription ointment are no more than packaging for knowledge.

Addressing the problem of information explosion, information science found a niche within the broader context in the evolution of the information society. In its various manifestations and attempted solutions, the niche is getting broader and bigger. But by no means does information science hold a monopoly in that niche. As the importance of information is increasing in society, more and more resources and expenditures are channelled into various information-related activities. More and more research funds, projects, and initiatives are devoted to information in various disguises. It is not surprising then that more and more fields, researchers, professionals, and businesses are turning to information, and even "discovering" information. There is gold in information. Information science has many competitors—it may be even swamped by them.

WHAT IS "INFORMATION" IN INFORMATION SCIENCE

In a scientific sense, the answer to the question is "We don't know." Yes, we can and do provide various lexical definitions of information, and we have an intuitive understanding of its meaning that we apply daily and widely. Thus, we do understand the message-sense in which we deal with information in information science. But that does not provide for a deeper and more formal understanding and explanation. Information is a basic phenomenon. For all basic phenomena—energy or gravity in physics, life in biology, justice in jurisprudence—the same "we-don'tknow" answer applies.

However, the investigation of the basic phenomena is proceeding—that is the basic point of all these fields. It is proceeding by investigating the *manifestations, behaviour,* and *effects* of phenomena under question. While we do not know what information is, or what some of its derivative notions, such as relevance, may be, over the years we have learned a lot about their various manifestations, behaviours, and effects. And we are continuing to learn about them through scientific investigations. "Information" has a variety of connotations in different fields. For instance, from the standpoint of physics and biology, a number of highly ambitious attempts have undertaken to explore information as a basic property of the universe.

In psychology, information is used, at times, as a variable dealing with sensory perception, comprehension, or other psychological processes. These senses of information are very different than the one in information science. In some fields, information science included, the notion of information is broadly associated with messages. For this sense, a number of interpretations exist, which are assumed in different theoretical and pragmatic treatments of information. We can present them as related, but differing manifestations of information in an ordered sequence or a continuum of increasing complexity.

Narrow Sense

Information is considered in terms of *signals or messages for decisions* involving little or no cognitive processing, or such processing that can be expressed in algorithms and probabilities. Information is treated as the property of a message, which can be estimated by some probability. Examples are information in terms of uncertainty in information theory, "perfect information" in game theory, or information as related to decision-making and market equilibrium in the theory of uncertainty and information in economics of information.

The latter has been surveyed by Hirshleifer and Riley, who provide this illustrative explanation: In the economics of uncertainty, an individual is assumed to act on the basis of current *fixed beliefs, e.g.,* deciding whether to carry an umbrella based on one's present estimate of the chance of rain, while in the economics of information a person typically is trying to arrive at *improved beliefs, e.g.,* by studying a weather report before deciding to take an umbrella.

Information may be considered as causing a difference between fixed and improved beliefs. The value of information is calculated as the difference between the decision maker's expected utility of the decision made without the information, and the expected utility of the best possible choice in decision made after receiving and analysing the information. The huge, and sometimes insurmountable, problem, of course, is estimating appropriate probabilities. A number of pragmatic applications follow this interpretation, such as computerized trading.

Broader Sense

Information is treated as directly involving *cognitive processing and understanding.* It results from interaction of two cognitive structures, a "mind" and a "text." Information is that which affects or changes the state of a mind. In cases of information services, information is most often conveyed through the medium of a text, document, or record, *e.g.,* what a reader may understands from a text or document.

The interpretation by Tague-Sutcliff fits:

- Information is an intangible that depends on the conceptualization and the understanding of a human being. Records contain words or pictures absolutely, but they contain information relative only to a user... Information is associated with a transaction between text and reader, between a record and user.

Broadest Sense

Information is treated in a context. That is, information involves not only messages that are cognitively processed but also *a context*—situation, task, problem-at-hand, and the like. Using information that has been cognitively processed for a given task is an example. In addition to other senses, it involves motivation or intentionality, and therefore it is connected to the expansive social context or horizon, such as culture, work, or problem at-hand.

In information science, we must consider the third and broadest sense of information, because information is used in a context and in relation to some reasons. The point was implicitly understood from the beginning of information science, particularly as reflected in the practice of information retrieval. This interpretation of "information" in information science is not new. Such a broad interpretation of information that explicitly incorporates cognition and context was, among others, elaborated by Wersig and Neveling and Belkin and Robertson. It is also implicit in the social role of information science.

THE BIG PICTURE: STRUCTURE OF INFORMATION SCIENCE

Any field is structured along some distinct, larger areas or subdisciplines of enquiry or practice. Think of a number of areas of medicine, computer science, librarianship, and so forth. Information science is not an exception. It has a distinct, two-partite structure. A number of authors observed that the work in information science falls in two large areas or subdisciplines, each, of course, with further subareas or specialties.

White and McCain conducted a monumental bibliometric study of the domain of information science by providing extensive analysis of co-citation patterns for 120 authors over a period of 23 years. Borrowing from White and McCain, visualize a map of information science as an ellipse with authors inside, distributed or clustered according to their connections. There are two large clusters at each end of the ellipse, with only a few authors spanning both. In other words, there are two major areas or subdisciplines.

I liked their metaphor:

- *As Things Turn Out, Information Science Looks Rather like Australia*: Heavily coastal in its development, with a sparsely settled interior.

In one of the coastal sections, fall authors that worked on analytical study of literatures; their structures; studies of texts as content-bearing objects; communication in various populations, particularly scientific communication; social context of information; information uses; information seeking and behaviour; various theories of information and related topics. As yet, there is no good label for that cluster. Some call it "information analysis." For simplicity, lets call this the *domain cluster,* as did White and McCain, although "basic" may be a good label. In the other coastal section are authors who concentrated on IR theory and retrieval algorithms; practical IR processes and systems; human-computer interaction; user studies; library systems; OPACs; and related topics.

Let's call this cluster the *retrieval cluster,* although "applied" may also be a good label. Basically, most of the areas in the domain cluster are about study of fundamental manifestations and behaviour of phenomena and objects that information science is all about. They are centred on the phenomenon of information and its manifestations in literature. The retrieval cluster deals, by and large, with a variety of implementations, on both practical and theoretical levels. It is about implementation, behaviour, and effects of the interface between literatures and people, including, of course, all kinds of retrieval aspects. Unfortunately, these two main clusters are largely unconnected. Only a very small number of authors spanned the two clusters. In other words, there are very few integrating works. The last text that undertook an integrative approach encompassing both clusters. A rare example of such an effort in research is the last work by Tague-Sutcliffe, where she related the notion of informativeness with evaluation of IR systems.

Several modern texts are specifically aimed at IR but none on information science as a whole. I dare to venture a prediction: fame awaits the researcher who devise a formal theoretical work, bolstered by experimental evidence, that connects the two largely separated clusters, *i.e.*, connecting basic phenomena with their realization in the retrieval world. And a bestseller is awaiting an author that produces an integrative text in information science. Information science will become a full-fledged discipline when the two ends are connected successfully. The two clusters are not equally populated. The retrieval cluster has significantly more authors, not to mention total number of works. As in many other fields, more effort is expanded on the applied side than on the basic side.

In part, this is due to availability of funds for given topics—not surprisingly, research goes after moneyed topics. By and large, over the last decade or so, major granting agencies funded only applied research in information science. For instance, I have been unable to identify a single grant addressing any of the topics in the domain or basic cluster from NSF Division of Information and Intelligent Systems since its preceding Division of Information Science and Technology was reorganized and included in the Directorate for *Computer and Information Science and Engineering* (CISE) in 1985. In de Solla Price's concepts and words, the domain cluster is "little science", while the retrieval cluster is "big science," and the connection between the two has presently no science.

PROBLEMS ADDRESSED

General

Webster routinely defines information science as "the science dealing with the efficient collection, storage, and retrieval of information." It is a general definition of problems addressed by information science. The definition follows pretty much an early and popular one given by Borko as a part of a wide discussion and controversy about the nature of the field in the 1960s. More specifically, information science is a field of professional practice and scientific enquiry addressing the problem of effective communication of knowledge records—"literature"—among humans in the context of social, organizational, and individual need for and use of information. The key orientation here is the problem of need for and use of information, as involving knowledge records.

To provide for that need, information science deals with specifically, oriented information techniques, procedures, and systems. To elaborate, the specific concentration of information science is on human knowledge records as *content-bearing objects*, in all forms, shapes, and media. The primary emphasis is on content of these objects, in terms of their potential for conveying information. "Literature" may be used as a generic term for these knowledge records, but "literature" has many other connotations, thus requiring a careful restriction in its use in information science. Because of these connotations, "literature" will not become popular in information science.

Realizing this, I am using the term here only as a shorthand, as did White and McCain, when they elegantly stated:

> "The proper study of information science is the interface between people and literature . . . modeling the world of publications with a practical goal of being able to deliver their content to enquirers on demand . . . While many scientists seek to understand communication between persons, information scientists seek to understand communication between persons and certain valued surrogates for persons that literature comprises.

In all of this there is a technological imperative, reflected in efforts to take advantage of modern information technology. While information science is not about technology, the problem of providing effective computer applications pervades the field. Following is a word on the extent and borders of information science.

Focusing information science on the content-bearing properties of literature, and on associated techniques and systems dealing with providing effective access to and use of literature, provides a restriction for information science.

Thus, the field does *not* deal with great many other information systems, such as payroll, inventory, decision support systems, data processing, airline schedules, and a zillion others, nor does it deal with direct communication among and between persons. Information science is about a specific manifestation or type of information that defines its scope and its systems. Information science, as many other fields, also involves a professional component. Starting in 1950s, the profession of information science grew from research and applications in IR, to become a powerful component of the field, and in many ways a leading one in respect to innovation.

As in many other fields, there is an uneasy relation between the scientific or research-oriented component and the professional or practice-oriented one. The profession is responding in its own way to needs of its users and organizations, and chartering its own technological applications, many times independently of research advances, and even in different directions. At present, the connection and feedback between profession and research in information science is not as well established as it is in older fields, such as engineering or medicine. This is a serious inhibitor for progress of both.

More Specific

A number of authors suggested a breakdown of specific areas of information science, beyond the structural analysis offered above. The breakdown among different authors is in significant agreement, although the labels differ somewhat. I will take the breakdown and labels provided by White and McCain. They provided a factor analysis of co-cited authors and extracted 12 factors as specialties.

In descending order of how authors loaded, they labelled the specialties as:

- Experimental *information retrieval* (IR);
- Citation analysis;
- Practical retrieval;
- Bibliometrics;
- General library systems theory;
- Science communication;
- User studies and theory;
- OPACs;
- General imported ideas—other disciplines;
- Indexing theory;
- Citation theory; and
- Communication theory.

While one may quibble with some of the classes and labels, these specialties provide a fairly accurate picture of problem areas in which information scientists worked over the past quarter of a century.

Over time, there were shifts in emphasis and there were movements between specialties. Nothing is permanent. But these are the specialties of information science. New areas are clearly on the horizon. For the 1990s, I would suggest that the major new areas include interaction studies; searching of the Internet; multimedia IR; multilanguage IR; and digital libraries.

These are prime examples of the new significant areas of concentration, not yet evident in the historical record. At the same time, the old area of experimental retrieval is blossoming like never before, courtesy of the *Text Retrieval Conference* (TREC), a government-sponsored mechanism for comparative evaluation of a variety of IR techniques and approaches that involves large test beds. IR was, and still is, the major and most populated area of information science. Thus, a separate discussion of IR follows.

INFORMATION RETRIEVAL

In the early and mid-1950s, a critical mass of scientists, engineers, librarians, and entrepreneurs started working enthusiastically on the problem and solution defined by Bush. By 1960s this became a large and relatively well-funded effort and organized activity. Often, there were heated arguments and controversies about the "best" solution, technique, or system.

These arguments brought on the tradition of evaluation, a major staple of IR research and development. What is now TREC started with Cranfield evaluations in the late 1950s and early 1960s. Remarkably, the basic evaluation principles developed then are still the underpinning of TREC today. Calvin Mooers, an active and highly visible pioneer of information science, coined the term *information retrieval* in 1951. The term took hold, and today is a part of the English language.

At that time, Mooers not only coined the term, but also defined the problems to be addressed:

> "Information retrieval embraces the intellectual aspects of the description of information and its specification for search, and also whatever systems, techniques or machines that are employed to carry out the operation.

Today, we would add that IR also and particularly involves interaction in all of these, with all the contextual-cognitive, affective, situational—aspects that interaction embraces. An expanded Mooers' conception is still valid. As it advanced, IR produced a number of theoretical, empirical, and pragmatic concepts and constructs. Numerous IR systems were developed and successfully deployed.

A great many historical examples can be given to illustrate the remarkable evolution of IR systems and techniques, adapting the ever-evolving information technology, from punch cards in the midcentury to the Internet at its close. Based on IR, an online information industry emerged in the 1970s, and grew through its own version of information explosion, as chronicled by Hahn. IR is one of the most widely spread applications of any information system worldwide. It has a proud history. Surely, information science is more than IR, but many of the problems raised by IR or derived from objects and phenomena involved in IR, are at its core.

Approaches and Paradigm Split

The approach taken by Mooers was to concentrate on the building of systems. This systems emphasis which was formulated early in the 1950s, was the sole approach to IR for some decades. It still predominates in a good part of IR research to this day.

Consequently, most of the IR research and practice concentrated on retrieval systems and processes. However, starting in the late 1970s and gaining steam in the 1980s, a different line of reasoning and research evolved-one that concentrates on the cognitive, interactive, and contextual end of the process. It addressed users, use, situations, context, and interaction with systems, rather than IR systems alone as a primary focus.

The retrieval cluster started splitting into subclusters, as noted by White and McCain, and before by others such as Saracevic and Harter. We now have two distinct communities and approaches to research in the retrieval cluster. They became commonly known as *systems-centred* and *user-centred.* Both address retrieval, but from very different ends and perspectives. The split is not only conceptual, looking very differently at the same process, but also organizational. The systemscentered side is now mostly concentrated in the *Special Interest Group on Information Retrieval* (SIGIR) of the *Association for Computing Machinery* (ACM), while the user-centred cluster congregates around the *American Society for*

Information Science (ASIS). Each has its own communication outlets-journals, proceedings, and conferences. There is less and less overlap of authors and works between the two outlets. We have two camps, two islands, with, unfortunately, relatively little traffic in-between. The systems-centered approach is exemplified by work on algorithms and evaluation based on the traditional IR model, a model that does not consider the users or interaction. The massive research that evaluates a variety of IR algorithms and approaches within TREC is a culmination of this approach.

In contrast, cognitive, situational, and interactive studies and models, involving the use of retrieval systems exemplify the human-centred approach. Following that approach, interactive models, differing significantly from the traditional IR model, started to emerge. Even in TREC, a group of researchers started an interaction track, but so far have a hard time conceptually and methodologically, thus demonstrating the difficulty in merging the traditional and interactive models and approaches. Let me characterize, in a simplified way, the relationship between the two approaches or subclusters addressing different sides of retrieval.

On the one hand, the human-centred side was often highly critical of the systems side for ignoring users and use, and tried valiantly to establish humans as the proper center of IR work. The mantra of human-centred research is that the results have implications for systems design and practice. Unfortunately, in most human-centred research, beyond suggestions, concrete design solutions were not delivered. On the other hand, the systems side, by and large, ignores the human side and user studies, and is even often completely ignorant of them. As to design, the stance is "tell us what to do and as suggested, do it." But nobody is really telling, or if telling, nobody is listening.

As a rule, in systems-oriented projects, people and users are absent. Thus, there are not many interactions between the two camps. Let me provide some examples. A rough analysis of the 1997 SIGIR proceedings found only 3 papers of some 34 that dealt in some way with people and users; in the ACM's Digital Libraries 1997 conference proceedings, of 25 papers only 3 mentioned people and users. If one reads authors such as Dervin and Nilan, and many of their successors, who champion the human centred approach, one gets the impression that there is a real conflict between the two sides and approaches, and that there is an alternative way to the "dreadful" systems approach.

In a way, this stance is a backlash caused by the excesses, failures, and blind spots of systems-centered approaches not only in IR, but also in great many other technological applications. Unfortunately, sometimes the backlash is justified. All of us who work on the humancentered side are not that dismissive of the systems side. But the issue is not whether we should have systems-*or* humancentered approaches. The issue is even less of human *versus* systems-centered. *The issue is how to make human* and *systems-centered approaches work together.* In this sense, a number of works have addressed integrating usercentered and systems-centered approaches in IR, but this has been discussed mostly by researchers from the usercentered side.

Examples are works by:

- Bates,
- Belkin,
- Cool,
- Stein,
- Thiel,
- Fidel
- Efthimidiadis,
- Robertson and
- Beaulieu.

To reiterate, it is not one camp against the other but how can we incorporate the best features of both approaches and make them work jointly. The issue is how to deliver and incorporate the desired design features that will improve systems orientations towards users, integrate them with systems features, and use advantages provided by both, humans and technology. In other words, the issue is *putting the human in the loop* to build better algorithms and to exploit computational advantages. Real progress in information science, and by extension in IR, will come when we achieve this. Lately, the NSF has championed human-centered design involving an interdisciplinary approach to information systems. Hopefully, this will go beyond rhetoric. It is not easy to do. But, that is what research is for—to address difficult, not only easy problems.

Proprietary IR

By the 1980s, the commercial information industry based on IR became successful and profitable. Out of academe, grants, and government, IR became a money-making proposition. This, of course, is another and important sign of success. Not surprisingly, a number of former IR researchers, practitioners, and graduates of IR programmes ventured out to become IR entrepreneurs.

Sure enough, throughout information science history there were many entrepreneurs, and they were highly significant in development of the field. But this generation of entrepreneurs was different. They ventured to develop and market a variety of IR procedures based on algorithms, applicable and scalable to large files, multiple applications, and/or various advanced technologies. It was knowledge industry at its purest. But, as in all commercial knowledge industries, the product was proprietary. While it was not that hard to guess the base of these various proprietary algorithms and how they worked—after all they were derived from publicly available knowledge and experiences, such as those that came from SMART experiments—they remain unpublished and "secret."

A new kind of IR evolved, separate from the rest, not communicating as to intellectual advances with the rest. None of these ventures became a high commercial success, as measured by Silicon Valley standards. But the World Wide Web, emerging in the first half of the 1990s, changed all this. The acceleration of the growth of the Web is an information explosion of the like never before seen in history. Not surprisingly then, the Web is a mess. No wonder that everybody is interested in some form of IR as a solution to fix it.

A number of academic-based efforts were initiated to develop mechanisms, search engines, "intelligent" agents, crawlers, and so forth, to help control the Web. Some of these were IR scaled, and adapted to the problem; others were a variety of extensions of IR. Many had few, if any original, developments, besides new packaging or labelling; and a good number were just the usual hype. The wheel was reinvented a number of times. But out of this, and fast, came commercial ventures, such as the pioneering Yahoo!, whose basic objective is to provide search mechanisms for finding something of relevance for users on demand.

And to make a lot of money. These enterprises pride themselves on having proprietary methods by which they are accomplishing the retrieval tasks. The connection to the information science community is tenuous, and almost non-existent. The flow of knowledge, if any, is onesided, from IR research results into proprietary engines. The reverse contribution to public knowledge is zero. A number of evaluations of these search engines have been undertaken simply by comparing some results between them or comparing of their retrieval against some benchmarks.

Some evaluations were done within, others outside of information science. Results were not complimentary. The Web-based proprietary IR is expanding and flourishing outside of the field. It is addressing a vexing problem, the like we have not seen before. But as yet, the success is elusive and questionable.

RELEVANCE

As information science pioneers developed IR processes and systems in the 1950s, they defined as the main objective retrieval of *relevant* information. Effectiveness was expressed in terms of relevance. From then to now, IR is explicitly geared not towards any old kind of information, but towards *relevant information.* Various IR approaches, algorithms, and practices were, and still are, evaluated in relation to relevance. Thus, relevance became a key notion in information science. It is also a complex phenomenon with a long and turbulent history in information science transcending IR, going back to early 1950s. Of course, there was a choice.

Relevance did not have to emerge as the key notion. Uncertainty was one choice suggested by a number of theorists to be the base of IR, and thus to reflect effectiveness. But it did not take. In contrast, uncertainty is the basic notion underlying expert systems. If the pioneers had not embraced relevance, but instead, let's say, uncertainty, as the base for IR, we would have today a very different IR, and probably not that successful. In general, relevance, according to *Webster*, means having significant bearing on matter at hand. As with many other concepts, relevance assumes related but more specific meaning in more specific contexts and applications.

In the context of information science, relevance is the attribute or criterion reflecting the effectiveness of exchange of information between people and IR systems in communication contacts based on valuation by people. With relevance as the criterion, and human judgements of relevance of retrieved objects as the measuring instrument, the measures of precision and recall are widely used in evaluation of IR systems. The strength of these measures is that they involve people—users—as judges of effectiveness of performance. The weakness is the same: it involves judgement by people, with all the perils of subjectivity and variability. Relevance indicates a relation. For relevance, many relations have been investigated.

An consensus has emerged in information science that we can distinguish between several differing relations that account for different manifestations or types of relevance:

- *System or Algorithmic Relevance:* Relation between a query and information objects in the file of a system as retrieved, or as failed to be retrieved, by a given procedure or algorithm. Comparative effectiveness in inferring relevance is the criterion for system relevance.
- *Topical or Subject Relevance:* Relation between the subject or topic expressed in a query and topic or subject covered by retrieved texts, or, more broadly, by texts in the system file, or even in existence. Aboutness is the criterion by which topicality is inferred.
- *Cognitive Relevance or Pertinence:* Relation between the state of knowledge and cognitive information need of a user and texts retrieved, or in the file of a system, or even in existence. Cognitive correspondence, informativeness, novelty, information quality, and the like are criteria by which cognitive relevance is inferred.
- *Situational Relevance or Utility:* Relation between the situation, task or problem at hand and texts retrieved by a system, or in the file of a system, or even in existence. Usefulness in decision making, appropriateness of information in resolution of a problem, reduction of uncertainty, and the like are criteria by which situational relevance is inferred.
- *Motivational or Affective Relevance:* Relation between the intents, goals, and motivations of a user and texts retrieved by a system, or in the file of a system, or even in existence. Satisfaction, success, accomplishment, and the like are the criteria for inferring motivational relevance.

Practically, IR systems assess systems relevance only-that is, they respond to queries-hoping that the objects retrieved may also be of cognitive relevance, and even more so of utility. However, a user may judge an object by any or all types of relevance-for a user they may interact dynamically. Difficulties arise when an object is of system relevance but not of cognitive relevance or utility, or conversely.

If items are of cognitive relevance or utility, but were not reflected in the query, they are not and cannot be retrieved. At the bottom of IR research is a quest to align systems with other types of relevance. People all over have a strong intuitive understanding of relevance, thus, they intuitively understand, without manuals, what IR is all about. This makes IR systems generally understandable and acceptable-a critical attribute in their widespread application.

DISCIPLINARY RELATIONS

Two things introduced interdisciplinarity in information science. First and foremost, the problems addressed cannot be resolved with approaches and constructs from any single discipline-thus, intedisciplinarity is predetermined, as it is in many modern fields. Second, interdisciplinarity in information science was introduced and is being perpetuated to the present by the very differences in backgrounds of people addressing the described problems. Differences in background are many; they make for richness of the field and difficulties in communication and education.

Clearly not every discipline in the background of people working on the problem made an equally relevant contribution, but the assortment was responsible for sustaining a strong interdisciplinary characteristic of information science. I will concentrate on interdisciplinary relations with two fields: librarianship and computer science. Obviously, other fields, most notably cognitive science and communication, have also interdisciplinary relations, but these are the most significant and developed ones.

Librarianship

Librarianship has a long and proud history devoted to organization, preservation, and use of graphic records and records in other media. This is done through libraries not only as a particular organization or type of information system, but even more so as an indispensable social, cultural, and educational institution whose value has been proven manifold throughout human history, and across all geographic and cultural boundaries.

Researcher defines the library as:

- . . .Contributing to the total communication system in society. . . Though the library is an instrumentality created to maximize the utility of graphic records for the benefits of society, it achieves that goal by working with the individual and through the individual it reaches society.

The common ground between library science and information science, which is a strong one, is in sharing of their social role and in their general concern with effective utilization of graphic and other records, particularly by individuals.

But there are also very significant differences in several critical respects, among them:

- *Selection of Problems Addressed and the Way they were Defined*: A majority of the problems were not and are not addressed in library science;
- *Theoretical Questions Asked and Frameworks Established*: The theories and conceptual frameworks in librarianship have no counterpart in information science, and *vice versa*;
- *The Nature and Degree of Experimentation and Empirical Development and the Resulting Practical Knowledge and Competencies Dderived*: There is very little overlap in experimentation and development between the two, and professional requirements differ as well to a significant degree;
- *Tools and Approaches Used:* A most telling example is the very different approach undertaken in relation to utilization of technology in IR and in library automation; and
- *The Nature and Strength of Interdisciplinary Relations Established and the Dependence of Progress on Interdisciplinary Approaches*: Librarianship is much more selfcontained.

All of these differences warrant a conclusion that librarianship and information science are two different fields in strong interdisciplinary relations, rather than one and the same field, or one being a special case of the other. This is not a matter of turf battles, or of one being better or worse than the other. Such arguments, while common between many fields, matter little to progress of either field. But differences in selection and/or definition of problems addressed, agenda, paradigms, theoretical base, and practical solutions *do* matter. Thus the conclusion that librarianship and information science, while related, are different fields. The differences are most pronounced in the research agenda and directions.

Interestingly, research on OPACs, now that they are incorporating more and more IR features, is bringing the two fields in closer relation. Probably, so will the research in digital libraries, but at this time, it is too early to tell. The conclusion is not without heated controversy.

Among other authors, Vakkari contends on information science and librarianship being one and the same field, with the now commonly used name of "library and information science." Does it matter? Administratively yes, very much so, particularly in universities and professional societies. Otherwise, no. The issue is, and always will be, in the problems addressed and solutions undertaken. I contend that they differ significantly.

Computer Science

The basis of relation between information science and computer science lies in the application of computers and computing in IR, and the associated products, services, and networks. In the last few years, this relation also involves research on the evolving digital libraries, with their strong technological base.

To illustrate the connection, we use a definition by Denning:

> "The discipline of computing is the systematic study of algorithmic processes that describe and transfer information: their theory, analysis, design, efficiency, implementation, and application. The fundamental question underlying all of the computing is: "What can be automated?"

Computer science is about algorithms related to information interpreted in the first, whereas information science is about the very nature of information and its use by humans, interpreted in the third or broadest sense. Computer science is about symbol manipulation, whereas information science is about content manipulation, where symbol manipulation is the indispensable infrastructure. The two concerns are not in competition, they are complementary—they lead to different basic and applied agendas. Computer science is also many times larger than information science.

A number of computer scientists have been involved in research and development on information and its many spin-offs, to the point of being recognized leaders in information science. Gerard Salton is a prime example. In addition, there are several streams of research and development in computer science that had no connection with the early evolution of information science, but have addressed information problems similar to those in information science. Among others, these include works on expert systems, knowledge bases, hypertext, and human-computer interaction.

More recently, this involves research and development on digital libraries, a "hot", financially heavily supported area by a host of government agencies in the U.S. and many other countries. Bolstered by heavy support, interest in digital library research exploded on the scene in 1990s, attracting the attention of computer scientists from a wide variety of streams, as well as people from many other disciplines. These areas have a significant informational component that is associated with information representation, its intellectual organization, and linkages; meta-information, information seeking, searching, retrieving, and filtering; use, quality, value, and impact of information; evaluation of information systems from user and use perspective; and the like-all traditionally addressed in information science.

Conversely, these streams of computer science research and development provide a different outlook, framework, and approach, and even a different paradigm, not only for information science research and development, but also for its academic and continuing education. Again, as with librarianship, the issue is not about turf. It is about paradigms, theoretical foundations, and pragmatic solutions; and ultimately, it is about their appropriateness to human information problems.

EDUCATION

That education is critical for any field is a truism that hardly needs to be stated. In particular, research lives by education, it cannot be better than the education that researchers receive and then extend and plow back into education. Unfortunately, education in information science has not received the attention that it deserves. This may explain the many difficulties in the field that I have discussed. Educational models that evolved differed to a degree or even substantially from country to country. I am concentrating here on the U.S. models only.

In the United States, two educational models evolved over time. I call them the Shera and Salton models, after those that pioneered them. Both have strengths and weaknesses. Jesse H. Shera was a legendary library school dean from the 1950s until the 1970s at Western Reserve University. Among others, he was instrumental in starting the Center for Documentation and Communication Research in 1955. Shortly thereafter, the library school curriculum started to include courses such as "Machine Literature Searching" and several other more advanced courses and laboratories on the topics of research in the Centre.

The basic approach was to append those courses, mostly as electives, to the existing library school curriculum, without modifications of the curriculum as a whole, and particularly not the required core courses. Information science became one of the specialty areas of library science. The base or core courses that students were taking rested in the traditional library curriculum. Information science education was an appendage to library science. A few attempts to spin off information science as an independent degree and curriculum were not followed widely. But Shera's model was. Library schools in the U.S. and in many other countries imitated Shera's model.

They used the same approach and started incorporating information science courses in their existing curriculum as a specialty. Out of this was borne the current designation "library and information science." Shera's model is still the prevalent approach in schools of library and information science. The strength of the Shera model is that it posits education within a service framework, connects the education to professional practice and to a broader and user-oriented frame of a number of other information services, and relates it to a great diversity of information resources.

The weakness is a lack of a broader theoretical frame-work and a total lack of teaching of any formalism related to systems, such as development and understanding of algorithms. The majority of researchers in the human-centered side, as I described earlier, came from or are associated with this educational environment. Gerard Salton was first and foremost a scientist, a computer scientist, and the father of modern IR.

As such, he pioneered the incorporation into IR research a whole array of formal and experimental methods from science, as modified for algorithmic and other approaches used so successfully in computer science. His primary orientation was research. For education, he took the time-honoured approach of a close involvement with research. Salton's model was a laboratory and research approach to education.

As Shera's model resulted in information science education being an appendage to library science education, Salton's model of IR education resulted in it being a specialty of and an appendage to computer science education. Computer science students that were already well-grounded in the discipline, got involved in SMART and other projects directed by Salton, worked and did research in the laboratory, completed their theses in areas related to IR, and participated in the legendary IR seminars.

They also published widely with Salton and with each other, and participated with high visibility in national and international conferences. From Harvard and Cornell, his students went to a number of computer science departments where they replicated Salton's model. Many other computer science departments in the U.S. and abroad took the same approach.

The strength of Salton's model is that it:

"Starts from a base of a firm grounding in formal mathematical and other methods, and in algorithms, and

- Relates directly to research.

The weakness is in that it:

- Ignores the broader aspects of information science, as well as any other disciplines and approaches dealing with the human aspects that have great relevance to both the outcomes of IR research and the research itself, and
- Does not incorporate professional practice where these systems are realised and used. It loses users.

Consequently, this is a successful, but narrowly concentrated education in IR as a specialty of computer science, rather then in information science. Not surprisingly, the researchers in the systems-centred approach came out of this tradition. The two educational approaches are completely independent of each other. Neither is connected to the other. Neither reflects fully what is going on in the field. While in each model there is an increase in cognizance of the other, there is no educational integration of the systems- and usercentered approaches. The evident strengths that are provided by Shera and Salton model are not put together. Their weaknesses are perpetuated.

It is high time for communities from each model to try to integrate education for information science. It is an open question whether the human- and systems-centered approaches can fruitfully work together as urged in all those calls for human-centered design until an educational integration occurs.

While library education receives formal attention from the *American Library Association* (ALA), and education for computer science from ACM, no such formal attention is paid by any professional/scientific society to education for information science, or for IR in particular. Neither ASIS nor SIGIR, as primary homes for information science, have been involved to any great extent in educational matters, such as setting of standards or devising model curricula. Clearly, there is a need and an opportunity for more substantive involvement by both organizations in educational issues.

INFORMATION SOCIETY

First, the general development of the information society is pushing to re-evaluation of all the institutions which work with information, data, and knowledge-indirectly also with culture. In this connection the roles of education and media have been discussed already quite largely also in the European Union. But libraries — as well as other memory institutions like archives and museums-have not been considered. Still, there is a clear need in the information society to maintain an institution which is concentrating in collecting and organizing information and offering general access to it.

Until now, this work has been underestimated, but I argue the situation will change! Libraries are especially important now when the whole idea of education is stressing more and more independent learning and acting. All citizens must be able to find and use information. It is the key raw material-but it is a zero resource, if there are no access points to it and if documents are in chaotic order.

Here we can see libraries enter the stage:

- The unique function of libraries is to acquire, organize, offer for use and preserve publicly available material irrespective of the form in which it is packaged in such a way that, when it is needed, it can be found and put to use. No other institution carries out this long-term, systematic work.

Culture must be nominated especially: it has an important and unique role in mobilizing resources of human beings. It has been described: *T*o some extent, culture makes its influence felt more indirectly than knowledge, but it is impossible to imagine how people's creative powers could be fully activated without the impact of culture, which extends into the depths of the mind. The challenge to modern societies is that the basic resource, knowledge, is developing from information in very individual, capricious and unpredictable process. It cannot be commanded.

Still, societies can support this development, *e.g.* by offering access to cultural and knowledge treasures. This can even be translated into economic language: to get out the best from the human resources in Europe, this resource must be feeded up with rich and various cultural and information contents! I would like to stress especially the idea of organising information by libraries. It is often shadowed by the second important side of library work: offering access. But in the life-long learning and new technology context just all forms of organising documents are getting more to the focus. This is clear to anybody who has tried to find something from not-so-often-used Internet websites.

NEW LINES IN THE EU AND IN THE UNITED STATES

In accordance with these phenomenons, there are new political lines in the

European Union (EU): The Maastricht Treaty in 1992 launched the cultural aspects. This was only after a long discussion, which made it clear that we have to remember to separate the national view and the European view. The Amsterdam Treaty in 1997 declared citizenship as an important theme. A significant part of this are a.o. granting information skills and access to information to every European.

In addition to this, the European future strategies need to meet the democratic aspects of the information society development. One of the crucial points is again general access to information. Libraries, especially public libraries, are a good tool in all of these new areas. But the European union does not support whichever cultural or citizen concentrated projects in Europe. In the interests of the European Union there is always to find the European element.

So, what can be done in library policy on the European level, taking in account that libraries are primarily a part of national education and cultural policies?:

> "The own-initiative report "The role of libraries in modern societies", adopted by the European Parliament in October 1998, is the first effort to answer these questions.

The same topics have been discussed in the United States. They have reached the point where especially the problems of those lacking access to digital resources have been studied. The report Falling Through the Net: Defining the Digital Divide by the U.S. Department of Commerce was released earlier in July 1999. The report finds that minorities, low-income persons, the less educated, and children of single parent households, particularly when they reside in rural areas or central cities, are risk groups.

The report calls for public policies and private initiatives to expand affordable access to critical information resources. But it also shows,, for the first time as far as I know, that libraries and community centres really can diminish the information gap between haves and not-haves. The 1998 data from the U.S. demonstrates very clearly that community access centers, primarily public libraries, are particularly well used by those groups who lack access at home or at work: *e.g.* unemployed groups used Internet in libraries three times as often as an average citizen.

EARLIER ACTIONS IN EU

In the European Union, there have been some efforts to mobilize "the treasures of the European libraries" since the mid-80'ies. These discussions and resolutions led to two special library programmes under the 3rd and 4th Framework programmes of research and development. The later programme has been known as "Telematics for Libraries".

They have been strongly concentrated in IT, because it has been seen as a good tool to produce better access to the existing, underused library resources. These programmes have had a clear impact in the European library co-operation and development.

Benefits of this work come to public libraries indirectly: common standards and working methods help in the end all kind of libraries. But a fact is, that nearly all the libraries active in these EU projects are national libraries or big research and university libraries.

Two main exeptions are PubliCA, a network of European public libraries, and ECUP, which was a copyright awareness raising project, and reached public libraries as well. A new beginning was the so called Morgan report in 1997.

In this report libraries were for the first time put clearly onto the place where they belong in the information society. As one result of the Morgan report, the European Commission informed that it will produce a Green Paper about the role of libraries in the information society.

For one or another reason, this was made quite ready but was never published. In this situation the Committee on Culture, Youth, Education and the Media in the European Parliament decided to produce an own-initiative report about libraries. The main reason was that they wanted to influence the big issues under work in the EU, first of all the copyright directive and the 5th framework programme, which will have a direct impact to libraries.

DECISIONS OF THE EP CONCERNING LIBRARY POLICY

In short, when adopting the own-initiative report, the EP (European Parliament) was calling the Commission and/or the member states to following actions:

- Libraries must be taken in account in national and EU information society strategies and in the respective budgets.
- Libraries need more resources for acquiring expensive books.
- The Green Paper on libraries by the Commission must be completed.
- The users position must be taken in account in the copyright directive process, the balance must be maintained-this was politically the most important decision in short run.
- Support to libraries was demanded from the 5th Framework programme of research and development, *e.g.* for networking, drafting standards, preserving, and transferring information; there is no more named library programme under the 5th framework programme.
- A clearing-house to solve problems of long-term conservation should be founded.
- Studies concerning permanent paper should be done on European level.
- The member states should take care of digitizing their cultural heritage for future.
- There should be studies and concrete support to libraries in licensing matters, which are–will be the next big issue in library work.
- The EU cultural and information budget should be opened to

libraries as well, libraries and their co-operation should be taken in account in planning new programmes.

- Problems of legal deposit in international and multinational materials, especially in electronic materials should be solved.
- The member states should provide all types of libraries with modern equipment, particularly with Internet connections.
- Free of charge use of public libraries, in the spirit of the UNESCO Public Library Manifest, was demanded.
- Free and easy access via libraries to material produced with the aid of tax revenues was demanded.
- The members states should organize for their library professionals up-dating education and training.
- A European Union focal point for libraries should be set up.
- The member states should found European information points at libraries in countries where they do not yet exist.
- Library statistics should be better and more comparable both on national and European level.
- The national Parliament libraries should be opened to the MEP's in countries where this is not yet the practice.

In addition to these, the report strongly stresses that the library financing must be re-thougt in the information society. Without new resources libraries are unable to do everything they are expected to do! After the EP adoption of this report, the European Commission informed that it will next prepare a communication about actions to do. It was stated that the report had already served as a discussion paper, and so the need for the Green Paper had disappeared. The communication is in summer 1999 still under work in the Commission DGXIII/2.

TRADITIONS AND NEW FORMS OF WORK IN THE SAME HOUSE

The European Commission R&D framework programmes have concentrated in IT matters. The three cultural programmes, Caledoskope, Ariane and Raphael, have not been very useful for libraries, because their scope has been quite narrow, *e.g.* the books and reading programme Ariane has concentrated in translations. In the coming framework programme Culture 2000 libraries will have more possibilities to get support also for their cultural actions. What then will be the fate of the traditional tasks of libraries in general? Will the information society wipe out book loaning and poems? These elements will survive, but will get completed by new media forms.

It was stated earlier that culture has a special role in building up the modern society and in mobilizing the capacity of its members The significance of reading is only growing in future. Demands to enlargen and deepen literacy skills get greater and greater. Literacy has a special role in guaranteeing the basic citizen competence to everybody. It is in general interests of the society to offer possibilities to all people for maintaining and developing their literacy. In library work new technologies offer new possibilities to raise service level, too. Good examples can already now be found all over the world, mainly of course in those countries where Internet is used largely.

Some models: Library catalogues are available via Internet, the patron can check her/his loaning data from Internet, and even renew the loans a country/areawide information service via Internet and e-mail; there are versions for link libraries or virtual libraries, where libraries collect and describe high-level link-ups discussion lists of librarians, where they can share their professional skills and knowledge, even take part in developing the library policy of the country/area.

There is one special comment concerning Internet which we have heard both from small libraries with rejected printed collections in Finland and from African libraries:

In case you got reach in Internet, the resources your library can offer to the patrons are suddenly multiplied. All of once we have exactly the same resource as British Library or the Library of Congress.

It is amazing, it is revolutionary, and we can use it! In the complicated modern society libraries have many kinds of answers to many demands of the society, as well as those of the citizens.

They have potential means to serve both the information society development and their traditional humanistic tasks. Maybe information technology will even make it easier to combine these elements in future than in the past!

ROLE OF INFORMATION IN PLANNING

WHAT IS PLANNING

Planning is a simple process used every day. In the process, one decides where he is, where he wants to be, and how he gets there. Getting to work every day, grocery shopping, preparing for a vacation or trip, and saving for retirement are examples of events that require planning. More formally, planning is an organizational process of envisioning a desired future and developing the necessary infrastructure to achieve it.

WHY PLAN

Overall, the purpose of planning is to achieve excellence in public library service.

Some specific benefits:

- Planning provides information to use in decision-making.
- Planning provides a blueprint for future library development.
- Planning guides decision-makers in setting necessary priorities about who receives what service with what efficiency.
- Planning provides information to use in the allocation of resources, particularly when they are scarce.

- Planning leads to structured positive change resulting in improved library service.
- Planning makes crises less critical.
- Planning encourages staff creativity and cooperation.
- Planning encourages accountability.
- Planning provides a basis for evaluating the library's performance.
- Planning can improve communication and give everyone who works with the library a sense of common purpose.
- Planning pays off—organizations that plan out-perform those that do not.

WHAT ARE THE STEPS IN THE PROCESS

There are many approaches to planning. Significantly, the Public Library Association published a new approach to public library planning; *Planning and Role Setting for Public Libraries: A Manual of Options and Procedures* is designed to meet the special needs of this community. The following is a summary of the eight major steps recommended.

PLANNING TO PLAN

- Organizes the planning process,
- Shapes the planning process to the library's needs and resources,
- Coordinates planning with other management activities,
- Defines the responsibilities of major planning participants, and
- Organizes and trains the Planning Committee.

LOOKING-AROUND

- Identifies information needed for planning,
- Collects information about the library and the community it serves, and
- Analyses information gathered for planning decisions.

DEVELOPING ROLES AND MISSION

- Describes eight distinct roles, or service profiles, that public libraries may emphasize in providing services to their communities;
- Describes a method of determining which roles are to receive a major commitment in the library and which are to be supported only minimally;
- Guides planners in writing a mission statement as a concise expression of the roles chosen for emphasis;
- Helps the library communicate its service focus to the public, elected officials, and staff.

WRITING GOALS AND OBJECTIVES

- Translates the library's role choices and mission into statements of desired ends or targets,

- Defines goals as long-range and representing a vision of excellence in library service,
- Defines objectives as specific, time limited, and measurable or verifiable, and
- Provides a framework for implementation and evaluation.

TAKING ACTION

- Produces tangible evidence of the library's planning,
- Identifies possible activities to implement the goals and objectives,
- Selects activities best suited to the library's circumstances and resources, and
- Leads to cycle of annual objective setting and updating of five-year plan.

WRITING THE PLANNING DOCUMENT

- Describes creation of a formal report of the library's planning activities, and
- Provides an opportunity for communication with the public, the library staff, and governing officials.

REVIEWING RESULTS

- Reviews the plan and its implementation activities after a period of time,
- Reviews extent to which objectives were accomplished, and
- Starts the planning cycle again.

"LEVELS OF EFFORT" AS A PLANNING TOOL

Planning and Role Setting for Public Libraries introduces the concept of "levels of effort," an approach that allows library planners to adapt the process to a particular library's needs, purposes, and resources. There are three levels of effort — basic, moderate, and extensive. Any of these will result in acceptable plans. Each library's level-of-effort choice reflects the interplay of several different factors.

- *Participants:* The more individuals and groups represented, the higher the library's level of effort for planning will be.
- *Resources:* Higher levels of effort call for a proportionally greater commitment of the library staff's time and larger expenditures from the library's budget.
- *Library Context:* Libraries serving a community with rapid growth or change, a complex and diverse population, shifting economic conditions, or libraries facing a major change in funding may need to plan at a higher level of effort.

- *Planning Purposes:* What the library expects the planning process to accomplish may affect the level of effort chosen for some planning phases.
- *Planning Structure:* Libraries planning at a basic level of effort may approach many planning activities informally; but as library complexity increases, the planning structure becomes more formal, thus increasing the level of effort.
- *Planning Schedule:* Some libraries may complete their first objectives cycle over a very short time period; higher levels of effort may require twelve to eighteen months to complete.

2

The Changing Nature of Reference and Information Services

In this first decade of the twenty-first century reference and information services are a vital yet changing part of the function and mission of the library institution. While the continually expanding availability of electronic resources and digitized materials has changed the nature of reference, the essential service remains central. Indeed, far from minimizing the need for reference services, the rise of the Internet, and with it the availability of a tremendous number of subscription and free online resources, makes this aspect of library service all the more crucial.

Librarians and their users are constantly bombarded with a wide range of information choices that must be evaluated for authenticity and accuracy. Whether at home on their computers or wandering through the stacks, many people feel as though they are drowning in a sea of information. New media and technologies are like tributaries leading to this great new body of knowledge, and each stream makes the waters deeper and more perilous. Reference services are at once a life raft, map, and compass to those who feel adrift.

In providing them with a combination of personalized service in a timely manner, libraries reaffirm their centrality as twenty-first century public institutions par excellence:

- For all its contemporary relevance, the concept of reference service is more than a century old. In 1876, Samuel Green, librarian of the Worcester Free Public Library in Massachusetts, developed the idea of having librarians assist the user in the selection of books to suit their needs. This served a dual function, increasing the use of his library's collection and thereby demonstrating the need for the library. Green saw the role of the public library as one of welcoming users by having a pleasant and cultivated female staff. Some forty years later, in 1915 at the thirty-seventh meeting of the American Library Association, a paper on reference work was delivered by W.W. Bishop, the superintendent of the Reading Room of the Library of Congress.

Bishop defined reference work as "the service rendered by a librarian in aid of some sort of study" holding that it was "an organized effort on the part of libraries in aid of the most expeditious and fruitful use of their books."

The idea of reference service was further developed by Charles Williamson in his 1923 report, "Training for Library Service: A Report Prepared for the Carnegie Corporation of New York," which included a course description for reference work:

- A study of the standard works of reference, general and special encyclopedias, dictionaries, annuals, indexes to periodicals, ready reference manuals of every kind, special bibliographies, and the more important newspapers and periodicals. Works of similar scope are compared, and the limitations of each pointed out. Lists of questions made up from practical experience are given, and the method of finding the answers discussed in the class.

Several authors, including James I. Wyer, Margaret Hutchins, William A. Katz, Richard E. Bopp, and Linda C. Smith wrote reference texts in which they continued to refine the role of the reference librarian over the subsequent decades. Perhaps the most important point to remember is that reference service seeks to fulfil the greater mission of the library by helping individual users. Despite the many transformations that have been wrought on reference work by both developments of our information society and paradigm shifts in the selfunderstandings of the library, much has remained the same.

First and foremost, it is still a service in which the librarian interacts with a patron on a one-to-one basis. This level of personal service has become even more important in the twenty-first century in light of the alienating and depersonalizing effects of many information technologies. On the other hand, the way such service is provided has changed considerably—it now extends beyond face-to-face assistance thanks to the availability of the telephone, e-mail, and the technology for chat and IM reference.

ETHICAL AWARENESS AND ENGAGEMENT

Ethical awareness and engagement is a crucial aspect of all library services, and the ideals that have been established for the profession generally apply fully to those working in reference services. Just as therapists would do their patients little good if they did not keep their information confidential, reference librarians must follow certain standards of behaviour if the service they provide is to be effective. The American Library Association's Current Code of Ethics, adopted in 1995, provides a useful guide. This code, composed of eight broad statements, upholds a variety of the principles essential to the modern library.

The first statement of the Code insists that librarians should provide the "highest level of service to all library users" and service that is equitable for all with information provided that is "accurate, unbiased and courteous." This statement is at the heart of good reference service, which strives to provide good quality information and information that can be documented.

Reference staff must understand what constitutes a good reference interaction and must strive to meet that standard with each user query. The second statement of the Code calls for the protection of the "principles of intellectual freedom" and resistance to "all efforts to censor library resources." Library selection is reflected in this statement, as librarians attempt to provide information on a subject from many points of view.

The third statement protects the user's right to privacy and confidentiality in requesting and using library resources. Reference librarians must be particularly cognizant of this professional obligation. They must respect the privacy of a user by keeping their reference interview and the resources used confidential. The fourth statement, intellectual property rights should be recognized and respected. It is important that librarians keep current with changes in intellectual property laws, especially copyright, and keep their users aware of these laws.

Librarians must know when copying is covered under the "fair use" provision of the law and when copying violates the copyright law. This is more than a good in itself; it also helps protect the institution, its employees, and its users from claims of copyright infringement and intellectual dishonesty. The fifth through the eighth statements of the Code all treat the relationship between personal interests and professional responsibilities. The fifth encourages the respectful treatment of coworkers and colleagues and the safeguarding of the rights of all employees. This is a statement that encompasses the whole library and its staff.

Every staff member should ensure that others are treated fairly. In the sixth statement, library employees are cautioned not to put private interests ahead of library interests. This means that employees should be circumspect in their dealings with library vendors and others outside the library so their decisions are made on professional merit and are not influenced by personal interest. The seventh statement cautions library employees not to put personal convictions or beliefs ahead of library interests. This is also of special significance to reference librarians.

Sometimes a librarian must help a user research an area that is personally against the librarian's beliefs or philosophy. But by putting professional duties first, the librarian can successfully assist the user and provide the information needed.

The eighth statement encourages all library staff to continue to grow in their knowledge and skills and to assist those entering the profession. We live in a time when change is constant, so all library staff must continue to learn and change. Other professional library organizations have their own codes of ethics. These include the *American Society for Information Science* (ASIS), the Society of American Archivists, the Medical Library Association, and the American Association of Law Libraries.

KINDS OF INFORMATION SERVICE

Information service, in the most general sense, is the process of assisting library users to identify sources of information in response to a particular question, interest, assignment, or problem. Sometimes referred to as reference service, the *Reference and User Services Association* (RUSA) of the American Library Association defines reference transactions as "information consultations in which library staff recommend, interpret, evaluate, and/or use information resources to help others to meet particular information needs". These reference transactions can take place in person or via the telephone, e-mail, or virtual reference technologies.

Librarians are also creating Web sites, answer archives, and links to answers to "frequently asked questions" all designed to anticipate user questions and help people find information independently. Traditional reference desk service continues to be highly valued by library users in many settings, but the newer forms continue to grow in popularity. Consequently, it is all the more important that librarians understand the range of enquiries that can be expected, allowing them to provide a full and ready answer, regardless of the form in which the query arises.

ANSWERING REFERENCE QUESTIONS

In light of the immense diversity and range of possible questions, being approached by a patron with a reference need can seem like a daunting prospect. Indeed, much of the difficulty of information services arises from uncertainty about the kind of service or breadth of information called for by a given question. Categorizing reference questions by type is a useful way to make sense of such concerns. Three common types of information service are ready reference questions, research questions, and bibliographic verification. *Ready reference questions* such as "Where was Abraham Lincoln born?" "Who won the 1992 World Series?" "What is the capital of Nicaragua?" or "Where can I find a copy of the United States' Declaration of Independence?" can be readily answered using one or two general reference sources.

The librarian may be tempted to tell the user the answer to simple ready reference questions. Yet here the old saying that "giving a man a fish feeds him for a day while teaching him to fish feeds him for a lifetime" is proven true. No matter how simple they seem initially, ready reference questions provide the possibility of teachable moments. Whenever possible, librarians should lead users through the process of looking up the information rather than simply providing the solution.

Librarians who assist users with ready reference enquiries on a regular basis sometimes choose to create a "ready reference" section of the most commonly used resources either in print or on the library's Web site to answer quick questions. Typically, such sections include a general all-purpose encyclopedia, dictionaries, almanacs, and handbooks. Care must be taken to keep the sources uptodate and to avoid depending so heavily on this subset of the collection that other sources are overlooked by library users and librarians.

Librarians may find that ready reference questions have diminished due to the ease of answering basic questions through online information portals such as Google. Nevertheless, ready reference remains a cornerstone of information services, and librarians should be primed to provide it at any time. *Research questions* are more complex, may take much longer to answer, and typically require multiple sources of information. These questions often require the user to consider a variety of sources and viewpoints and to subsequently draw conclusions.

Sometimes questions that initially seem like ready reference questions are far more complex as previously hidden facets of the user's enquiry are revealed. Here, the variety of possible sources increases with the complexity of users' questions. Librarians should, for example, guide the user in the use of bibliographic sources, citations, and the back-of-the-book bibliographies. Likewise, users with complex questions may need to be taught how to find or request the full text of articles for which only citations are given in a search of electronic databases, allowing them to move beyond cursory surveys of the literature.

Research questions, especially if the user is unable to fully articulate the nature of his or her query, require librarians to ask questions of their own, trying to get at the nature of the request before setting out to help the patron answer it. The librarian may, for example, have to determine how much information is needed, what level of information is needed, and what other sources have already been consulted. Information services call for mutual engagement, especially with more complex questions.

Reference librarians should never be passive participants, pointing the way to an answer. Instead, they should play the part of dynamic guides, joining users on their journeys to knowledge. Naturally, the extent of such engagement may vary from one circumstance to another. Different types of libraries tend to have their own standards for how long librarians should spend with users on research questions. Many public libraries recommend that users be given five or ten minutes of personal assistance and then asked to return if more help is needed.

A university library may have a similar standard, or depending on the institution, may be able to invite the user to make an appointment for more in-depth research assistance. Some libraries may suggest that users call or e-mail ahead of their visit so the librarian can be prepared to offer the best possible assistance. Other libraries, including special libraries, may only be able to provide a basic level of help during the first visit. Libraries may refer users to other libraries with more specialized materials in the area of the user's research or may offer to call back if additional information is found.

Finally a library user may seek *bibliographic verification* when he or she has already obtained the information needed but must verify the sources. Sometimes this service is a matter of fact checking, whereas on other occasions users may have completed their research but lack full citation information. As users increasingly depend on electronic databases for information, compiling and formatting bibliographic citations becomes easier. Verifying and citing material found on Web pages is more difficult since the information needed for the citation is not always easy to find.

READER'S ADVISORY SERVICE

Reader's advisory service, sometimes considered a type of information service, is the quest to put the right book in the hands of the right reader. Librarians are increasingly expected to provide an answer to the dreaded question, "Can you help me find a good book?" Fortunately, as demand has increased, so too has the ease of providing this service. Although there is no substitute for one's own knowledge or experience, many new technologies serve to make the reader's advisory far easier than it was in the past. Many online databases, for example, have functions that automatically recommend other books for those who like a given title. Others have searchable lists of works by genre, helping readers match their favourite books to others like them.

As always, however, remember that reader's advisory, like other reference work, is predicated on the interaction between librarian and library user. Asking directed questions, listening carefully to the users' responses, and tailoring assistance accordingly is the basis of excellent, truly helpful service. The reader's advisory service is generally associated with public libraries and tends to be employed primarily by those looking for fiction. In academic libraries, it is far less common as users rarely come in searching for a mystery to read. Even so, reader's advisory may be needed to help lay researchers looking to deepen their knowledge of a particular field.

A patron who has read and enjoyed Stephen Ambrose's *Undaunted Courage,* but is troubled by allegations about Ambrose's questionable accuracy and academic honesty, may want to know the titles of books about the Lewis and Clark expedition that are both reputable and engaging. Successful reader's advisory librarians are skilled at asking users questions that enable them to assess users' reading level, language, or educational background. They must know a great deal about various genres of fiction and non-fiction and be intimately familiar with their library's collection. Significantly, it is important that they be able to convey their expertise in a friendly and conversational manner.

INFORMATION LITERACY

User instruction, which is now usually referred to as *information literacy,* may range from showing an individual how to use the library's online catalogue and basic print reference sources to formal classroom sessions about conducting research in the library. The basic component of information literacy includes demonstrating how, when, and why to use various reference sources in an integrated way that will capture the user's attention at the teachable moment. In today's educational settings, the ease of using electronic resources often results in a failure to teach more traditional research strategies. While finding superficial information has grown easier, in-depth information has become increasingly obscure for many students.

In the library too, approaches to instruction may vary and librarians often question whether to simply answer questions posed by users or to teach users how to employ the available resources. This may be contingent on the mission or purpose of the library. Academic institutions may call on their librarians to help students understand how to engage effectively and independently in the research and information evaluation process. Public librarians, by contrast, may try to teach users about reference sources in a more informal manner as they lead users to the answers they seek.

Thus, while instruction is always an important part of reference work, the degree to which they go about providing it is highly contingent on the circumstances. In any case, all reference librarians must be skilled at helping users find information and answers quickly and be ready to teach users how to use the reference sources that are available. The best reference librarians develop an intuition for when to be information providers and when to be bibliographic instructors.

In some libraries, only specific, designated librarians are charged with conducting library instruction courses. Nevertheless, an increasing number of librarians are required to participate in their libraries' bibliographic instruction programme, and library school graduates are expected to be capable of teaching basic classes on the use of library resources. As should be clear, even those librarians not charged with providing formal instruction have the opportunity to teach those they serve.

SELECTING AND EVALUATING PRINT AND ELECTRONIC INFORMATION

Selecting and evaluating print and electronic information for the library's collection can be as professionally rewarding as providing expert information service. Reference librarians' involvement in evaluating and selecting titles for the collection helps them develop rich knowledge of the sources at their disposal, increasing their effectiveness. The responsibility for selecting reference materials depends largely on the size and scope of the library. In large academic libraries, selecting reference materials may be assigned to subject bibliographers whose work may be limited to collection development responsibilities.

On the other side of the continuum, the evaluation and purchase of resources in very small libraries may be the work of a single reference librarian or coordinator of reference. A range of shared evaluation and selection possibilities between these points include reference materials selection committees or group assignments. The question, "What makes a book a reference book?" has long been debated in our profession. For the purpose of this discussion, reference books are those texts set aside to be consulted for specific information rather than to be read as a whole. In other words, reference books contain content meant to be "looked up".

Typically, one turns to a reference source in search of something in particular rather than to the text as a whole. Another common characteristic of reference books is that they do not leave the library premises. This ensures that all works in the reference collection are always on hand, making for a consistently available body of knowledge. Note that labelling narrative or non-reference books as "reference" to deter theft or ensure that a popular volume is always available may lead to bloated reference collections, and it is not generally recommended.

Finally, with the addition of electronic reference sources, which are increasingly available to remote library users from their homes, dorm rooms, offices, and elsewhere, reference collections encompass much more than print books and serials and may be available twenty-four hours a day.

As the present trend towards shrinking budgets for reference collections, lean reference collections, and the elimination of duplication among print and electronic collections continues, the careful evaluation and selection of reference materials is essential. Libraries should determine the criteria that will be used in selecting sources for its reference collection. The following criteria may help determine whether an item is a worthy addition to a library's collection: scope, quality of content, appropriateness for audience, format, arrangement, authority, currency, accuracy, ease of use, unique coverage and cost.

Criteria for selecting electronic resources may vary, though all of the criteria used to evaluate print resources should be considered, especially in libraries that aim to avoid redundancy in their print and electronic reference collections. Some libraries select reference materials by reading reviews in the library professional literature such as *Library Journal* and *Choice* and *Booklist*'s "Reference Books Bulletin." Other institutions insist on physically reviewing reference sources at trade shows or through special arrangements with publishers of reference materials. Most libraries employ a combination of these two.

CREATING FINDING TOOLS AND WEB SITES

Another strategy employed by many reference departments is the creation of finding tools and pathfinders for library users. Here, librarians act as cartographers, mapping out the best routes through familiar territory and pointing out interesting sites along the way. Pathfinders are often prepared for commonly requested subjects such as high school and college assignments about capital punishment, drug abuse, and the history of Native American tribes. Similarly, public libraries may prepare pathfinders that address frequently asked questions of a quotidian nature such as: finding job information, checking the credentials of a health care provider, or researching a family tree.

Depending on the topic, audience, and needs, the path-finder may guide the user to a selection of appropriate reference books, relevant databases and search terms, a selection of current and authoritative Web sites, and tips for searching the library's *Online Public Access Catalogue* (OPAC) for additional materials. Librarians also create Web sites of carefully evaluated links organized by topic, sometimes known as "webliographies" that serve as finding tools. Who better than librarians to organize the World Wide Web of information, pointing the users to "the best" sources and helping them steer clear of the dubious? Web-based finding tools offer several advantages to print pathfinders.

They are available to users 24/7, they can be updated as often as needed, and they can include direct links to Web sites and electronic reference tools. Depending on the circumstance and the nature of a library's Web presence such webliographies can be either general, providing direction to broadly targeted reference resources, or subject specific.

General all-purpose lists of librarian-selected Web resources include the *Internet Public Library* and the *Librarians' Internet Index*. Examples of library subject-specific webliographies include The New York Public Library's *Best of the Web* and the University of Washington's *Information Gateway*. Larger libraries, whether academic or public, often produce indexes of both types. Smaller libraries may be better served by developing webliographies for specific areas in which they have subject specialists and linking to a general reference site like the *Internet Public Library* or the *Librarians' Internet Index*.

PROMOTING AND MARKETING LIBRARIES AND REFERENCE SERVICE

Paying attention to promotion and marketing of libraries and reference service is becoming more important than ever. Without support from the community, the library will not stay viable. Promoting reference services among individual library users can go a long way towards achieving this goal, especially insofar as it demonstrates how the library can serve them. In large communities—urban public libraries, for example-promoting the library through individual users is not enough to attract new users and major marketing or publicity campaigns become important. In academic libraries, school libraries, and special libraries, promotion and marketing are equally essential. Use of print and online newsletters, Web sites, and opportunities to meet with faculty and staff can provide opportunities to promote the library's resources.

EVALUATING STAFF AND SERVICES

Libraries may seek to routinely evaluate their reference collections or reference service. In her book *Evaluating Reference Services: A Practical Guide*, Jo Bell Whitlatch wisely emphasizes the importance of defining the purpose of the evaluation before setting a strategy. "The most important questions you must ask," according to Whitlatch, are these: "Why am I evaluating reference services" and "What do I plan to do with the study results?" The quality of the reference interaction, from either the user's or the librarian's perspective, may be assessed to help determine how effective the reference service is. Evaluating reference staff is one way to help determine how effective the reference service is, and is one way to help assure quality reference service.

The American Library Association's Reference and User Services Association has developed "Guidelines for Behavioural Performance of Reference and Information Service Professionals," which are intended to be used in the training, development, or evaluation of library professionals and staff. The performance of reference librarians is typically evaluated on both the information conveyed to users and the satisfaction of the interaction on the library user.

The following factors are covered by the ALA Guidelines:

- *Approachability:* Are users able to identify that a reference librarian is available to help?
- *Interest:* Does the librarian demonstrate a high degree of interest in the reference transaction?
- *Listening/Enquiring:* Does the librarian identify the user's information need in a manner that puts the user at ease? Are good communication skills used throughout the transaction?
- *Searching:* Is the librarian skilled at creating search strategies that yield accurate and relevant results?
- *Follow-up:* Does the librarian determine if the user is satisfied with the results of the search/interaction?

These performance guidelines may form the backbone of a library's staff evaluation instruments, whether the instrument is a simple self-evaluation checklist, a peer-evaluation tool, or a formal evaluation system influencing earning potential. In addition to evaluating staff, the library may measure its productivity or efficiency with quantitative measures that include the number of questions answered and the frequency with which print and/or electronic sources are consulted. Smaller libraries may continuously count the number and type of in-person questions answered by the reference staff.

In larger libraries, quarterly one-week periods are frequently used to estimate the number of questions answered over the course of a year. Depending on the available resources, data may be recorded using hand-held computers, by making hash marks on a form, or by any means in between. Avariety of other evaluation strategies are also available to libraries: Assessing the quality of the resources available may, for example, be another useful measurement. Issues of resource allocation may also be incorporated into departmental evaluations, if one includes how the library's budget allocates for library staff, print and electronic resources, computers and networks, and buildings.

Evaluation methods frequently used to gauge users' satisfaction with reference services and sources include questionnaires, surveys, focus groups, observation and interviews. It is crucial that library administrators determine what is to be measured and against what standards before choosing the preferred method of evaluation. Many sources are available for detailed information on designing evaluation instruments for libraries. Selecting the best method, developing and field testing the instrument, administering the survey, questionnaire, or interview, planning the observation, avoiding interviewer bias and scores of ethical issues should be carefully considered. Analysing data and developing conclusions and recommendations may require advanced training and in some cases evaluation experts are hired.

THE CHANGING NATURE OF REFERENCE

As the form of the library has evolved in the years since Samuel Green's seminal pronouncements in 1876, so too has the nature of reference services. Today it stretches far beyond the walls of the library and strives to far loftier ends than welcoming users to the library with a "cultivated female staff." Academic libraries in particular have already seen a slowing of traffic to the physical library and the increasing use of the library's online resources. Users can ask questions 24/7 through virtual reference and expect an immediate response. Likewise, they can access electronic resources that the library provides through its Web site.

Virtual reference is growing quickly; the appeal of instant messaging and like services point to a generational paradigm shift ahead. These online reference services have the advantage of being convenient and necessary in our fast-paced world. In numerous forms and fashions, technology continues to change reference services. Libraries must be ready to learn new technology and adapt to the needs of users unable to imagine a world without technology. Like few other professionals, librarians must be willing to ride the waves of such change, adapting to meet the needs of their users. Whether it is the cell phone, the Palm Pilot, the MP3 player, or the iPod, users will want to receive and read their information on this new technology.

New models of reference are also developing to meet different user needs. Libraries are adding more points of service. For example, an information desk near the front of the library, a reference service point combined with other library services or an in-depth reference center where a user can sit down with a librarian and work out a plan for researching a paper have all been instituted to positive effect at libraries around the world.

In other situations, librarians rove the reference area to help users who do not approach the reference desk. These and other new strategies are changing the way information services are offered. As we look ahead, we must be aware that reference work will no doubt be based increasingly on electronic means of communication. It will at the same time continue to be a personal service although not necessarily face to face. There will be more emphasis on electronic materials while some older materials will still need to be consulted in print format. Even so, the way we find information and convey it is as fundamental today as it ever was.

INDEXING AND ABSTRACTING SERVICE

An abstracting service is a service that provides abstracts of publications, often on a subject or group of related subjects, usually on a subscription basis. An indexing service is a service that assign descriptors and other kinds of access points to documents. The word indexing service is today mostly used about computer programmes, but may also cover services providing back-of-the-book indexes, journal indexes and related kinds of indexes. An indexing and abstracting service is a service, that provides shortening or summarizing of documents and assigning of descriptors for referencing documents.

The product is often an abstract journal or a bibliographic index, which may be a subject bibliography or a bibliographic database. Guidelines for indexing and abstracting, including the evaluation of such services, are given in the literature of Library and information science.

CENTRAL AUTHENTICATION SERVICE

The *Central Authentication Service* (CAS) is a single sign-on protocol for the web. Its purpose is to permit a user to access multiple applications while providing their credentials only once. It also allows web applications to authenticate users without gaining access to a user's security credentials, such as a password. The name *CAS* also refers to a software package that implements this protocol. The CAS protocol involves at least three parties: a *client* web browser, the web *application* requesting authentication, and the *CAS server*. It may also involve a *back-end service,* such as a database server, that does not have its own HTTP interface but communicates with a web application. When the client visits an application desiring to authenticate to it, the application redirects it to CAS. CAS validates the client's authenticity, usually by checking a username and password against a database. If the authentication succeeds, CAS returns the client to the application, passing along a security ticket. The application then validates the ticket by contacting CAS over a secure connection and providing its own service identifier and the ticket. CAS then gives the application trusted information about whether a particular user has successfully authenticated. CAS allows multi-tier authentication via proxy address. A cooperating *back-end* service, like a database or mail server, can participate in CAS, validating the authenticity of users via information it receives from web applications. Thus, a webmail client and a webmail server can all implement CAS.

SERIAL DIGITAL INTERFACE

Serial digital interface (SDI) is a family of video interfaces standardized by SMPTE. For example, ITU-R BT.656 and SMPTE 259M define digital video interfaces used for broadcast-grade video. A related standard, known as *high-definition serial digital interface* (HD-SDI), is standardized in SMPTE 292M; this provides a nominal data rate of 1.485 Gbit/s. An emerging interface, commonly known in the industry as dual link HD-SDI and consisting essentially of a pair of SMPTE 292M links, is standardized in SMPTE 372M; this provides a nominal 2.970 Gbit/s interface used in applications that require greater fidelity and resolution than standard HDTV can provide.

A more recent interface, 3G-SDI, consisting of a single 2.970 Gbit/s serial link, is standardized in SMPTE 424M that will replace the dual link HD-SDI. These standards are used for transmission of uncompressed, unencrypted digital video signals within television facilities; they can also be used for packetized data. Coaxial variants of the specification range in length but are typically less than 300 meters. Fibre optic variants of the specification such as 297M allow for long-distance transmission limited only by maximum fibre length and/or repeaters. SDI and HD-SDI are currently only available in professional video equipment; various licensing agreements, restricting the use of unencrypted digital interfaces to professional equipment, prohibit their use in consumer equipment. There are various mod kits for existing DVD players and other devices, which allow a user to add a serial digital interface to these devices.

DIGITAL SERVICES

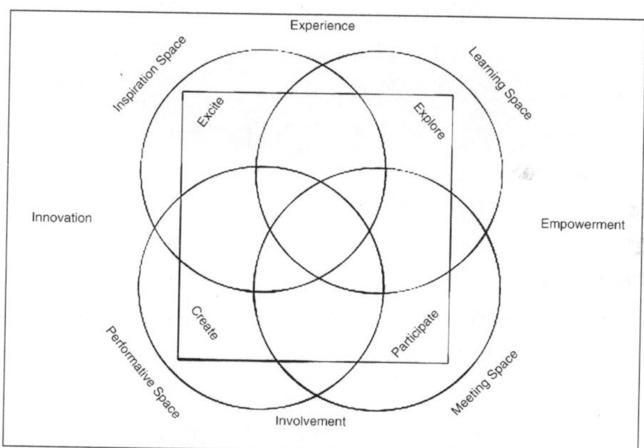

Fig. A New Library Concept.

Do we agree on the vision:

- To establish a coherent digital library covering all fields of media and library services from baby-to researcher level.
- Corresponding with the library space.
- Aiming at all citizens with segmented services and building on partnerships of all kind.

How do we get there:

- Establish a convincing strategy.
- Demonstrating capability by good working examples on new services.

- Lobbying and marketing for a new political under-standing of a library concept meeting the needs in the knowledge-and innovation society.

Digital means 'change' and 'divide':

- The gap between analogue and digital media is growing.
- The 'traditional' library still works well but we loose more and more users if we do not move faster building digital libraries.

The digital media landscape is part of a bigger agenda:

- The knowledge and innovation society.
- The changed economic balance between Europe and the new economies.
- The fragmentation of social life and growing tension
- Needs for better skills.

A European agenda:

- Knowledge societies imply globalization and a new competition pattern–jobs are moving east.
- The answer to the challenge is 'innovation' based.
- On more research, better education, lifelong learning, a strong identity and cohesion in society.
- We are in badly need of all these elements facing illiteracy, social tension in a more and more multi-cultural society.
- The fragmentation and cultural changes in the 'late modern society' are roaring for counter strategies.

E-book service is also part of a bigger agenda:

- An e-book platform is not enough.
- Developing a new library concept.
  - Public service concept: services for all citizens, segmentation.
  - Competing with other information services: the library niche.
- Creating new organizational frames
  - No library is an island: (inter)national development
  - Partnerships.
  - Break up of traditional library collection oriented organization.

Analogue and digital services should be integrated:

- The library space is for public libraries still the hub.
- The activities in the four spaces of the new library concept are virtual and real.
- The programmes support the agenda of society, from innovation to democratic inclusion and participation.
- Partnerships basic for organization.

3

Towards Equality of Access: Library Services and Technology

INTRODUCTION

Libraries across India, as in other parts of the world, are facing sweeping changes on account of the media in which information is generated, transmitted, disseminated and archived due to the increasing presence of electronic formats. There is no doubt that information in electronic form is a potential asset, and that it can be vigourously applied in any environment.

The advent and spread of electronic formats has made a major difference in the information processing and service environments in libraries, especially after the emergence of the Internet and Web as the dominant pathway and repository of electronic information resources.

In an increasingly networked world, it is possible that universities may be able to take back control of scholarly information, and libraries may risk being cut out of the author-publisher-dissemination loop. Libraries act as facilitators to provide the right information to the right user at the right time. Users visit libraries to borrow identified documents, or to take photocopies/ printouts of those documents from reference collections or journals not issued out normally.

The advent of Web-enabled information resources, such as e-journals, e-books and e-reference sources, and their access through networks has taken the library to the users and a significant amount of information access is now taking place beyond the four walls of the library. In many cases users want a 'pinpointed precision' in the information search process whereas the library attempts for an 'exhaustive recall' to comply with the various ways in which an information source is approached and to satisfy each user's diverse interests.

This information overload may cause doubts in the users regarding the relevance of information services as perceived from a professional angle. Along with quantifying use, it is equally important to assess the qualitative attributes of implicit and explicit use and examine the difficulties of users in properly framing their requests for information. The limitation on the part of library professionals to perceive and represent what is demanded by users in information systems, and the dilemmas of information organisation and retrieval to handle these demands must be effectively addressed. Libraries and professionals are equally concerned about the emergence of Internet as an information repository beyond the library's walls, as amply demonstrated by enhanced citations of Web resources.

As library acquisitions are falling, information sources are increasing, and a single site library satisfying the user's needs is a doubtful proposition; users are forced to look beyond the library for their information needs. Thus the only option for the libraries is to enter into collaborations, networking and consortia and to reorient their roles as information services and access centres from their previous roles as information warehouses.

At the same time, the technical advances resulting from enhanced research in science and technology have made it possible to reduce drastically the time involved in information collection and identification. Also the extra time required in adapting printed information to client service through cumbersome manual routines of classification and cataloguing is considerably reduced by the availability of electronic information, leaving the professionals to concentrate more on tasks to support the extensive teaching and intensive research environment.

ACADEMIC AND RESEARCH LIBRARIES

The application of computing to library work in India has a history of at least three decades because since, the time the computer entered premier academic institutions and selected R & D facilities, it has been explored for improving information processing and management routines. Information technology (IT) enriched library services arrived initially for science and technology (S&T) information handling and for the special libraries attached to research and development (R&D) centres and academic libraries in higher education institutions. In comparison to other libraries, academic and research libraries have better infrastructure and skilled manpower in greater numbers, making them able to offer information services comparable to advanced countries. Like qualified teaching and research personnel and well-equipped laboratories, the right information service is another vital element in the trinity which completes a fruitful academic or research environment.

MARKET-DRIVEN COLLABORATION

Academic and research libraries, especially in developing countries, are passing through a very challenging phase in their existence due to unfriendly trends in the emerging information market. On the one hand, these libraries are still left with many of the old problems such as poor budgetary support and weak infrastructure, as well as staff in fewer numbers and often with less expertise. But the new information marketing techniques, like the possibilities of delivering and accessing electronic information in diverse channels, force these libraries to be very vigilant and cautious in their approach towards information acquisition and services. Libraries and professionals in India were quick to understand the emerging information environment was forcing their users to depend largely on those resources, which are becoming more expensive day by day due to the rise in production costs, fall in subscriptions and inflationary trends of Indian currency.

When individual libraries found that alone they are not in a position to satisfy the information requirements of their clients, they formulated various collaborative arrangements with other libraries such as, interlibrary loan (ILL) services, document delivery services (DDS), resource-sharing, and consortia-based subscriptions.

PRESENT PRACTICES AND EMERGING GOALS

The special libraries attached to research and higher education were lucky enough to garner resources to automate their in-house routine operations and for hosting online public access catalogues (OPACs); some of them also set up facilities to search electronic databases. A few of them evolved the desired infrastructure for Internet surfing, for hosting of full-text database access, and for setting up digital libraries. The major advantage of the progress in computerisation is a considerable increase in the amount of information available online.

We have experienced that at the start of computer applications only the surrogates existed online, but some full-text content has been made accessible online in recent years. These libraries are experiencing the virtues of electronic information in different forms such as e-journals, e-books, bibliographic/full-text electronic databases on CD-ROMs and through Web access. Due to publishers' 'electronic plus' policies, libraries are able to access electronic versions of printed sources such as journals either for free or by paying an additional fee. However the goal these libraries in specialised research and academic centres should have set for themselves is to enhance their information facilities to fully functional digital libraries, comparable with similar facilities in the developed countries.

CULTURES AND CONFLICTS FACED BY LIBRARIES

The fixed roles suggested by Levy for researchers, publishers and libraries are either overlapping or changing in the electronic scene. There are cases where an author or a library is acting as electronic publisher, and there are publishers providing a wide variety of information packages beyond the contents of printed journals. The real question is: has the library really lost ground in the emerging information scene? Even the critics will not say so.

The concerns expressed are only to revitalise the professional skills of librarians, rejuvenate the style of working and reorient the library towards its rightful place in effective dissemination of information. Maybe the common feeling that the library is a central place in the institution visited everyday by large numbers of users, like any public utility, has lost some ground in the electronic scene. Non-etheless, apart the continuing provision of information services for print sources, the electronic revolution has reaffirmed the library more as an information service and access centre than as an information storehouse.

TECHNOLOGY-ENHANCED LIBRARY SERVICES

TECHNOLOGY ADVANCES

The major technology breakthroughs in the context of libraries include:

- Advent of printing press and mass production of printed documents enabled democratisation of information. Libraries had a major role in the print era, as no one can own a large number of books on a particular subject whereas libraries by their very purpose concentrated on doing so.
- Microforms helped to preserve less used information in a compact space and as a smoother delivery option for voluminous sources. Libraries had their unchallenged role even in the microform era as the special purpose readers for microfilms and microfiche were costly and exclusively housed in the library.
- The economical and affordable copying technology revolutionised the concept of information use as it spearheaded the trend of owning copies of relevant portions of library resources. The copying technology freed the user from sitting in the library for long duration for reading, since, one can simply get a copy quickly and leave.
- Computing is the biggest technology revolution so far, as it is a major enabler in the information dissemination chain; also it is not a stand-alone technology unlike earlier technologies and can be networked and integrated with a whole lot of other devices and technologies. It not only revolutionised the production of books and microforms but also brought the arrival of online and CD-ROM databases, electronic information resources, Internet and the digital revolution.

PRODUCTS AND SERVICES

Adapting IT for library applications is an ongoing process, right from procuring or developing IT enabled information products through computer aided processing and management to delivering IT-enriched services. Library professionals in India are already exposed to the different offshoots of IT for library organisation and information services.

LIBRARY AUTOMATION PACKAGES

The availability of a wide variety of library automation software to suit the varied needs of libraries themselves is a reflection of the progress libraries have made in automating the operations of procuring, processing and providing information sources. Procurement is the end of the story for many other software/databases used in a library, whereas library automation systems will open a floodgate of issues. What the vendor provides is a structure to build information concerning the collection and users, to conduct various aspects of organising the collection and offering information services.

Thus software needs to be evaluated for its suitability for the target library before purchase. This may include case studies from other libraries using the software, evaluation of hardware and operating system required, computer awareness among staff and users, network as well as computer infrastructure in the institution, and all estimation of cost and charges for after-sales support. Using suitable software for library automation will significantly reduce manual operations and enable professionals to dedicate more time for professional jobs.

CD-ROM AND ELECTRONIC DATABASES

Due to the poor communication infrastructure prevalent in India and to the immense costs involved, online database services were used only by few institutions. The distribution of the same content of online data repositories subsequently in CD-ROMs made it affordable to a larger number of institutions. While the library automation package gave search-and access facility to information sources present in the local collection, CD-ROM databases attempted consolidated access irrespective of holdings to the bibliographic data of publications in a discipline. CD-ROM databases have also freed library professionals from conducting searches and allowed the end user to conduct the searches. CD-ROM is so common nowadays that a library holds a good number of them not only for bibliographic, numeric and full-text databases, but also those received along with printed books and other reference sources. Managing and serving these high capacity discs was a problem earlier due to the stand-alone software required, whereas the onset of networking and hard-disk cached solutions provides an effective and functional way to enable access to them through the intranet.

WEB

Since, the 1990s, the Internet has changed the dissemination of information, such as electronic copies of traditional paper-based journals and conference proceedings, free electronic-only refereed journals, haphazard copies of all kinds of material on home pages and a handful of electronic preprints archives. Most libraries in India now have a web site and they use the site to present the basic strengths of the library and to host services such as the OPAC and Web access to electronic information. The 'size of the catalogue card' and the field lengths of primitive database technology are surpassed in the Web era. Types of information resources on the Web also vary from authentic primary information about the latest research results to ephemeral product catalogues. Issues worth consideration are often the content of the sites that are deleted, modified or changed to new machines without proper redirection and the extraction mechanism through search engines, when a flood of sources is retrieved against a query, of which few are relevant.

The Internet and Web demonstrate that a large amount of electronic information can be hosted in a decentralised fashion in a cost-effective manner. The Web has also freed the user's dependence on library resources for finding information related to address and contact details of a person/institution, contents pages of books, journals, etc. As far as possible, especially for reference and information services, looking at the Web has become an innovative trend in the reference service to complement dated print sources.

Many publishers visibly feel the benefits and reach of the Web, and have considered it as an alternate medium for delivering information sources; some publishers even permit unrestricted access of tables of contents and abstracts of their primary journals. As a result of these initiatives, the 'print and distribute' paradigm is challenged by 'distribute and print' paradigm.

CONSORTIAL LICENCES

The term 'consortial licences' designates library groupings to negotiate access rights to (print and) electronic information with publishers and vendors aiming at enhanced access to more resources at better pricing. "Consortia can be a means to introduce products to a previously untapped market" for vendors and "consortia provide shared expertise, access to new electronic and print resources, professional development, new sources of funds, and safety in numbers" for libraries. In contrast to earlier library collaborative arrangements such as ILL and resource sharing, the publisher and trade community are parties in the consortial agreements. In resource-sharing, libraries concentrate on collaborative subscriptions by avoiding duplication, where as in consortial licences, the emphasis is to strike the 'best deals' even if the library suffers some duplication.

The publisher community experience is that increased subscription costs lead to a reduction in the total number of subscriptions, further raising the subscription cost every year. Publishers also found it difficult to enforce ownership rights with electronic sources, even after adopting the latest technology tools and forcing libraries to sign the toughest of the legal clauses. The good marketing wisdom of the publisher and trade community prevailed to open up information access rights through consortial licences for a large part of the product spectrum to at least those libraries or groups of libraries which procure products beyond a certain threshold value.

The Indian National Digital Library in Engineering Science and Technology (INDEST) is the first and the major consortium in India. It is under the aegis of the Ministry of Human Resource Development (MHRD). Before the creation of the consortium, access to electronic journals in these institutions remained at 60 per cent of subscribed titles, but the number of online journals has increased 10 times after the establishment of the consortium.

The rates for access offered to the consortium are lower by 50 per cent to 90 per cent depending upon the category of institution and the consortium paid only 11 per cent of the list price to access these resources. Info net, another consortium, floated by the University Grants Commission (UGC) for Universities, is also gaining strength. Similar consortia are also operational for research institutions under the Council of Scientific and Industrial Research (CSIR) and the Department of Atomic Energy (DAE).

DIGITAL LIBRARIES

Libraries in India are engaged in the development of prototypes of digital information resources, as influenced by developments in other countries. There are certain types of content which lie inaccessible or less used in their present physical forms that can be put to more visible and enhanced use through digitisation. Also heavily used content presently available in limited numbers of copies can be identified for conversion to electronic format.

The linear text in many of the print sources presents difficulties for providing a hypertext approach or a multimedia feeling, for simulating learning by doing; sustaining attention and interest for long duration calls for using electronic technologies to enable content to be more functional. The static content in printed sources fails to attract users who are increasingly exposed to the widely appealing features of broadcasting and IT-intensive presentation tools. Multimedia-enabled digital information will be useful to a large percentage of illitreate and older population also. There are cases such as papers in journals and conferences in print form that never get their deserved visibility and often end up with out reaching the target population.

The digital dissemination of this content may lead to very effective teaching and more focused research in most areas. To demonstrate the efficacy of digital libraries and collections, libraries must be able to identify materials in the public domain, sources generated in-house, and similar materials to overcome the constraints of copyright. Digital library (DL) development needs a two pronged strategy to digitise local content as well as to devise options for providing access to external resources obtained as free or as part of existing subscriptions or access licences.

The typical academic or research library in-house digital library on an Intranet must include the following components:

- Consortial access to electronic journals and electronic databases.

- Free/paid Web access to journals subscribed in print format.
- Subject gateways and virtual libraries.
- Free/paid e-books from publishers and portals.
- Intranet access to bibliographic and full-text databases, and CD-ROM publications.
- Local archiving of free and paid e-books.
- LAN serving of e-supplements of purchased books.
- In-house digitisation of copyright-owned and copyright-free printed books in the collection.
- Born-digital in-house publications such as research reports, annual reports, convocation reports, teaching materials, theses and dissertations, in-house journals, proceedings of conferences, seminars, workshops, etc., conducted by the institution.
- Preprints and post-prints of research papers sent for publication to journals, conferences, and books, especially with respect to the Open Archives Initiative gaining ground to provide further access to research published in toll journals and to make the results of publicly funded research available to those who need them.
- Publications in the public domain, such as government publications, publications from non-profit institutions, etc.

But many libraries are unable to provide these components due to lack of awareness or due to the hurdles invariably faced by libraries in India. The lack of interest on the part of parent institutions and the absence of action plans or priorities is the major hindrance. Though computer and communication infrastructure is improving, their availability for information work is not appreciated in many organisations. Paschoud commented how several of the speakers and many of the delegates at the International Conference on Digital Libraries (ICDL) 2004 conference in New Delhi focussed on addressing what most European libraries would consider very basic issues such as network/Internet connectivity and management.

Even in places where infrastructure is available, there is an acute shortage of competent labour to take up the task of digitising local content and evolving digital information repositories. The students, faculty, curriculum and training methodology at the disposal of library schools have to be improved visibly to meet this challenge. Coupled with this is the need for continuing education for retraining the working professionals. Institutions, individuals, or private publishers have rights over content, and motivating them to ease these rights when they are not inclined towards digitisation is not a simple task. Levying charges for access is a distant proposition; instead sponsorships from institutions, government bodies and library suppliers can be explored.

Even when hosted as a free facility, enough security mechanisms must be evolved to prevent any trespassing by hackers. Selecting useful content requires careful review and evaluation by subject experts, as digitisation will only help to preserve the record, and not its enhanced and continued access.

Internet bandwidth in India has to be sufficiently augmented to allow faster access to Web content as more content is being hosted on the Web. The different funding agencies, research councils and institutions are not currently offering monetary support to the desired extent for digital library development.

CULTURE AND CONFLICTS FACED BY USERS

MANUAL AND ELECTRONIC SEARCH

Searching for manual sources required scanning catalogue cards or indexing and abstracting sources. As cross-references often increase the number of cards or pages, there was a difficulty in being very exhaustive. Conducting selective dissemination of information (SDI) services had been extremely difficult as the document profiles must be matched with user profiles with the aid of semi-mechanical systems. Most of these limitations are easily eliminated in the electronic environment due to the very nature of information processing and organisation in electronic form.

The inherent advantages of indexing electronic information help the user to search for any or all the fields in a timesaving manner. Since, document profiles are already stored in the database and search software supports creation of user profiles, current awareness services (CAS) and SDI services are achieved more easily. The concern for end-user searching was dominant right from the beginning of early CD-ROM database systems since, the time spent for searching does not involve communication costs as is the case with online searching. Also with the universe of knowledge getting increasingly complex as a result of continuing advances in research in intra and interdisciplinary areas, vitiating the search conducted by a generalist like a librarian may not be effective in amassing the user's information requirements completely or not achieving the desired results expected by the user.

The convoluted information requirements of present day researchers require sufficient knowledge of their disciplines and since, the users are increasingly exposed to the computerised work environment, they feel very confident to conduct information searching on electronic systems. The professional ethos and egos also plays a part as users find more satisfactory results from electronic systems than manual systems, and in a relatively easy and convenient way. The librarians should recognise the confidence and maturity of users to conduct searches on their own as they have better knowledge of their disciplines, more exposure to the different keywords and their relationships and because of the inherent advantages of locating related sources serendipitously while scanning the retrieved results.

There should be closer interaction and effective communication between library professionals and users to understand each other's views about information needs and use. Library user meetings, orientation sessions for new users, special help for research scholars, training programmes about usage of print and electronic resources, a help desk at reference counter, holdings locator services, interacting with users through phone and e-mail, encouraging users to approach the librarian, ask a librarian, and user friendly web sites are some options practiced in libraries in India.

INFORMATION USE

Information services provided by a library are primarily based on subjective input from users and hence, justify users commenting about misses or noise in electronic information service outputs. An information need is what an individual ought to have; an information want is what an individual would like to have; an information demand is what an individual asks for; an information use is what an individual actually uses; and an information requirement denotes what is needed, what is wanted or what is demanded.

Information needs are affected by a variety of factors such as the range of sources available, the uses to which information will be put, individual characteristics of the user, social, political and economic systems surrounding the user, and the consequences of information use. Accessibility of information resources is usually assumed to depend on a range of cognitive, social, and physical factors, such as whether a person is aware of a resource, has the knowledge and skills needed to access it, and has the resource close at hand. Scientists spend 50–60 per cent of their time communicating. The computerised environment has increased the quantum of information available nearby, but it has not enhanced a person's information consumption skills.

There is a burden of effort in information storage and retrieval that may be shifted from author to indexer to index language designer to searcher to user. Though the user is exposed to more microfilms, Xerox copies, and electronic information on desktop/ Intranet/Web, ready to display at the touch of a button, the more time one spends in searching and collecting information, the less time s/he gets to use the information. Scholarly articles are identified for reading in five basic ways: browsing, automated searches, citations found in the litreature, mentions by other people, and current-awareness tools. How much information one requires to work on a particular problem is also subjective as human beings observe the 'principle of least effort'. Perhaps one may easily deal with an information crisis by identifying a part of the total references and by using few of what is identified.

USER BYPASSING

Though libraries in India are progressing well on the automation and information access front, there is a definite case of fewer users present in the library due to different reasons. The real question is whether electronic services of libraries have in any way affected the user interests or have the users found more confidence in an information superhighway beyond the library. The same proportions of scientists still browse to identify scholarly articles to read, but more are using online searches and the proportion of readings identified through online searches appears to be increasing. Library acquisitions suffered a serious setback in recent years unable to withstand the price rise and these budgetary constraints forced users to look beyond the library for their varied information requirements.

Hence, research publications in some disciplines now cite more Web resources. Librarians are not yet acting as true consumers and hence, cannot blame predatory publishers for taking advantage of the situation. Another issue involves the very large and rapidly increasing number of articles obtained through photocopying, interlibrary loan, document delivery, preprints, and reprints. The right step in assessing whether there is a depleted user interest in libraries is to study use patterns over the years and, in a populous country like India, just going by the numbers will not address the qualitative aspects.

There has not been much reduction in book issues in an academic library, but are the new acquisitions being used to the same extent? But what is seen is the fall in library attendance, as observed and reported by many library managers. It is evident that fewer users actually visit the library, and very few still spend more time, a lot of others use the library through lending, photocopies, electronic access through networks, etc. It becomes difficult to quantify use as the library has statistics only about explicit use, but there are also implicit uses through browsing or reading inside the library, which are difficult to quantify.

There are also vital questions about whether mere issuing a book or taking a photocopy of a journal article attribute to use and hence, comes the need for a qualitative assessment of use. Perhaps professionals are afraid to look at these issues as the results of such assessment may force the authorities to examine critically the investments in a service institution like the library. Like Reenen's comment about false consumers, it seems that librarians fear self-assessment of library usage or to undergo a performance audit.

THE LIBRARIAN'S IDENTITY CRISIS

EDUCATION AND TRAINING

The students, faculty, curriculum and training methodology at the library schools have to be visibly improved to meet the challenges posed by electronic information and impatient, highly demanding users. There are also problems of infrastructure and a directionless attitude in the teaching and research sector often forgetting the interdisciplinary aspect of the subject. Working librarians have good exposure to new databases, their acquisition and use, pragmatic implementation of various routines, etc., which are not accessible to library schools. Thus apart from teaching faculty, expert practitioners in the discipline would also be involved in education programmes to bridge the gap between preaching and practice.

The existing courses must always look at the sweeping changes in the library workplace and adapt well to enable the students to face the challenges with confidence, giving ample opportunities for improving reasoning, communication skills, general awareness, and other characteristics identified for a multi-tasking service organisation. The age-old teacher-centric teaching has to be circumvented by student oriented and professional (job)-centric teaching.

JOB OPPORTUNITIES

Though the major employer, the government, is not recruiting many, more and more universities/institutions are offering library courses in the regular and distance modes. And this upheaval in quantity does not contribute in any way to the quality of these courses. For a prospective student/parent, the job advertisements provide an impression of plenty of jobs in the field, as library jobs at different levels in different institutions do not follow standard designations. But only when one finishes the course and looks for job openings, does the actual state of affairs come to light. Actually the increase in library-related jobs is merely additive, and not multiplicative, like computers, management or engineering, and should not show an exponential rise at any point of time.

CONTINUING EDUCATION

Since, the mode and rate at which information is generated, organised and used is witnessing sweeping changes in the perfectly wired information age, a continuously evolving discipline like LIS is meant to tackle the intricacies of information for societal development; thus it shall not be learned effectively and practiced perfectly by exposing students to a framed curriculum in formal education only. The discipline has changed drastically from being based totally on print sources; aware of the increasing richness of information in electronic forms and available over networks thus is leading to embracing vigourously other disciplines like computers, management, and information and communication technology.

It is imperative for the information practitioners to continuously monitor and augment their professional skills through continuing education (CE) to discharge their duties to users, employer and profession. The present initiatives on CE are generally being made by national institutions and suffer limitations such as: they are of short duration, generally infrequent, claiming comparatively high fees, working professionals finding it difficult to get sponsorship from their institutions, involve travelling to far off destinations hampering their regular work, etc.

CULTURES AND CONFLICTS FACED BY LIBRARIANS

Gone are the days of close-minded librarians and the quality of candidates entering the profession is continuously improving. As technology-intensive librarianship is gaining ground in the country, working librarians are getting much exposure to new technology tools for providing better information products and improved information services. Working librarians in at least the major academic and research institutions have better computer infrastructure and possess better expertise on the latest information products and services.

It is quite natural in the emerging print plus electronic hybrid library scenario that a library professional right from first job is expected to be conversant with the electronic apart from the manual means of information collection, processing, management and servicing. But there are also apprehensions about the level of technology appropriate to conducting well in the challenging and demanding academic and research setup.

A library professional must be distinct from a computer professional due to the very nature of their profession and the expected deliverables. But the acute emphasis on technology has created a situation that a professional can hide many of his/her professional ignorance by a little computer knowledge which is not going to be good either for the profession or for the libraries. Google cannot and will not be replacing libraries because both can co-exist with their diverse functionalities catching the attention of users at different occasions.

The professional nature of the librarian's job always motivates him or her to help the users unlike administrative staff in the institution who are always rule-based; sometimes this may lead to not so proper upkeep of administrative procedures and records, and in some cases cause unnecessary rivalry with the administrative staff. There are also personnel problems as the librarians fail to command a leadership role in many institutions thereby eclipsing their role in strategic planning.

Institutions attach prime importance to libraries but are they doing the same towards the personnel in their libraries? It is a strange case of all the virtues are of the system and the problems are due to the staff. Largely a service wing in many institutions, not enjoying the power, visibility, service conditions, and career prospects of the research and teaching staff, the status of library professionals in many of these institutions is not a morale booster, leaving many of them underperforming. It is not uncommon to see non-professionals heading many libraries, maybe just because they are senior teachers or good administrators or researchers and not because they are good as librarians.

There are also problems of the lack of a peer group in the profession resisting such attacks on the profession as many senior professionals have become self-centred, and professional associations compete for minor issues. The professional staff members working in many libraries in developing countries are totally engrossed in administrative and routine jobs related to library operation and administration. Many institutions do not demand their library professionals to pursue an offensive role. The users always need quick services and they never respond to any of the reasonable operational or managerial delays.

The real situation is that the libraries have very little control over their suppliers whereas their consumers have too much control over them. Users are not patient enough to interact constantly with the library staff to tune their profiles to improve the relevance of information services, maybe due to time constraints on their parts. Again by a rough assessment, it seems that less than 10 per cent of the users usually respond to SDI results and the remaining are either using it as it is or rejecting it straightaway. Out of those responding, only a few show their willingness to give feedback to modify their keywords to improve the utility of such services. Users may sometimes get so arrogant with the helpful nature of library staff and doubt it as their weakness.

CONCLUSION

Like building collection and providing services, improving access to information should be the guiding criteria for libraries in the electronic era. Apart from hosting external information, they should also evolve local digitisation ventures to give more visibility to internal information. We have to design a new set of parameters to judge operational efficiency and performance effectiveness of libraries. Traditional libraries boasted that they attracted a lot of users to stay inside their premises for comparatively longer duration whereas a modern librarian will be more concerned about carrying information to users' desktops.

No library, no matter how rich its budget allocation and collection may be, is in a position to satisfy all the information needs of its users. As a person well versed in the intricacies of the emerging information market, the librarian should be frank enough to admit that the information needs of all users are not met by the library alone. Collaboration with other libraries through consortia or networks increases the amount of resources available to users. Most academic and research libraries spend a lot of public money for information needs of a small percentage of the population and optimising that spending for the benefit of more number of users is the need of the hour. Library professionals have a major role in the emerging print plus digital hybrid information environment that is looming large in many academic and research libraries.

This role can be properly identified and refined only through constructive interaction of administrative heads of institutions, library professionals and professional associations. There is no doubt that we are passing through a severe phase and this is the right time to have a close introspective and critical look at collections developed, services offered and professional skills required in the light of complex user needs, hazy use patterns and the ever-increasing spread of Internet, electronic databases and digital libraries.

4

A Global Approach to Digital Library Evaluation

When an animal bred in captivity runs, flaps or slithers into the wilderness for the first time, scientists do not simply wave goodbye, wish it well and move on to the next project. Usually the animal is tracked and observed for a long time thereafter—the point of release is where the research really begins.

However, this has been less true for grant-funded digital library projects. Administrative and institutional barriers tend to confine evaluation to the funding period when the system is being designed, and when its uses and effects can only be guessed at.

In this short paper I will discuss a digital library project in environmental science where some of these evaluation issues arose, the value of eliciting narrative data from users, and some ways to take better advantage of existing but underused mechanisms for long-term evaluation of digital libraries.

Viewing information technologies and society as inextricably co-determined makes it necessary to gather data both on the design process and on how the finished systems are used by people—often in quite unexpected ways.

Iterative design and formative evaluation are ways to introduce user feedback into ongoing design, but while these strategies can serve as an effective translation layer between users, designers and builders, the focus is on how an evolving system *might* be used.

How it is *actually* used can be more accurately determined when the system is in the wild, when the designers and their formal evaluation instruments have gone away. Digital libraries are social entities. They tell stories about a culture, a science, a place or a time, through the items represented and organized in the collection, and in use, they help generate new stories as well.

Manovich has advanced the idea of database and narrative as two ends of same continuum; both structure information, but where a database aims for access, a narrative aims for psychological immersion in the story. From an institutional standpoint, digital libraries are rarely ends in themselves.

The social missions of the funding organizations—the stories they wish to tell— often drive the creation of digital libraries, but how well a finished system supports the mission can't be fully evaluated until the digital library has had some time to develop a user base.

This line of research began with a participant observation of the design of a digital library of environmental science collections. Funded by an Library Services and Technology Act (LSTA) grant, the project involved diverse designers, content, metadata and institutional participants.

As one of the participants in the environmental science digital library noted, "Part of the art of grant writing is interpreting vague language in a way that lets you do what you want to do," or in other words, making project proposals and achievements dovetail with the mission and goals of the funding agency.

These goals included outreach and evaluation, so a usability component was included in the grant proposal. My initial role in the project was to develop the instruments and conduct the evaluation.

Understandably, digital library designers tend to create evaluation instruments that demonstrate in a measurable way the work they've done, a tacit statement of the value produced for the grant funds received. For example, the design of the interface, the appropriateness of descriptive metadata, and user success at canned search tasks are classic evaluative measures.

However, in an analysis of the Perseus Digital Library (PDL), Marchionini writes: "Operational data are powerful components in a chain of inferences that address impact but the PDL evaluation illustrates the value of anecdotes and "stories" that illustrate new effects, *i.e.*, how DLs augment existing capabilities with new ones. These augmentations garner public support for a DL and should not be underestimated in assessing impact.

Integrating multiple views is more naturally done with narratives than summary statistics and integrating these forms of evidence can aid in assessing complex change." In the evaluation, statistical and demographic data were not hard to come by.

Observation, interviews, document analysis, narrative analysis and social network analysis were effective ways to construct as complete a picture as possible about the interactions of the designers. But the usability component needed to be completed at the same time as the digital library, in time for the results to be included in the final LSTA grant report (though the exact LSTA grant regulations vary by state, most LSTA grantees must submit a final grant report within 15-30 days of project completion).

Participants in the usability study were evaluating a still evolving system, and had to project potential uses into their responses to open-ended interview questions. By the time they might integrate the collections into their professional lives, and perhaps surprise themselves with unexpected dimensions of usefulness, the evaluation would be long over. This is certainly not to say that there is no such thing as continuing evaluation of grant-funded digital libraries.

But the mechanisms for long-term evaluation are usually little more than Web forms or e-mail links, not organic components of the digital library. In practice, designers are more concerned with present and future digital library projects than with continuing evaluation of those of the past.

Digital library researchers have an opportunity to conduct this longer-term research, to question and reveal the impacts of digital libraries as social entities, and to apply the resulting knowledge to future projects.

The good news is that in some situations, a mechanism for longer term evaluation already exists. For example, the State Library of Ohio's LSTA grant process makes use of a "year-after" evaluation form (http://winslo.state.oh.us/publib/lstayraft.html), which includes questions such as "Did the project produce any unexpected results?" and encourages narrative ("Please provide a success story of how your project has impacted someone's life or had a positive impact on the community.").

This is precisely the sort of openended data collection instrument that can reveal how a digital library is actually being used—but even this document is only the length of a one-page questionnaire. Subsequent research will attempt to evaluate the usefulness of this and other longer-term evaluation instruments, and how they might be expanded.

While longer-term evaluation should include quantitative data such as transaction logs and perhaps a list of external sites that link to collection content, evaluation instruments should also be open-ended, designed to encourage narrative expressions of unexpected use, the kind of data that reveal to funding agencies the real impact of their grants.

Iterative digital library design philosophies have always had at their core the sense that user input should feed back into ongoing system design. I propose here simply a wider iterative design circle, one that allows for more naturalistic data about longer-term use to be fed back into future systems.

In sum, lessons learned that will be explored in future research include an increased emphasis on:

- Long-term evaluation of digital libraries
- Narrative data; allowing users to tell stories
- Unexpected uses
- Evaluating social outcomes, not just the design process or product
- Linking findings more directly to the higherlevel goals of funding agencies

DIGITAL LIBRARY INFORMATION APPLIANCES

Although digital libraries are intended to support education and knowledge work, current digital library interfaces are narrowly focused on retrieval. Furthermore, they are designed for desktop computers with keyboards, mice, and high-speed network connections. Desktop computers fail to support many key aspects of knowledge work, including active reading, free form ink annotation, fluid movement among document activities, and physical mobility.

This chapter proposes portable computers specialized for knowledge work, or *digital library information appliances,* as a new platform for accessing digital libraries. We present a number of ways that knowledge work can be augmented and transformed by the use of such appliances.

These insights are based on our implementation of two research prototype systems: XLibris, an "active reading machine," and Tele- Web, a mobile World Wide Web browser.

Fig. XLibris Prototype in a Reader's lap.

The standard platform for accessing today's digital libraries is a desktop computer with a keyboard, a mouse, information retrieval software, and a network connection. Unfortunately, desktop computers are not suitable for many types of knowledge work.

Studies of people using electronic and paper documents show that desktop systems fail to support four important activities:

- Active reading
- Free form ink annotation
- Fluid movement among document activities
- Physical mobility

As a result of focusing on the desktop, today's interfaces for accessing digital libraries support retrieval in isolation, without addressing these broader work practices. We propose a new platform for accessing digital libraries: specialized portable computers designed for knowledge work, or *digital library information appliances.*

In this chapter, we draw on our experience designing and building two research prototype information appliances— the XLibris "active reading machine" and the TeleWeb mobile Web browser— to show how these devices can support a broad range of activities in the digital library.

READING AND DIGITAL LIBRARIES

The first and most fundamental document activity is reading. "Reading" encompasses a broad range of complex and poorly understood practices involving documents, including skimming, searching, browsing, speed-reading, surfing, reviewing, and rereading. Although we often take it for granted, reading can be hard work. We use the term *active reading* to distinguish this rich collection of activities from simply looking at words on a page.

Desktop computers do not support active reading. Once expected to create a paperless office, computers have instead produced ever-increasing quantities of paper documents. Dataquest predicts printers and copiers will generate over 1012 pages in the U.S. in 1997.

This statistic suggests that people do not use computers to read. The reason for this is obvious: paper supports extended, focused, deep reading practices better. Current research on digital libraries does not address a broad range of reading activities. Instead, as David Levy points out, digital libraries support shallower, more fragmented, and less concentrated reading.

The research focus in this field is on tools for search, selection, and distillation, tools that promote identification and extraction of information fragments. Because digital library interfaces do not support active reading, people search online and then print documents to read them. This "search and print" reality contrasts with the "search and read" ideal held by researchers.

Although a dual online/paper system is not *a priori* undesirable, we will show the many advantages of an online system that enables a variety of reading practices. The XLibris active reading machine supports a broad class of reading activities by employing a "paper document metaphor" (as opposed to the desktop metaphor) that imitates the physical experience of reading and marking on paper.

The paper document metaphor follows lessons learned from a number of studies comparing reading online to reading on paper, summarized below.

TANGIBILITY

Readers often move paper documents to avoid glare, to speed up handwriting, or to adjust their perspective of a text. In contrast, most computer displays are stationary while in use, so that readers must move themselves— their heads, their bodies, and their arms— rather than their display. XLibris supports paper document-like tangibility by running on tablet displays. Although XLibris has not been deployed for real use, people say that holding a page-sized display in their lap and being able to easily reposition it changes their online reading experience. The tangibility of paper documents also supports navigation. Turning paper pages seems easy and natural, and the weight and thickness of a paper document convey length and location.

In XLibris, pressure strips on the case of the device provide a tangible interface for page turning: pressing on one side of a sensor moves to the next or previous page, and holding down initiates riffling through pages. The harder you press, the faster you move. A quick animated transition indicates the direction of turning.

Beyond Paper: Supporting Active Reading with Free-form Digital Ink Annotations

Bill N. Schilit, Gene Golovchinsky, Morgan N. Price
FX Palo Alto Laboratory, Inc.
3400 Hillview Ave., Bldg. 4
Palo Alto, CA 94304
+1 650 813-7322
{schilit, gene, price}@pal.xerox.com

ABSTRACT

Reading frequently involves not just looking at words on a page, but also underlining, highlighting and commenting, either on the text or in a separate notebook. This combination of reading with critical thinking and learning is called *active reading* [1]. To explore the premise that computation can enhance active reading we have built the XLibris "active reading machine." XLibris uses a commercial high-resolution pen tablet display along with a paper-like user interface to support the key affordances of paper for active reading: the reader can hold a scanned image of a page in his lap and mark on it with digital ink. To go beyond paper, XLibris monitors the free-form ink annotations made while reading, and uses these to organize and to search for information. Readers can review, sort and filter clippings of their annotated text in a "Reader's Notebook." XLibris also searches for material related to the annotated text, and displays links to similar documents unobtrusively in the margin. XLibris demonstrates that computers can help active readers organize and find information while retaining many of the advantages of reading on paper.

Keywords

Paper-like user interface, reading online, affordances of paper, pen computing, dynamic hypertext, document metaphor, information retrieval

INTRODUCTION

Computers, once expected to create a paper-less office, have instead produced ever-increasing quantities of paper documents. Dataquest predicts that 1,344 billion pages will be generated by printers and copiers in the US in 1997 [13]. This statistic suggests that people are not using computers to read. Whereas paper is lightweight, inexpensive, and easy to annotate, interfaces for reading online typically involve clumsy interactions with bulky desktop monitors.

Although reading online presents a number of problems, we will show that integrating computation with reading also presents novel opportunities for improving the reading process. Thus there is a tension between the advantages provided by computation and the advantages provided by paper: the choice depends on the reader's goals. For reading a romance novel at the beach, low weight and portability are essential, and it is unlikely that computation could provide any real benefit. For other, more dynamic, types of reading, however, computation may be desirable.

Active reading is the combination of reading with critical thinking and learning, and is a fundamental part of education and knowledge work. Active reading involves not just reading *per se*, but also underlining, highlighting and commenting, either on the text or in a separate notebook [1]. Readers use these marks to organize information for later review and retrieval. In addition, active reading often requires readers to move from one text to another to satisfy their information needs.

We have built an "active reading machine," XLibris, to explore the premise that computation can enhance active reading. XLibris has three major features: the paper document metaphor, a "Reader's Notebook" for organizing annotated documents, and margin links for serendipitous discovery of related material.

XLibris emulates the physical experience of reading a document on paper. The metaphor of a paper document pervades the design: the hardware approximates the form factor of a stack of paper, and the software supports a paper-like interface. Readers hold a lightweight pen tablet that displays one page of a scanned or printed document at a time. As on paper, readers can use a pen to mark anywhere on the page.

To go beyond paper, XLibris monitors free-form ink annotations that readers make as part of their existing reading practice. These annotations, replete with meaning to the reader, can also be meaningful to the system. The system can use the extent of the annotations to determine

Finally, "location guides" of varying thickness drawn in the top cor- ners of each page provide feedback about the length of the document and the reader's current location.

Page Orientation and Fixed Layout

Paper documents are laid out on fixed-size pages. The page layout often communicates the type of the document (*e.g.*, business letter versus technical article) and where to find important information (*e.g.*, a return address). The fixed layout also supports spatial memory and helps readers find old information. In these and other ways, paper pages give readers an excellent "sense of the document." This sense of the document is often lost online.

Most CRT monitors cannot display a full page of text legibly, leading to awkward scrolling and zooming. Word processors and Web browsers commonly re-flow the text on a "page." And hypertext versions of paper documents can lead to disorientation and a sense of being lost. XLibris respects pages by displaying the image of a single page at a time.

Because the LCD panels we use are designed for landscape viewing, XLibris rotates the image 90º to approximate the portrait orientation of a typical printed page. XLibris stores the image of each page and the underlying text; this "image + text" file format is compatible with printed and with scanned documents.

Multiple Displays

People often work with multiple pieces of paper simultaneously, either with several pages from one document or with several documents. Most of today's computers provide multiple virtual displays through use of a windowing system. Unfortunately, the effort of managing window layout and switching among windows can interfere with reading.

Therefore XLibris displays a single page image and does not support windows. Since limiting the digital library information appliance to a single page image is problematic, we have considered a number of ways to address the need for collateral displays. Presenting two full-page images side by side, as in Book Emulator, makes text unreadable on current tablet displays, but may be feasible as LCD technology evolves. A form factor with multiple physical displays is another approach.

(Bush's vision of a Memex desk included multiple displays). In our case, to maintain mobility, a book (instead of a tablet or desk) with two opposable LCD panels may be appropriate. Weiser presents an enticing vision of ubiquitous computing with devices so cheap they can be scattered and used as paper. In the near term, however, a small number of pen computers in conjunction with nearby desktop displays or even paper may provide the most practical solution to the problem of collateral document work. In summary, XLibris employs tangibility, page orientation, and fixed layout to provide an online reading experience comparable, in many ways, to reading from paper.

FREE FORM INK ANNOTATION

"Until we provide support for smooth integration of annotation with reading, it is likely that people will continue to annotate paper materials, even as they read materials in a digital library." – Cathy Marshall The second key document activity is annotation.

Knowledge work involves reading combined with categorizing, speculating, remembering, judging, or, more broadly, critical thinking.

This active reading process is facilitated by underlining, highlighting and making notes on the text or in a separate notebook. Marking on paper helps readers "make the text their own" and is a common practice associated with deep understanding of written information. In a nutshell, readers write.

Unfortunately, annotation online is quite different from its paper-based cousin. Interfaces for annotating often involve selecting a command, pointing with a mouse, and typing on a keyboard. They generally require much more effort than scribbling with a pen.

Text annotations are not as visually distinct as ink marks, and online annotations often cause changes in the layout of the document.

We believe that the ability to make unstructured, free-form, idiosyncratic ink marks is a crucial feature of any interface to digital libraries.

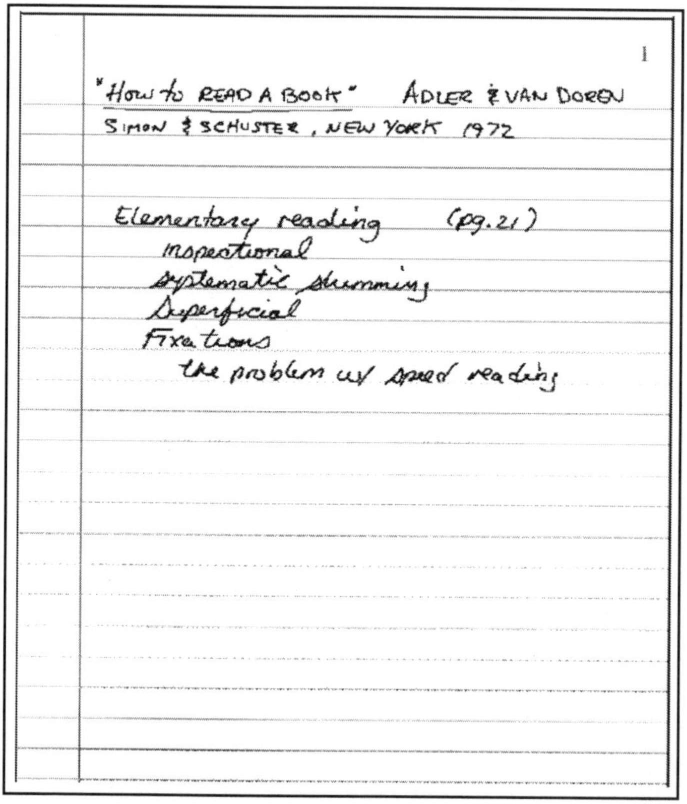

Fig. A Notebook page from XLibris.

Although such marks may not have explicit meaning to the computer, they have rich semantic meaning, supporting visual and episodic memory.

An essential aspect of ink on paper is its lack of modality: users can write anything they want, anywhere on the page.

In XLibris, we followed this principle by letting users scribble notes, draw figures, highlight, or annotate text, all without switching modes or applications. Readers highlight and mark-up document page images as they read or flip to a blank page in a lined notebook for more space. XLibris provides several colours of ink, several highlighter pens, and a stroke-based eraser.

FLUID MOVEMENT AMONG DOCUMENT ACTIVITIES

The third key aspect of knowledge work is fluid movement among different styles of reading and different document activities. As an example, consider the process of "information triage" where an analyst skims through a pile of search results and reduces them to a manageable set.

The current practice is to fire off a query to a search engine, retrieve the 100 top-ranked documents, print them out, mark them up with highlighters, and put them into piles. Analysts then read the most relevant passages to answer the original question. Consider an alternative scenario where the analyst owns a digital library information appliance.

After conducting a search, the analyst skims the documents online. The appliance enhances skimming by emphasizing important material. As on paper, the analyst marks up important information as it is found. Instead of reviewing the collected information by thumbing through piles of paper, the analyst views a concise collection of his or her text annotations.

If any of the annotated material is worth reading in greater depth, the analyst can do so comfortably online. If the analyst needs more information, the text that has already been highlighted can be used to generate the next query. At a high level, this scenario demonstrates fluid movement among document activities. The analyst quickly moves among searching, skimming, annotating, reviewing, and deep reading.

There is no waiting for a printer. Because skimming and deep reading are tightly integrated with retrieval, analysts can determine if the information they are collecting is useful before they invest much effort. This scenario also demonstrates how computation can enhance skimming, reviewing, and searching. Because the interface is based on a paper document metaphor, the reading and annotation activities remain much the same as on paper. In our design, the "computer" remains in the background and, when requested, rises to the surface to assist the reader with the tasks of skimming, reviewing, and searching. Below we describe how XLibris supports and augments these three activities.

Skimming Mode

Skimming is one way readers gain a quick impression of a text. When skimming, the reader's eyes typically search for and alight on key words or sentences and take in short passages before moving on. Sometimes the reader becomes engaged and shifts into deep reading, or is distracted and moves into quicker skimming or into riffling.

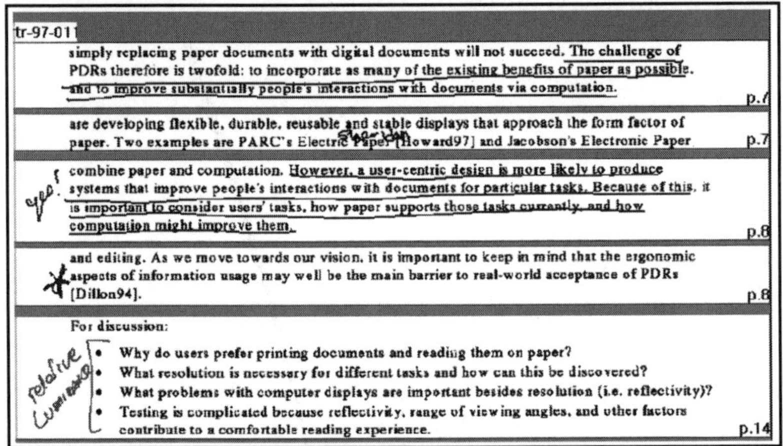

Fig. The Reader's Notebook shows annotated clippings of documents laid end-to-end. Clippings are labeled with document title and page number and are linked to the corresponding pages.

XLibris' "skimming mode" highlights phrases and sentences that are characteristic of the document being skimmed. We call out key phrases because they can be read at a glance and tend to reflect the topic of the nearby text.

This assists with the activity of scanning the text for relevant portions to read. The *Wall Street Journal* and *People Magazine* use a similar technique of boldfacing company names and Hollywood celebrities' name to help readers find information. We also highlight summary sentences to support a speedreading– like activity. Skimming mode uses a commercial text summarizer to identify summary sentences that are emphasized. Skimming through a document of highlighted summary sentences provides a narrative overview that is not available by just reading key phrases.

Both of these highlighting techniques permit a smooth transition from skimming to deep reading: key terms and sentences can help readers decide whether a passage is worth reading and are likely to be appropriate places to transition to deep reading. Skimming mode uses shades from gray to black to indicate term importance. Meaningful terms are identified by heuristics that select noun phrases.

The shade for each term is then based on a statistical information retrieval measure: terms that occur frequently in the document but occur rarely in other documents are colored black, while terms common to many documents are colored light gray. For example, the term "digital library information appliance" would be colored black when it appears in this document. Skimming is a common practice: a study of college students' reading habits reported that skimming occupied 32 per cent of their reading time, and that "86 per cent of the descriptions of skimming strategies mentioned a selection process based on key words and/or particular sentences and paragraphs in certain text locations". Although our design requires empirical evaluation to confirm its utility, from our experiences thus far, we are optimistic that computers can improve the skimming activity and that augmented skimming is a useful function for a digital library information appliance.

Reviewing the Reader's Notebook

Reviewing paper documents is facilitated by the marks made during reading: marks not only record information but are also used to organize it for later review. There are three common venues for marking: annotating on the page, taking notes in a notebook, and writing on loose-leaf paper. Annotations on the page highlight key information but tend to be lost in piles of paper. Notebooks are compact and can be reviewed quickly, but taking notes can be tedious and error-prone.

Unbound notes can be reorganized flexibly, but require even more effort by the note taker. XLibris' Reader's Notebook combines the best features of annotating directly on the page, of taking notes in a separate notebook, and of organizing index cards. As with paper documents, readers mark on the page in the context of the document, yet without the laborious and imprecise step of copying.

As with a bound notebook, readers can review concise annotations by time. Finally, as with note cards, flexible filtering and sorting of the view allow readers to reorganize their information as needs change. The Reader's Notebook extracts "clippings" of annotated text and lays them end to end in a separate, multipage view.

Each clipping is linked to the corresponding annotated page, so readers can move fluidly between notes and documents. Each clipping includes some surrounding text, and is labeled with document title and page number to help readers understand the meaning of the marks. In designing clippings, we had to decide how much of the document should be shown for each annotation.

Starting with the bounding rectangle of each ink stroke, we expand it horizontally to the width of the page and vertically to include complete words. Snippets that overlap are merged together resulting in reasonably sized clippings of annotated text.

The Reader's Notebook can display, sort, and filter clippings from one document or from all documents. By default, clippings are sorted by document page number, which is analogous to rummaging through a pile of paper, but should be faster because readers do not see the less important (*i.e.*, un-annotated) information. Clippings can also be sorted by time so that new information appears at the end, as in a paper notebook.

Finally, readers can filter the clippings by ink colour to search for different kinds of marks or to group related items together. Many readers already use different pens to mark different types of information. For example, some lawyers highlight "pro" information in green and "con" information in red.

Finding Information Related to Readers' Annotations

Readers often search for related material and move from one text to another. For example, an ecology student studying the effects of acid rain in the Appalachian Mountains decides to search the Internet for information on the economy of West Virginia. A doctor reading up on a drug she has never prescribed decides to follow a reference to a study of its side effects.

Unfortunately, in both online and offline situations, finding related materials and reading are not well integrated. Typical information retrieval interfaces force users to stop reading, to identify related documents, and then to print them.

References found in paper documents are even more timeconsuming to track down. Although hypertext was designed to address some of these problems, authors cannot anticipate the information needs of all readers. Ironically, despite the fact that readers' interests may change rapidly, interfaces for moving from reading to finding and back to reading again are time consuming and disruptive.

Clearly this is another example where fluid movement across document activities is desirable. XLibris facilitates fluid transitions among reading, searching and browsing by creating a dynamic hypertext from readers' marks.

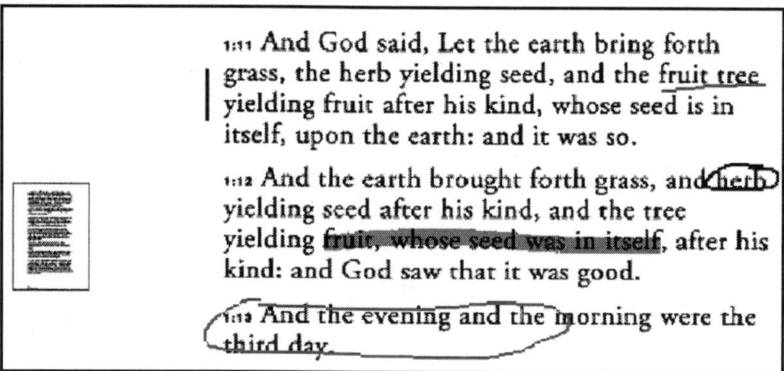

Fig. Examples of Highlighting, Underlining, Circling, and margin Annotations. Each Annotation Generates a Query. If a good match is found, XLibris adds a margin link (Rectangle on the left) that shows the thumbnail of the Destination page.

The system observes readers' annotations and the text of the underlying document and generates hypertext links (margin links) to related documents: no additional effort from readers or authors is required. Because XLibris suggests links of interest to particular readers at particular times— based on the passages they are marking— people can discover useful information *serendipitously*. This type of serendipitous retrieval is a benefit of paper libraries: as people walk to the shelf for a particular book, walls of related books surround them, making it possible to find interesting material accidentally. Although serendipity in the library is often a rewarding experience, it is generally lacking in online systems. XLibris provides two user interfaces that integrate reading, searching, browsing, and serendipity. These are described below.

MARGIN LINKS

Margin links provide serendipitous access to related documents *during* the active reading process. As readers mark up passages, the system finds related documents and presents links unobtrusively in the margin; our intent is to provide a modeless link suggestion mechanism. Because margin links persist, readers can follow links at their leisure.

We use thumbnail images of the target page as anchors. The reader taps on an anchor to move to that page. For the most part, link creation does not disrupt the reading process since the reader is free to disregard the suggestion and to continue reading. In the current design, however, margin links intrude on the reading process more than we would like. One problem is that XLibris computes a separate query for each stroke (although strokes often do not result in margin links because of a similarity threshold). We have begun to address this by adding a button to turn links off and by designing ways to manage the frequency with which margin links appear.

FURTHER READING LISTS

When readers reach the end of a document, they often want to know more. The document may not emphasize the topic they are most interested in, or it may spark an interest in a new topic without providing enough depth or detail. Sometimes this need is addressed.

Further Reading

LEGALLY SPEAKING: REGULATION OF TECHNOLOGIES TO PROTECT COPYRIGHTED WORKS. Pamela Samuelson in *Communications of the ACM*, Vol. 39, No. 7, pages 17–22; July 1996.

FORUM ON TECHNOLOGY-BASED INTELLECTUAL PROPERTY MANAGEMENT: ELECTRONIC COMMERCE FOR CONTENT. Edited by Brian Kahin and Kate Arms. Special issue of the *Interactive Multimedia News*, Vol. 2; August 1996.

LETTING LOOSE THE LIGHT: IGNITING COMMERCE IN ELECTRONIC PUBLICATION. Mark Stefik in *Internet Dreams: Archetypes, Myths, and Metaphors*. Edited by Mark Stefik. MIT Press, 1996.

SCIENTIFIC AMERICAN March 1997 81

Fig. A Further Reading list from *Scientific American*

For example, articles in *Scientific American* typically describe an area of research at a high level, without providing much technical detail. To help readers go into more depth, the editors create a further reading list at the end of each article.

The *Scientific American* example illustrates the limitations of authored reading lists. The article describes a technological vision for protecting digital copyrights. Consider a reader with a narrower interest, such as "how digital copyright affects librarians." The reference to a six-page article on digital copyright law may help track down this information, but the reference is unlikely to answer the question directly. Furthermore, by the time the reader scans the further reading list, more appropriate articles may have been written. XLibris augments this traditional editorial practice by automatically generating further reading lists for each document.

Unlike static references, these lists reflect the interests of a specific reader at a specific point in time. As with margin links, the reader's interests are inferred from annotations, and no additional intervention from the reader is required.

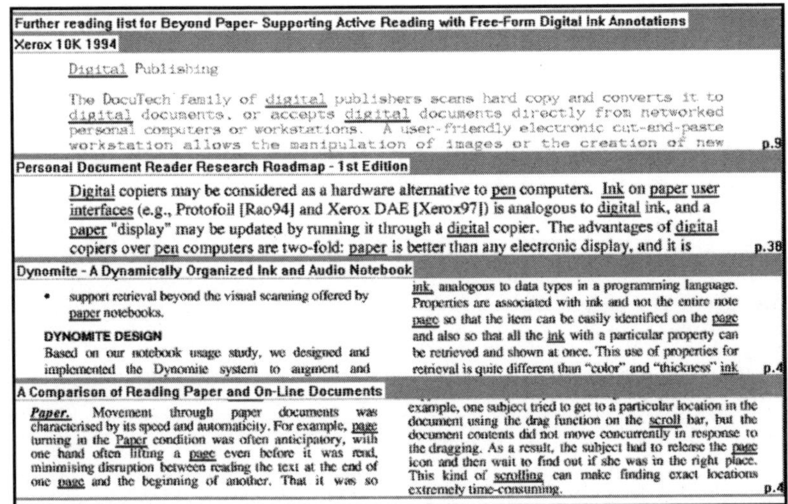
Further reading list for Beyond Paper- Supporting Active Reading with Free-Form Digital Ink Annotations

Xerox 10K 1994

Digital Publishing

The DocuTech family of digital publishers scans hard copy and converts it to digital documents, or accepts digital documents directly from networked personal computers or workstations. A user-friendly electronic cut-and-paste workstation allows the manipulation of images or the creation of new p.9

Personal Document Reader Research Roadmap - 1st Edition

Digital copiers may be considered as a hardware alternative to pen computers. Ink on paper user interfaces (e.g., Protofoil [Rao94] and Xerox DAE [Xerox97]) is analogous to digital ink, and a paper "display" may be updated by running it through a digital copier. The advantages of digital copiers over pen computers are two-fold: paper is better than any electronic display, and it is p.38

Dynomite - A Dynamically Organized Ink and Audio Notebook

- support retrieval beyond the visual scanning offered by paper notebooks.

DYNOMITE DESIGN

Based on our notebook usage study, we designed and implemented the Dynomite system to augment and ink, analogous to data types in a programming language. Properties are associated with ink and not the entire note page so that the item can be easily identified on the page and also so that all the ink with a particular property can be retrieved and shown at once. This use of properties for retrieval is quite different than "color" and "thickness" ink p.4

A Comparison of Reading Paper and On-Line Documents

Paper. Movement through paper documents was characterised by its speed and automaticity. For example, page turning in the Paper condition was often anticipatory, with one hand often lifting a page even before it was read, minimising disruption between reading the text at the end of one page and the beginning of another. That it was so example, one subject tried to get to a particular location in the document using the drag function on the scroll bar, but the document contents did not move concurrently in response to the dragging. As a result, the subject had to release the page icon and then wait to find out if she was in the right place. This kind of scrolling can make finding exact locations extremely time-consuming. p.4

Fig. A Further Reading list in XLibris. Each related Document is Presented as a Clipping of the most Relevant Sentence with key Phrases Underlined.

Further reading lists are presented as a separate set of pages, or *view*, associated with each document. Readers can access this view at any time, whether or not they have annotated the current document.

Of course, the more annotations the user has made, the more focused the resulting list is on the reader's interest as opposed to the document as a whole. Visually, the further reading list looks like a Reader's Notebook of annotations except that each clipping is a segment of a related document obtained from a search engine.

These clippings, with matching terms underlined, help readers understand the destination of the link and also make the target passage more recognizable if they choose to follow the link.

Query-mediated Links

Both margin links and further reading lists use a technique called *query-mediated links*. Query-mediated links derive a query from a user's interaction with a document and use that query to identify related documents. Golovchinsky has shown that query-mediated links based on explicitly selected words and passages are effective in supporting information exploration tasks.

XLibris computes margin links from the words, phrases and passages that are implicitly selected by the reader's marks. (We do not expect readers to make marks for querying explicitly, but rather as part of their existing annotation practice.)

Marks are converted into text selections, which are then expressed as full-text queries that yield a best-matching passage. The system adds a margin link to the best match if its similarity value (or belief score) is above a threshold. For further reading lists, each annotation is interpreted as a text selection and is transformed into a list of word scores.

The scores for each word are then summed across all annotations. If several annotations select the same instance of a word, then the maximum score for that instance is used.

The words along with their scores are used to generate a query. If not many words have been included, then terms that are most characteristic of the document can be added.

This padding reduces the chance that a query based on a small number of annotations will return documents that are entirely unrelated.

Ink Annotations as Queries

XLibris recognizes several distinct ink patterns from which queries are computed. These include underlined words, highlighted words, circled words, circled passages, and margin annotations. We emphasize that there is no "vocabulary of marks" that readers must learn; rather, our heuristics are based on general annotation practices. Each type of annotation results in a slightly different query for the search engine. Marks that select specific words translate into queries that retrieve other instances of the same term. Marks that select longer passages generate queries that search for similar passages.

PHYSICAL MOBILITY

The fourth and final document activity supported by digital library information appliances is mobility. Until now we have discussed reading in XLibris; in this section we describe mobile information access in TeleWeb. Desktop access to digital libraries is not adequate for mobile workers.

A doctor making hospital rounds has no desktop with her to access a digital library. This could have grim repercussions: a recent study concluded that patients for whom prompt MEDLINE searches were conducted have significantly lower costs and shorter hospital stays. Mobile work is not limited to physicians and traveling salespeople; even office workers often work with documents away from their desks. For these people, portable information appliances can provide access to digital libraries anywhere, anytime. Unfortunately, it is not possible to give mobile people the same network access that they would have in their office. Compared to wired desktop networks, wireless networks are slow, expensive (with different billing schemes), and only intermittently available. As workers move from place to place, they are likely to experience three levels of connectivity: high quality connectivity from an office network, lower quality connectivity from a wireless network, and no connectivity at all when disconnected. How can people use digital library appliances to access distributed information sources across this range of operating conditions? Aside from the variable networking conditions, there are two other issues that affect mobile access to digital libraries.

First, downloading a document over a wireless network can be very expensive, and current interfaces for search engines and Web browsers do not help people manage these costs.

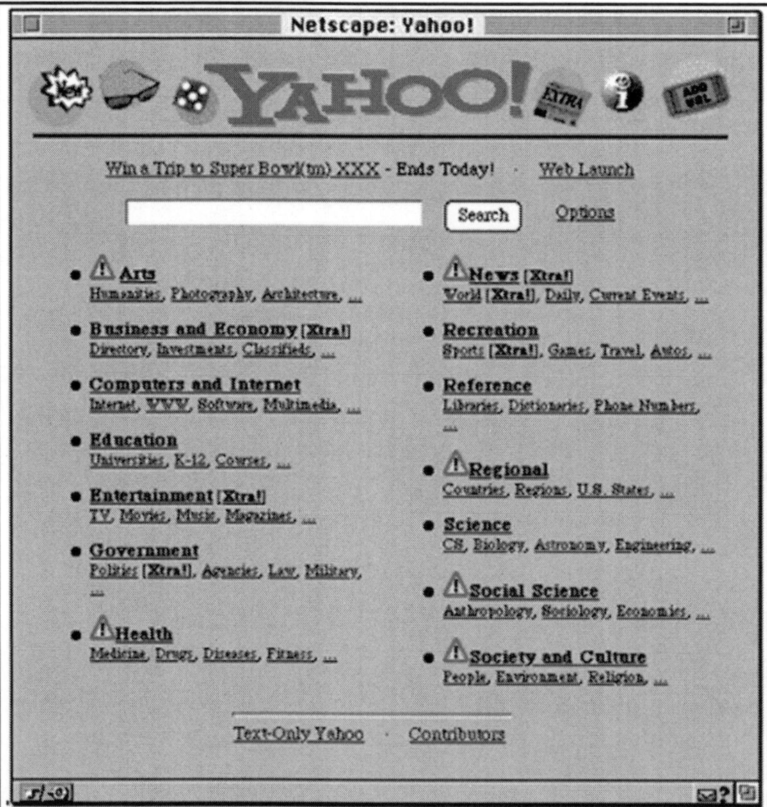

Fig. A Document Annotated with road sign icons to show Hypertext anchors Absent from the cache. *Networking not ubiquitous*

Second, user interaction is punctuated by surprises: an information request may return right away (when data is locally stored), take a while (when data is remote), or take forever (when the network is down). The TeleWeb mobile Web browser was designed and built to explore these three issues. TeleWeb runs on a laptop computer with multiple communication channels: it may be docked to an office Ethernet, used from home over a telephone line, used while traveling over a wireless network such as a cell phone, or operated while not connected to a network. The lessons learned from TeleWeb apply not only to the Web but also to digital libraries.

In the design of TeleWeb, we assumed that at least some of the time users would be disconnected but would still want to browse the Web. Some mobile networks are so limited in bandwidth compared to office networks that users may feel like they are disconnected. How can people browse the Web when disconnected? TeleWeb uses "caching for availability," the standard solution for this problem. This means that the system loads documents into a local cache when fully connected.

Later, if the user needs the document while the network is not available, the locally cached copy is returned. Caching for availability only works if the system knows the user's information needs ahead of time. The system can use past history to predict future needs. In addition, the user can tell the system what documents belong in the cache; unfortunately, in practice people find it difficult to articulate which documents they need. Furthermore, both techniques share the drawback that information needs often change in unpredictable ways. Overall, caching for availability often works, but is frustrating when it does not.

An alternative solution is to replace synchronous interaction (a user request followed immediately by a response from the network) with asynchronous interaction. For example, when the user requests a document not in the cache, TeleWeb asks the user if the system should download it later. If so, Tele- Web downloads the information the next time the user connects and adds the document to a "to read" list that the user can browse. This interaction style is analogous to sending a request for a book from an out of state library, and eventually receiving it in the mail. There are other reasons to postpone downloading a document. For example, if a user is connected over a cellular telephone, downloading a large document is going to be expensive, and can tie up the network connection for hours. Given the choice, the user might be happy to download this document overnight or upon returning to the office. There is a tradeoff here between how urgently people need information and how much they are willing to pay for it in time and money.

With a mobile information appliance, users should be able to decide how much they are willing to pay for each document and how quickly they need that document. With this principle in mind, TeleWeb includes a budget monitor that sits between the user and the network. If a request is made for a document that is not in the cache and downloading the document will break the user's budget, then TeleWeb presents a "conditional download" form instead of the document. Users can override their budget to fetch the document immediately, or they can request that the document be fetched at a later time.

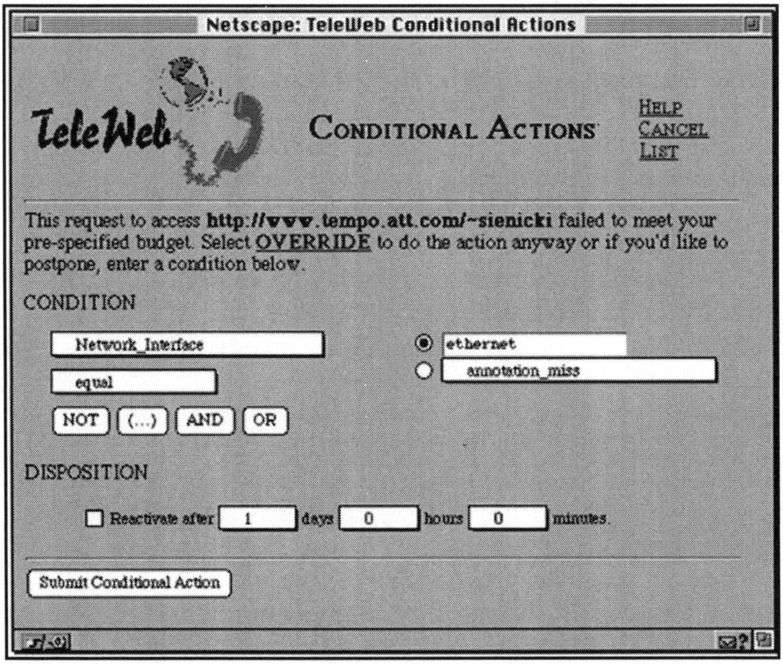

Fig. Creating a Conditional Download to fetch documents when Reconnected. *No feedback on cost*

Unpredictable Systems are Frustrating

The third problem of mobile appliances is unpredictable behaviour. Those using computer networks already know this problem: sometimes they hit a key and nothing happens. In wireless computing, this experience is magnified many-fold. TeleWeb's solution is to show the user what is going on inside the cache and network manager. Specifically, Tele- Web labels links that will be slow to download with a "road work" icon.

If there is no road sign, then either the link destination is cached, or a high-speed connection to the information superhighway is available. This simple change— essentially exposing the state of the system— makes mobile Web browsing much more predictable. This contrasts with the traditional approach of trying to simplify the user's view of the system by concealing the state of the network.

THE FUTURE

The development of tomorrow's digital library information appliances is an iterative process. Our current cycle, however, is not complete until we evaluate the ideas presented in this chapter. Towards this end, we have begun a series of laboratory user interface experiments and are in the planning stage for a real-world deployment. One experiment suggests that free-form ink marks made while reading are better for query formulation than traditional relevance feedback.

People who have tried XLibris agree that our approach of taking a work practice and augmenting it— rather than redefining it— makes the system immediately accessible. Information *appliances* must be accessible. The digital library community must decide whether digital libraries should, as we propose, support users throughout the process of turning information into knowledge.

If so, there are many issues that must be addressed.

One reviewer of this chapter asked: "Where is the digital library?" We purposely avoided describing protocols, services, and architectures because we believe infrastructure should *support* the vision of working with a digital library information appliance, not *define* it.

The next step is to understand how users of digital library information appliances should interact with external repositories. For example, should users pay authors to cache documents on their devices, even when they do not read them? How should users search repositories that are not always accessible?

How should searches be distributed between local and remote databases? These and other issues require further investigation. We have shown how information appliances based on the paper document metaphor can support active reading. Because these systems allow people to work on digital documents much as they would on paper, this provides an alternative to the standard "search and print" model of digital libraries.

Furthermore, by integrating a wide variety of document activities, and by allowing fluid movement among them, disruptive transitions between paper and digital media can be eliminated.

The combination of the paper-like and the digital allows us to augment these activities without redefining them. Finally, the mobility of a digital library information appliance supports work away from the desk.

With all these benefits, digital library information appliances can create a rich, universally accessible, digital library experience that improves the way we work. Clearly there is an exciting future for digital library information appliances in the digital library.

5

Building and Sustaining Digital Collections: Models for Libraries

The starting point for a study of economic models of the digital library such as this must be an understanding of the meaning of the term 'digital library'. Numerous definitions of the term have been proposed. They vary considerably with regard to their proximity to the concept of a traditional library. The latter classifies, catalogues, and provides access to quality-controlled information resources. It also offers related services and tends to restrict access to a well-defined user group.

The term digital library is used less precisely and may refer to anything from a limited list of hotlinks to the entire content of the Internet. The only common factor in these definitions is the idea of digitisation.

A study of economic models of the digital library requires a definition. Although the UK Electronic Libraries Programme (eLib) and the US Digital Libraries Programme have done a great deal to progress the concept of digital library and, latterly, the hybrid library, a clear and universal concept is still lacking. Before an economic model of a digital library could be tested, not only would a clear definition be required but considerable progress should have been made towards development and implementation. Such progress has been made with regard to specific digital library resources and services. Thus, with a view to exploring economic models of the digital library in a systematic and useful manner this study focuses on models of specific digital library resources and services. It takes as a starting point the different areas of the eLib programme.

This chapter will review and compare economic models of the academic digital library. Until now, empirical testing of economic models of digital libraries has been limited. Economic issues tend to be tested after solutions have been found to the more pressing technical, cultural and legal issues because no library manager or user would consider paying for a service that had not been shown to be technically sound, legal and useful to its target audience. The pace of development of different elements of the digital library has varied over the last two decades. This document will include models of aspects of the academic digital library that are sufficiently developed to be modelled. As electronic alternatives to traditional library services are developed, shifts occur in the roles and activities undertaken by different stakeholder in the academic information delivery chain.

Consequently, there have been sometimes unanticipated changes in the apportionment of costs and benefits to those stakeholders. Many roles are still fluid and change will continue until effective models are established.

There will be no attempt here to predict the future. This report evaluates and compares only models that have been proposed or tested. A useful economic model of the digital library must accurately represent all stakeholders in the academic information delivery chain, their relationships to the supply and delivery of digital resources, and the associated costs and benefits. The principal stakeholders involved in digital libraries are:

- Academics as authors; · academics as editors and referees;
- End users (inc. academics as researchers, students, and clinical, professional and industrial users of electronic academic information);
- Academics as teachers and recommenders of texts;
- HE librarians;
- HE computing support departments;
- Publishers of both primary and secondary literature (commercial, not for profit, University presses, etc.) and other electronic content suppliers (such as museums);
- Booksellers;
- Funding bodies;
- Subscription agents;
- National libraries;
- Document suppliers such as the British Library Document Supply Centre (BLDSC);
- Reproduction rights organisations;
- Intermediaries such as the National Electronic Site Licence Initiative (NESLI) and Higher Education Resources ONdemand (HERON);
- Internet service providers and other aggregators and distributors (including companies such as CatchWord and Ingenta which provide Internet publishing for publishers);
- The Higher Education Digitisation Service (HEDS).

These stakeholders are both individuals and organisations of both present and future generations. Some groups have a more direct stake than others.

Arguably, the most important are academics as authors; academics as users of scholarly information; academics as teachers; HE libraries and librarians; publishers; and information brokers (including subscription agents and document supply agencies).

Economics of Digital Library Services

When considering the economics of digital libraries it can be tempting to focus on financial factors that are directly related to digital library services, for example the price of resources and infrastructure. It is important, however, to be aware of other economic factors.

These include the cost of downloading bandwidth-hungry images and time spent filtering information in an environment where the signal-to-noise ratio is minuscule. While the authors acknowledge the importance of these factors it was beyond the scope of this project to determine their economic impact.

Electronic Journals and Electronic Individual Article Supply

The Serials Crisis

Much of the incentive for the development of electronic journals and electronic individual article supply (eIAS) services has arisen from the financial pressure on libraries caused by:

- Budget restrictions;
- An explosion in scholarly information;
- The fact that, over the last two decades, journal prices have consistently increased well above the general rate of inflation.

Librarians have become increasingly critical of publishers, focusing on journal subscription prices as the significant factor in the serials crisis. It may be argued that this single contributing factor is over emphasised in discussion of the serials crisis. The problems faced by academic libraries as a result of budget restrictions is significant.

The explosion in scholarly information is not only a key factor but one driven from within HE. However, library budget cuts are one element of a larger problem facing the HE sector which cannot be addressed within the scope of this study.

Furthermore, attempts to address the problems associated with the scholarly information explosion tend to focus more on alternative and cheaper formats for publication than on reducing the quantity of published research output. Librarians continue to focus on journal subscription prices and they appear to have legitimate cause for complaint.

There is evidence that the market for commercial journals is anti-competitive and at the very least, does not show much price elasticity. Furthermore, rationalisation, in the form of mergers, has occurred and although users may expect this trend to drive prices down, it has resulted instead in significant price rises.

Publication Costs

The advent of electronic publishing has been hailed by some as an opportunity to overcome these problems. It is argued that electronic publication is much cheaper than publication of hard copy. Proponents of this argument maintain that the cost to print and distribute a journal represents a significant proportion of the total publication cost.

Content is received and refereed free of charge and typically, the author assigns copyright to the publisher who is then free to package the material in any appropriate format and distribute it for a fee.

In an electronic environment, the cost of distributing content is negligible and thus, the total publication cost for an electronic journal should be significantly lower than it is for a print journal. Publishers, among others, argue that fixed costs (or first-copy costs) represent at least 70 per cent of journal production costs and thus that a change in delivery medium could save at most 30 per cent of total costs.

Furthermore, libraries expect publishers to supply electronic journals in multiple formats and end users expect additional functionality from electronic journals, for example multimedia elements, hot links to references, links from abstracting and indexing services or from OPACs to full text.

Clearly, to succeed, any move to replace print journals with electronic journals must be supported by end users and those users will not invest time and effort in learning to use electronic journals unless there appears to be clear advantage in doing so; added functionality, or speed of delivery are examples. However, additional features require time and personnel with expensive skills which adds to production costs.

It is argued that this makes electronic journals at least as expensive to produce as print. A publisher distributing an electronic journal for a fee must also meet the additional cost of controlling access. This is likely to be small if a well-established system such as ATHENS is used (http://www.athens.ac.uk). ATHENS is a JISC-supported service which provides a single password to HE users for accessing new datasets and services within the UK HE community and manages password accounts for the service suppliers. However, although ATHENS is clearly valuable to the HE community, its use may not be consistent with a publisher's commitment to supply statistics on usage to libraries. Another consideration is that libraries consider it important, having paid for a subscription to a journal, that the volume is still available to their users even if they cancel the subscription at a later date. A publisher can fulfil this requirement by supplying the basic journal content on a portable medium such as a CDROM or by granting permission to the library to create and/or archive a digital copy.

If a publisher itself were to guarantee online access in perpetuity it must migrate such content to new technologies when current technologies become obsolete. These additional costs make it less likely that electronic journals will be cheaper to produce than print journals. To date, publishers have found electronic publishing to be even more expensive than anticipated (Albert Prior, personal communication, 8 February 1999).

The Relationship Between Cost and Price

On balance, it seems that the additional costs associated with publishing a new valueadded product outweigh the costs of reproduction and distribution that are saved. Nevertheless, the argument that journals are overpriced remains valid.

It is important that journals are priced at a level sufficient to recover costs. In a print environment this has never been a problem. On the contrary, commercial journal publishers make large profits, and are sometimes more profitable than companies like Microsoft. Correlation between cost and price is not strong.

As an example, Odlyzko cites the 'three most prestigious maths journals' which are published by a commercial publisher, a university and a scholarly society respectively. Prices vary by a factor of seven, suggesting that first-copy costs are not the primary factor determining price.

Journals are priced according to what the market will bear and, until recently, the market has been relatively inelastic; academic journals are considered to be 'must have' items and one cannot easily be substituted for another should the latter become too expensive. Thus, profit margins in print commercial academic journal publishing generally fall within the range 40–60 per cent.

When compared with, for example, school text publishing at approximately 12–15 per cent, database publishing at approximately 18–20 per cent, or fiction publishing at approximately 5 per cent, it is clear that commercial publishers of print journals have continued to extract large profits despite the financial pressures facing libraries.

There is a clear need for academic libraries to demonstrate to publishers that the demand for scholarly journals is not inelastic. However, while there are no alternatives to the 'must have' material offered by publishers it is very difficult for libraries to do so.

Non-commercial Electronic Journal Publication in Higher Education

As a solution to the serials crisis various stakeholders within the HE sector have proposed that academics bypass commercial companies and publish electronic journals themselves.

There has also been an initiative in the US called the Scholarly Publishing and Academic Resources Coalition (SPARC) which aims to facilitate origination and publication of affordable journals which compete with expensive commercial journals.

SPARC will support sympathetic publishers by guaranteeing a market for their journals. Alternative journal publication models such as these often focus on cost savings gained by:

- Automating the editorial function;
- Dispensing with desk editorial work such as marking up and proof reading; and of course,
- Distributing the material electronically.

Whether costs are reduced or not, a viable economic model must include a costrecovery mechanism. Furthermore, that mechanism should be transparent as users and contributors will consider a publication to be unstable if it has no apparent means of recovering costs.

The additional costs associated with charging subscription fees (*e.g.* maintaining accounts and restricting access) combined with the 'gift culture' of the Internet that effectively requires most content to be available free of charge, make it difficult to recover costs directly from users.

An alternative to the traditional subscription model recovers costs from authors in the form of page charges and makes journals available to users free of charge. An important element of this model is that page charges should be levied at a rate acceptable to authors as a fee for widespread distribution of their papers; Harnad and Hemus suggest 'dozens rather than hundreds of dollars per page ... $400 for a 20-page article'.

Clearly, papers that are refereed and then rejected must also be paid for by the model. Variations on this model would recover costs by charging only for submission and/or acceptance. In common with the models of others who propose to bypass publishers, Harnad's model and variations of it require a reduction in publishing costs when compared with print journals.

The Institute of Physics Publishing Publishing (IoPP) and Deutsche Physikalische Gesellschaft (DPG) have recently launched a new pure electronic journal, the *New Journal of Physics*, that is based on this type of model (http://www.njp.org/).

The journal was started after widespread international consultation with librarians and physicists. It is available on the Internet free of charge to users. Authors are required to pay $500 on acceptance of their papers. A discount is available for IoP or DPG members.

Authors are invited to submit only articles of 'outstanding scientific quality; likely to be widely read and highly cited'. Presumably, this criterion is intended to keep the rejection rate low so that the publication fee can cover the costs of papers that are refereed and rejected. The rejection rate of papers in science disciplines tends to be much lower than in social sciences at rates of around 10–30 per cent.

This initiative suggests that IoPP and DPG consider it viable that the *New Journal of Physics* be financed by author acceptance fees of only $500. A journal consisting of, say, 120 papers would be produced for only $60 000.

If a journal produced at this cost were to adopt subscription as a price mechanism it could recover costs by selling 1000 subscriptions for only $60 or 500 subscriptions for only $120. Either rate would be very cheap for a physics journal.

This comparison suggests either that:

- Those publishers who claim that 'no-frills' electronic publishing is almost as expensive as print publishing are wrong;
- That the cost of journal production in either format bears no relation to the subscription price and that many commercial publishers are determined to maintain high margins.

Economic Characteristics of the Academic Information Delivery Chain

Authors and Editors

Among these models, there are undoubtedly some that accurately represent the economics of publishing electronic journals at reduced cost. However, the journals produced would almost certainly not incorporate the additional functionality demanded by users as it would be too costly to do so.

The incentive for authors to submit their papers to these 'bargain basement' publications and for academics to leave the editorial boards of quality commercial journals to sit on the boards of these journals is unclear.

The importance of academics in their capacity as authors and editors must be recognised if a useful economic model of electronic journals is to be developed. Authors are not simply content originators; they drive the information explosion by seeking the most prestigious outlets for their increasing quantities of journal articles.

Both authors and editors then apply pressure to ensure that their institutional libraries hold the journals to which they are affiliated either as authors or as editors. Thus, academics as authors and editors effectively represent demand in this 'market'.

Libraries

The economic model of electronic journal publication proposed by Andrew Odlyzko identifies library costs as the significant element in the 'serials crisis'. Odlyzko argues that a system-wide perspective reveals that the serials crisis is a library cost crisis.

Libraries have focused on subscription prices as a visible problem which contributes to library budget crises but, in fact, for every $1 spent on journal acquisition, $2 is spent on processing, storing and handling print journals.

Furthermore, if publishers were to include many library functions in their delivery systems, libraries subscribing to their electronic journals would save so much in operating costs that they could afford to pay subscription fees at or above their current levels.

Comparative cost–benefit analyses of a hard-copy journal collection and access to an electronic archive, conducted at the University of Michigan supports Odlyzko's arguments that holding a traditional journal collection is an inefficient use of library resources.

However, the cost to publishers of compensating for the relative lack of information skills among end users when compared with librarians is not insignificant. 'Ease and relevance of retrieval is directly proportional to the work put into the data beforehand', and that work represents additional cost.

One reason why publishers have found electronic publishing to be more expensive than anticipated is that they have included in their systems some functions that, in a print environment, were undertaken by other information professionals (Albert Prior, personal communication, 8 February 1999).

A controversial element in Odlyzko's model is his explanation of how publishers will make available in digital form archives of previously published volumes. Odlyzko claims that digitisation costs are small (as low as $0.60 per page) and suggests that publishers digitise their back runs and make them available to libraries.

This, he says, would be a one-off investment for a publisher migrating to the digital environment. Experience of projects in the UK electronic libraries programme (eLib) indicates that creation of accurate, searchable digital text is much more expensive than Odlyzko suggests.

Furthermore, the cost of this activity would not be recovered quickly. The cost of digitising journal archives is a major market entry problem for existing commercial publishers of academic journals (David Worlock, personal commununciation, 9 February 1999).

Odlyzko acknowledges that costs vary significantly depending on what level of functionality is required. He claims that the last 20 per cent of functionality accounts for 80 per cent of the costs. Reports suggests that, for users, a primary interest in electronic journals arises from the added functionality of the new medium.

Odlyzko's model requires users to differentiate essential functions from those that are nice to have. At present this distinction is likely to be arbitrary. The SuperJournal project found use of electronic journals to be 'an essential pre-condition for answering the question of what readers really want'. Until exploitation of functionality has been developed and explored, it will be difficult for anyone to identify the essential functions of electronic journals in the 21st century.

Users

A system-wide view of the costs and benefits of producing and delivering journal articles must acknowledge the costs and benefits to users. Some of these are referred to above, for example additional functionality is an added benefit as is access to users' desktops; time taken to visit the library is directly related to use of library resources. However, the time that it takes to identify high-quality information and to download it to the desktop is a cost as is time spent learning to use a new interface.

This is demonstrated by the fact that users will not invest time learning to use a new system unless a critical mass of material is available using that system. All of these factors will affect users' uptake of electronic journals but many of them are fluid and are difficult to quantify.

Pricing Mechanisms

The pricing mechanism in traditional journal publishing (annual subscription per title) creates a very low-risk market for journal publishers.

The consumer base is widespread and payment is made in advance. In an electronic environment, it is unnecessary to bundle articles into issues before distributing them; it is possible to distribute individual articles on-demand at very low cost to the publisher.

It is possible also to reconfigure bundles to better meet the needs of researchers in specific disciplines and subject areas, *e.g.* to include in a bundle articles from a variety of journals which may be published by a range of different publishers.

Bundling

For electronic journals, a very low-risk pricing mechanism from the publishers' point of view is a site licence arrangement whereby a publisher's entire list is licensed to one or more institutions as a single product.

This is known as bundling. This not only guarantees payment in advance; it also secures payment for low-use journals which subscribing institutions might otherwise cancel. The UK Pilot Site Licence Initiative (PSLI) is a high-profile example which used bundling as a pricing mechanism.

Pricing schemes adopted by publishers participating in the PSLI varied but all represented some form of bundling. Several of the publishers effectively extracted more revenue by offering as a single product all of the titles on their lists. Institutions valued these titles differently; *i.e.* on a single subscription basis institutions A and B would have subscribed to different titles but during the PSLI both institutions paid for a collection of titles which included their selected journals among others.

The PSLI represented an opportunity to introduce electronic journals to large numbers of users throughout the UK. However, its value as a means of testing the pricing mechanisms and pricing levels was limited. Not only were the costs subsidised by the JISC but publishers were not necessarily testing realistic pricing models.

The Institute of Physics Publishing, for example, made electronic copy of its journals available free of charge to institutions that subscribed to hard copy of those titles.

An IoPP representative at that time described this pricing strategy as unrealistic and said that charges would be introduced. The PSLI was criticised for propping up the 'serials crisis'; not only did it mask the effect of rising subscription prices, it also sustained circulation levels of high-cost, low-use journals that many libraries would otherwise have cancelled. For the duration of the initiative, use of PSLI journals was limited; the PSLI resources were used heavily at only six institutions.

It was possible however, to identify 'core' materials that were heavily used and a large number of titles that were used only occasionally. HEFCE suggested that, in future, institutions may use these data to negotiate different rates of discount on titles published by a single publisher. If institutions succeed in these negotiations, one of the benefits of a bundled site licence may be lost to those publishers. When the PSLI ended, the National Electronic Site Licence Initiative (NESLI) was established. NESLI is a service rather than a project. It was established with JISC funds but the cost of content provided to institutions is not subsidised and NESLI must become self financing.

NESLI will attempt to address the issues raised by the PSLI with a view to meeting the needs of libraries and end users in the UK HE community. A model licence has been developed with a view to agreeing standard terms with publishers.

Not all publishers will agree to all of these terms, but the journals of those that do will be offered through a seamless interface which allows users to access the journals of a range of publishers. The variety of proprietary systems required to access PSLI journals proved to be frustrating for users.

The formal launch of the NESLI service is expected in October 1999. Institutions will also be granted ownership of the electronic copy of journals to which they subscribe; *i.e.* access will not be withdrawn when subscriptions are cancelled. Other issues being explored include the facility to subscribe to subject-based clusters of journals from a variety of publishers, the facility to link to NESLI journal articles from library OPAC entries, and supply of useful management information in the form of statistics on 'hits' at various levels including table of contents, abstracts and full text.

An important difference between NESLI and the PSLI is that the latter tied the price of electronic copy of journals to the price of hard copy offering subscriptions only to parallel publications. NESLI aims to offer access to the electronic format alone if publishers are willing and institutions wish to subscribe on those terms.

Thus, if Odlyzko is correct and the 'serials crisis' is largely related to the cost of handling and storing print journals, NESLI will enable libraries significantly to reduce the costs associated with journal subscriptions.

Price Differentiation

As well as facilitating sale of products in bundles that vary in size and content from an article to a publishers' entire list, the electronic environment facilitates price differentiation, *i.e.* varying the price of information with willingness to pay. An example of the potential for price differentiation was identified by researchers working on the ACORN project at Loughborough University.

It was suggested that if charges for journal articles from the electronic reserve service were introduced, they may be escalated towards the exam period. This would effectively reduce the load at peak times by charging a higher rate to students who cram for exams.

Price differentiation can be implemented only if differences in user types are easily observable. In a print environment, it is possible to differentiate between different types of journal subscriber, for example professional vs. educational or library vs. individual.

However, it is very difficult to observe user characteristics beyond this, *e.g.* to observe the quantity of articles read by any researcher or their relative use of tables of contents, abstracts, and full-text articles. In an electronic environment, it is feasible to observe different types of use.

Thus, it should be possible to differentiate between users based on the quality and quantity of the information that they require or for which they are willing to pay. For example, some users may be willing to pay for additional functionality such as hotlinks to all citations in a paper, while others would be willing to forgo this facility to access the text at a cheaper rate.

It is increasingly common for authors to publish the text of their research papers on the Internet despite publishers' attempts to protect their exclusive right to publish. It has been predicted that when publishers have to cede exclusivity on individual papers, they will begin to trade in added value, for example retrieval services tailored to individual needs.

PEAK: Exploring bundling and price Differentiation

The PEAK project at the University of Michigan is a collaborative venture with Elsevier Science which aims to test three different pricing models for electronic journals. The models are based on the economic theory on bundling and on price differentiation.. It is argued that:

- 'Non-linear pricing is facilitated by lower transaction costs for fine-grained purchases and feasible direct usage monitoring' by publishers or libraries;
- That bundling can extract revenue from those who value content differently. A key research objective of PEAK is generalisability to other user populations.

The number of possible dimensions which can be manipulated when defining a bundle is very large, for example, the 'article component (abstract, references, text etc.); time limit on usage (unlimited, per use, per year etc.); and usage rights (read only, read and print etc.)'.

To infer anything from data gathered during PEAK, it was necessary that the variables be limited. Only three different pricing mechanisms are being tested. These are described below.

- The electronic journal is supplied on the same terms as a traditional print subscription, *i.e.* articles are made available on an issue-by-issue basis to all authorised users at a subscribing university.
- The Institution pays in advance for a specific number of articles and may then access articles from any of the 1100 titles available from Elsevier in electronic form. The fee paid is $5.46 per article. If the institution has used these 'vouchers' and wishes to purchase more it must pay for them at the higher rate of $7. Thus, Elsevier and the institution share the risk. Note that both the reduced voucher price of $5.46 and the higher rate of $7 are very low and when

converted at the current exchange rate ($1.571/£1 on 19 May 1999) both are cheaper than the price of an interlibrary loan request from the British Library (£4.95).

- Articles are ordered as required and are paid for either by the institution or by individual users within institutions. Articles are more expensive to order in this way than they are in model.

When an individual has ordered an article through PEAK, it is made available to all users at that individual's institution and use of that article is then monitored. On average, each article has been accessed 2.5 times.

The three pricing mechanisms operated by PEAK are effectively two-part tariff schemes as institutions are required to pay $25K to the University of Michigan to join PEAK and then they incur fees for journals and/or articles.

Although there are three discrete pricing schemes, participating institutions need not restrict themselves to one. They may, for example, subscribe to 'core journals' and buy vouchers for additional provision.

Ten institutions are participating in the PEAK project. Very few results have been reported by PEAK researchers but initial results indicate that the traditional subscription is the least popular pricing model. The PEAK project is due to end in August 1999.

Electronic Individual Article Supply

One of the pricing mechanisms being tested by PEAK is electronic individual article supply (eIAS). This mechanism effectively disintegrates the traditional product and increases the publisher's risk. The publisher is no longer paid in advance for a package of around 120 articles to be delivered in 6 or 12 issues throughout the year. The publisher can no longer focus marketing effort on the 120-article bundle and its identifiable market; each article must sell on its own merits and thus is an individual product.

The eIAS model characterises access or 'just-in-time' provision as an alternative to holdings or 'just-in-case' provision. Users can benefit from access to a much wider range of titles than the institution could afford if it maintained journal subscriptions.

Furthermore, comparison of the costs of access and holdings models indicate that the former is economically efficient for libraries and is popular with end users. However, to date, the scale of comparative studies conducted has been limited; there may be economies or diseconomies of scale inherent in a large-scale access model which are not yet evident.

IAS in those studies was not a seamless process whereby the end user searched, identified and received articles directly from the supplier and had them delivered electronically to her desktop. Although end users had access to the OPACs of collaborating universities and thus were able to identify the location of requested items, orders were made via librarians at the borrowing and lending libraries and documents were supplied in hard copy by post or courier.

To date, access models have tended to rely on library privilege whereby libraries are legally permitted, without paying a copyright fee, to supply an individual with a single copy of a document for the purposes of research or private study. However, users must sign a print request before they receive their copy of the requested document. Thus, the process whereby the end user searches, identifies and receives the required resource is necessarily interrupted and this interruption represents a significant additional library administration cost.

Furthermore, widespread adoption of an access model which relies on library privilege would undermine the economic incentive to publish as libraries would cancel journal subscriptions thus reducing subscription bases and publishers would receive no alternative revenue from article supply. Publishers are unlikely to comply with library requests for permission to fulfil ILL requests electronically. Alternative copyright-cleared sources of individual articles in electronic form are available. It is difficult to assess their relative costs and benefits when compared with subscription, however, as services offering copyright-cleared articles tend to operate complex price differentiation policies. These policies can be based on several of the following variables: the country from which a request originates; the type of user; the number of requests; the type of delivery; and the speed of delivery.

Most services offer at least two alternative payment mechanisms, including, most commonly, pay-as-you-go schemes based on credit card payment and payment in advance based on deposit accounts or pre-paid forms. One drawback of pricing electronic articles individually is that the facility to hotlink to citations is less attractive when every link incurs an additional fee.

It is worth noting that JISC has agreed in principle to provide sums to help launch an eIAS service in the UK under JISC/PA auspices, but the details of the Tender call have yet to be concluded.

Scholarly Communication and the Market

A recent eLib supporting study compared different models for pricing electronic scholarly journal articles including those based on bundling, price differentiation and IAS. Fishwick *et al.* consider the current academic information delivery chain to be inefficient due to a number of distortions in the supply–demand chain. Among these are that:

- Authors represent a principal source of demand for publication but make no contribution to publication costs;
- Those consuming the information, *i.e.* the readers, seldom pay for it, preferring instead to obtain it from libraries;
- Much of the journal publication work is undertaken by editors and referees without payment, or with minimal honoraria.

Fishwick *et al.* propose an alternative model which introduces 'normal' market feedback mechanisms into the academic information delivery chain with a view to overcoming the serials crisis and developing an efficient market for scholarly articles.

The most efficient pricing mechanism would be determined by the market; a number of alternatives would be available in the first instance. Publication would be funded by authors and users both of whom contribute to demand. The publisher would receive usage-based payment at a level sufficient to sustain the model.

Editors and referees would be paid to encourage efficiency, and authors would receive royalties to encourage them to submit for publication only material of the highest quality.

Papers would then be available individually or in customised bundles from the publisher database. Included in the system would be a mechanism to support authors who cannot afford to pay a submission fee. Furthermore, payment by authors would facilitate publication of papers that may be important scientifically but are unlikely to be popular among readers at their time of publication.

The current system for selecting papers to be published in a journal, peer review, assesses them based primarily on quality rather than wholly on their likely popularity at the time of publication.

The contents of a journal issue will contain a selection of papers, some of which will be widely read at the time of publication and some of which will attract very few readers. In economic terms the former subsidise the latter.

When the journal is disaggregated and electronic copy of each article sold ondemand this cross-subsidisation will end and publishers may find it difficult to recover the publication costs of lesser-read papers.

The authors of the study acknowledge that publication of such papers may not be guaranteed, and suggest that public support be available to ensure that all important developments are recorded through publication; the merit of all papers would continue to be gauged by peer review. The basic product would be unsophisticated electronic text.

Additional functionality would be available for a higher fee. An important element of this model, it is claimed, would be generation of management data based on usage which would be useful to library managers and publishers. This type of feedback is most useful if users are required to prioritise between materials that are available to them. Thus, it is argued that access should be rationed, even to material obtained by site licence.

Printing and additional functionality are approached in the same way, *i.e.* it is suggested that if users are required to pay for prints they will filter before, rather than after they print. This argument suggests that end users waste resources by gathering information that they do not really need.

Time, for any student or researcher, is a scarce resource and it takes time to gather information. If end users do need all of the information that they acquire, it may be argued that rationing would prejudice their ability to work effectively.

Fishwick *et al.*'s model incorporates elements from many different economic models including Harnad's model. However, in spirit, the model is the antithesis of Harnad's.

Harnad argues convincingly that scholarly communication differs from other types of publication in that it is not a commercial market. Authors of journal articles are not motivated by the promise of royalty payments; they want their papers to be distributed as widely as possible and, in the past, have often paid to acquire offprints so that they could contribute to this dissemination process.

This view is reinforced by a recent study of what authors want from publication. Fishwick's argument that structural problems in the current system preclude the introduction of an efficient system that would benefit all stakeholders is compelling but uncomfortable for those who consider scholarly communication necessarily to be qualitatively different from trade commodities.

Whether or not the principle of introducing normal market economics into the scholarly communication chain is valid, certain elements of the model proposed by Fishwick *et al.* are problematic:

- Like many other HE proponents of alternative models for scholarly communication, Fishwick *et al.* claim that print and distribution represent the most significant costs in the journal production process and thus, that distribution in an electronic environment should be significantly cheaper. This would be an important factor in maintaining authors' publication fees at an affordable level. The proportion that print and distribution contribute to publication costs is a contentious issue. However, it may be less important than many authors suggest as publication costs may well be low even though current prices are very high.
- The basic product proposed by Fishwick *et al.* is unsophisticated electronic text. It may be difficult to persuade authors and editors to abandon print journals in favour of such a 'bargain basement' publication. However, if submission fees are introduced, and thus submission in high-quality journals is expensive, those authors not in receipt of large research grants may find that they cannot afford to publish in a high-quality publication.

Thus, the result could be a two-tier system whereby research that is not grant funded is published in the Fishwick *et al.* alternative system and grant-funded research is published in a more sophisticated format.

This problem could be overcome only if all authors, including those in receipt of large grants, are prepared to publish in and thus to support 'alternative' journals that are cost effective for HE such as those proposed by SPARC.

This would require a massive attitude shift among important authors. At present authors publish in the most prestigious journals because to do so carries more weight with regard to research assessment and tenure awards. Authors would have to be persuaded of the utilitarian benefits of publishing in 'alternative' cost-effective journals. It is difficult to imagine how such an attitude shift would come about.

International co-operative agreements resulting in HE policy directives may solve the problem but co-operation at a national level let alone at that level is notoriously difficult to achieve. Because this model differs radically from that proposed by Harnad and his ilk, it was also evaluated in the research reported later in this report.

THE MODELS

A variety of different approaches to publishing cost effective electronic journals have been proposed in recent years. Many have common characteristics. Four models will be tested here. The second models non-commercial production of a journal that is available for use free of charge on the Internet as described by Harnad.

The third is a non-commercial journal funded by users by a combination of subscription and eIAS.

The fourth is an alternative non-commercial journal model proposed by the authors which differs from the third model only in that costs are recovered through a combination of a modest submission fee and sales of subscriptions and individual articles. None of these models assumes that the production process will be conducted entirely by academics or other stakeholders who have neither experience nor expertise in publishing.

User studies show that professional design is important to user acceptance. Journal production and related tasks such as marketing are undertaken more efficiently by publishing professionals; this is reflected in the models. Tasks that can be automated effectively are automatic in all of the models.

The Conservation Ecology (CE) project has demonstrated that all administrative tasks in the editorial process can be automated and, in an international enterprise, that an automated system can be more effective as it is not constrained by a time zone. Furthermore, the cost of copy editing *Conservation Ecology* is much cheaper than the equivalent cost in a print environment because the bulk of formatting is done automatically1.

Conservation Ecology is published by two permanent employees, a parttime production editor and a part-time systems administrator. All versions of each manuscript are archived by the software. Metadata can be amended at minimal cost as standards change by using a formatting template.

The whole process can be decentralised because all actors in the chain can access files remotely from any networked PC throughout the world. There is no reason why any of the models described here should differ from the others with regard to exploitation of this type of system so editorial costs for each of the models will be based on the CE model.

Variables in the Models

All evidence to date suggests that people prefer not to read at length on screen. They may use the electronic medium to search and identify resources and they will read small portions of text on screen but having established that they wish to read a substantial amount of text such as a journal paper, users obtain a print.

Often electronic journals are not even published in a format suited for reading on screen; electronic versions of journals published in parallel print and electronic form tend to be made available in PDF, a format that is cheap to produce in a parallel production process but is designed to be printed.

The models explored here will be used to examine the economic implications for users and/or their institutions of tending to print or read on screen. One variable with a very significant impact on costs for electronic journal production is the degree of functionality required by users. Most of the models described here require a reduction in production costs.

This implies a lack of additional functionality. It has been suggested that users not only want additional functionality but are unwilling to learn to use new systems unless there are clear functional advantages.

However, despite their expressed interest in additional functionality, in practice end users are most interested in content, browsing (including linking), and printing. Odlyzko asserts that cost-effective journal production requires users to discriminate between those functions that they need and those that they would like.

However, although it is claimed that added functionality will significantly increase journal production costs there are no published data which differentiate the costs of different functional elements. Odlyzko estimates that the last 20 per cent of functionality will incur 80 per cent of the total cost but does not attempt to apply this with reference to different functions.

Variations in electronic journal production costs should be explored but it is beyond the scope of this project to do so. Generally, it is assumed that scholarly journal articles have a limited audience. This characteristic contributes to the expense of publishing such articles.

First copy costs are inevitably spread across a relatively small number of potential users. However, some recent work has suggested that the market for journal articles can be expanded. Odlyzko forecasts increasing use of journal articles by pressure groups. This is plausible given the recent shift in political activity among ordinary citizens towards single-issue politics. Researchers at Project Muse found that institutions that had not subscribed to John Hopkins University Press titles in print did subscribe to journals in electronic form.

MONOGRAPHS AND TEXTS

For the purposes of this report, a monograph is defined as a low-volume work intended for library purchase and use as a resource by researchers. The market for monographs is 'global and export driven'. In contrast, a textbook is defined as being intended to be used as a teaching resource and for student use. If successful, a textbook may be reprinted or new editions may be issued.

Textbooks usually depend on the home market; they are 'developed or adapted in the local market'. However, the distinction between textbooks and monographs is not always clear cut. In any case, it is difficult for publishers accurately to predict the size of the market for a work.

Some works commissioned as textbooks sell so few copies that perhaps they should be categorised as monographs and some commissioned as monographs are far more successful than anticipated and may reasonably be categorised as textbooks. There may be a greater rationale for supplying a textbook in electronic form than for a monograph.

The former is likely to be required by large numbers of students at the same time, while the latter is likely to be consulted by individuals and demand is unlikely to be concentrated to specific time periods. As people do not like to read more than a small amount of text on screen, a monograph in electronic form is unlikely to meet user needs. It would be too expensive, both financially and in time, to print the work.

However, if a textbook were required by all students in a large undergraduate class it may be viable as an electronic product as all students in the class could access it at any time, perhaps from their residences, and select those parts that they wished to print. Experience on the ELINOR project suggests that students do not use electronic text in this way; they use it to identify useful materials which they then borrow from the library shelves.

This experience may however, have been due to design, screen resolution and similar factors. As these factors are constantly improving, so a similar experiment run today may generate different results.

Developments towards electronic books for individual use that are portable and facilitate book marking, annotation etc. in the form of Rocket eBook and other similar tools while important, are not library developments and will not be explored in this study.

Monographs

The obvious advantage of digital publishing of monographs is that there is no requirement to invest in inventory (David Worlock, personal communication, 11 February 1999). Nevertheless, digital publication requires investment in first copy costs and, as in most publishing ventures, these represent the most significant proportion of monograph publishing costs. Developments in digital publication of monographs is at a very early stage.

The experience of University presses in the US is that if monographs are made available free of charge over the Internet, sales of hard copy increase 2–3-fold. This is attributed to the reluctance of users to read on screen or to spend time and money downloading and printing substantial quantities of text which are available in a more convenient format from booksellers. These early projects have explored the market for digital analogues of print monographs. Studies with journal users suggests that it is inadequate simply to deliver in a digital environment material which has been designed for print; to be useful, digital resources should be designed for the medium.

Those publishers attempting to explore the utility of the digital environment for monograph publishing have come to question its suitability and suggest that this environment may change the very nature of the format. For example, use of open review pre-publication may, ultimately, result in a new format: a hybrid between a journal and a monograph.

Publishers are aware that for digital monographs to succeed added value is likely to be important. However, they argue that any additional functionality will increase the cost, and therefore, the price of monographs.

In recent years, 'monograph publishing has almost disappeared in many disciplines because short print runs and library budget problems have made it untenable'. Any increase in cost and price is likely to exacerbate rather than alleviate this problem.

Texts

Publishers have used digital technology to offer university and college teachers the facility to customise texts. For example, Wiley's custom publishing service offers teachers the facility to select chapters from a CD-ROM database of large general texts in a specific subject. Chapters must be drawn from a minimum of two titles and the teacher must order a minimum of 30 copies. The material is collated, bound and delivered to the campus bookseller for sale to students. Perhaps custom publishing by the publisher precludes alternative means for students of obtaining the information. Thus, by adapting to the market, Wiley is more likely to maintain its customer share and profitability. Furthermore, when texts represent good value, students may be more prepared to buy them and become less reliant on library provision for core materials. Developments at Wiley use digital technology for production but not for delivery and thus this experiment has limited relevance to the digital library.

There is no evidence to date to suggest that texts are being produced for electronic delivery. Development work in this area suggests that, as yet, there is no market for digital texts. The Internet can, however, be used effectively to facilitate sale of peripheral products such as self-marking tests for certification of professional skills such as nursing. Such tests are also delivered free as an value-added supplement to a print publication, *i.e.* effectively as an incentive to buy/use the associated text.

As with journals, publishers are working with academics to explore ways of utilising the digital medium for teaching. A good example is ChemConnections, a Wiley collaboration with the University of California and Beloit College which is grant-funded by the National Science Foundation.

ChemConnections comprises a number of modules which can be used over a period of weeks for teaching on a variety of different areas of chemistry. Evidence to date suggests that, as yet, publishers are only exploring the utility of the medium for both text and monograph publishing.

Economic modelling is likely to be explored much later in the development cycle, after products have been shown to be sufficiently useful that libraries and/or academic departments would pay for them. At that time, publishers expect developments such as the digital object identifier (DOI) to be important in facilitating commercial transactions. '

As yet use of metadata by monograph publishers is inconsistent and ad-hoc. Given the embryonic state of electronic monograph publishing it is likely that a more consolidated approach to charging models will emerge in the future'. No economic model for producing and delivering electronic texts has been published. Therefore, this area is not the subject of a modelling exercise here.

ELECTRONIC DATASETS

The economic model for electronic reference works is better established than for most other areas of the digital library. A database or dataset consisting of a number of databases is generally supplied on licence either on CD-ROM or online. Where both formats are available the price tends to be similar.

Negotiation of licence terms can be undertaken by institutions individually or by consortia. Economic factors related to licence negotiation are covered below in the section on licensing.

In the UK, the Combined Higher Education Software Team (CHEST) negotiates with dataset suppliers on behalf of the JISC to secure favourable access terms for UK Higher Education Institutions (HEIs) and to standardise terms and conditions of use wherever possible.

Standardised terms reduce costs for all parties including individual institutions which must adhere to those terms. Networked access to these commercially supplied datasets from one of JISC's data centres (BIDS, EDINA, and MIDAS) is then offered to the HE community.

Each individual institution can choose which of the available datasets it wishes to pay for and, for an annual fee, it obtains a site licence. Institutions then supply end users with access to these datasets free at the point of use.

CHEST licences are usually agreed for five years so institutions subscribing to a dataset commit to take it until the end of the CHEST agreement. The five-year commitment has been cited by several institutions as a reason for not taking JISC datasets.

The price of a dataset is obviously important to institutions when deciding whether or not to subscribe but it is not the only factor. Some JISC datasets are made available to the community free of charge but uptake is still not universal. One reason may be that use of datasets by end users can increase demand for journals and ILLs, and thus increase pressure on the workload of library staff. Another is that even a 'free' dataset involves the HEI in some opportunity costs. An economic advantage to institutions of supplying datasets to end users is a reduction in mediated online searching. Furthermore, as more datasets become available online rather than on CD-ROM, technical support and maintenance costs are reduced. The current annual subscription with a minimum commitment, usually of five years, does not suit many UK HEIs, especially smaller institutions.

A recent survey of attitudes to pricing of JISC-funded databases found that institutions would like the option of usage-based payment.

There was also a call to render prices more equitable by allowing a number of small institutions to subscribe as a consortium which would pay at the same rate as a large institution; institution size would be based on student numbers. It is difficult to model provision of datasets to the UK HE community as:

- The term dataset covers a wide range of different types and volumes of content;
- The contribution of the JISC and the terms that it demands from suppliers are unclear. As this is not a controversial area and economic relationships are established and work effectively it is not modelled and explored here.

6

Availability and Accessibility of Information Sources and the Use of Library

INTRODUCTION

Information is power and an essential ingredient in decision-making. To obtain timely, relevant and quality information for your study or research work, you need to know the various sources of information available. This module is expected to deepen your knowledge of sources of information in print, non-print and electronic formats. It presents the definition, originators/producers, types, formats, and categories of information sources. The module also shows where information sources could be found *e.g.* archives, libraries and the Internet.

PRODUCERS/ORIGINATORS OF INFORMATION

There are four main producers/originators of information, these are:

- Government Agencies
- Academic institutions
- The private Sector
- Individuals

GOVERNMENT AGENCIES

Government departments and agencies publish lots of information in print and electronic formats. In various countries of the world, governments at all levels play an important role in producing information for the society they serve. In many occasions, government officials may need information about the society in order to make decisions relating to economic, social and political issues. Some of the information produced by government is grey literature comprising reports such as National HIV/AIDS reports, gazettes, population statistics, census data, government notices, policy documents etc. Since government documents are generated with public funds, they are made available either free of charge or at low cost. This can be done through the various government agencies including the public libraries or the government Websites.

In Nigerian for instance, some government departments and agencies Websites include:

- National Agency for the Control of AIDS (NACA),
- National Bureau of Statistics (NBS),
- Federal Ministry of Information and Culture (FMIC).

ACADEMIC INSTITUTIONS

Academic institutions such as universities and colleges are major producers of information in a society or country. Academic institutions around the world especially those in the United States, United Kingdom, Africa have conducted extensive researches in various specialties including the health sciences. Numerous publications and knowledge materials are generated from these research studies as technical reports, books and articles in peer reviewed journals. Academic institutions also have other publications such as Newsletters, Magazines, Technical reports, Manuscripts, Maps and lots of other Grey literature.

Web addresses of some academic institutions in Africa are listed below:

- University of Ibadan, Nigeria;
- University of Zambia;
- Kenyatta University, Nairobi, Kenya;
- University of Zimbabwe;
- Makerere University, Uganda; and
- University of Bamako, Mali.

PRIVATE SECTORS

A third major producer of information in a country is the private sector. This consists of print and electronic media organizations, commercial business outfits, publishers/vendors and aggregators, performing/film industry that publish and or make their information products and services accessible on the Web either free or by subscription.

Others are:

- Non-profit professional organizations.
- Profitable organizations and commercial agencies.
- International Agencies.
- Professional Associations or organizations.
- Private institutions.
- Corporate laboratories.

Unlike government departments and agencies, published reports of research carried out by most organizations, agencies and commercial outfits in the private sector are not made available for public consumption. However, non-profit organizations and agencies do make their publications available to those that need them.

Some examples of agencies in the private sector or non-profit category are:

- The World Health Organization (WHO).

- Joint United Nations Programme on HIV and AIDS (UNAIDS).
- Elsevier Publishers.
- Cables News Network (CNN).

PRIVATE INDIVIDUALS

Individuals also create information. Many print and web documents available today are created by private individuals, some of whom have their own Websites/pages. Some individuals disseminate information through Facebook, Twitter, Blogs, You-tube etc, while others publish information in print as text books, monographs or articles in journals, magazines or newsletters. On the other hand, some important information is not published rather, it is passed on from generation to generation. For example, some parents pass information to their children by word of mouth on how diseases were treated using traditional unorthodox methods in their communities.

DEFINITION OF INFORMATION/ INFORMATION SOURCES

Information is processed data. An information source is where you got your information from; this can be a book or a Website. Information sources are the various means by which information is recorded for use by an individual or an organization. It is the means by which a person is informed about something or knowledge is availed to someone, a group of people or an organization. Information sources can be observations, people, speeches, documents, pictures, organi-zations. Information sources can be in print, non-print and electronic media or format.

TYPES OF INFORMATION SOURCES

Information can come from virtually anywhere: personal experiences, books, articles, expert opinions, encyclopedias, the Web. The type of information needed will change depending on its application. Individuals generate information on a daily basis as they go about their work. In academic institutions, staff and students consult various sources of information. The choice of the source to consulted is usually determined by the type of information sought.

The three types of information sources are:

- Primary;
- Secondary; and
- Tertiary.

PRIMARY SOURCES

Primary sources are original materials on which other research studies are based. Primary sources report a discovery or share new information; they present first-hand accounts and information relevant to an event. They present information in its original form, not interpreted or condensed or evaluated by other writers. They are usually evidence or accounts of the events, practices, or conditions being researched and created by a person who directly experienced that event. Primary sources are the first formal appearance of results in print or electronic formats. Examples of primary sources are: eyewitness accounts, journalistic reports, financial reports, government documents, archeological and biological evidence, court records, ephemerals, literary manuscript and minutes of meetings etc. The definition of a primary source may vary depending upon the discipline or context. A diary would be a primary source because it is written directly by the individual writing in the diary. Interviews are primary sources because the individual talks about the topic directly from what he/she knows about it.

Other examples are:

- Video of the inauguration of the first female president in Brazil.
- A scientific publication reporting the development of a new medication to manage patients with sickle-cell anemia.

A newspaper article reporting the bomb blast in Abuja, Nigeria, during the celebration of the country's 50th Independent Anniversary.

Note: The types of information that can be considered a primary source may vary depending on the subject discipline, and how the material is being used.

For example:

- A research article in a peer-reviewed journal that proved the effectiveness of a newly developed vaccine for the prevention of HIV virus would be a primary source.
- A magazine article that reports the development of a new vaccine for the prevention of HIV infection would be regarded as a primary source.
- Information in a magazine article that reports a study of how compact fluorescent light bulbs are presented in the popular media could be considered a primary source.

SECONDARY SOURCES

A secondary source of information is one that was created by someone who *did not* have firsthand experience or did not participate in the events or conditions being researched. They are generally accounts written after the fact with the benefit of hindsight. Secondary sources describe, analyse, interpret, evaluate, comment on and discuss the evidence provided by primary sources.

Secondary sources are works that are one step removed from the original event or experience that provide criticism, interpretation or evaluation of primary sources. Secondary sources are not evidence, but rather commentary on and discussion of evidence. A secondary data are one that has been collected by individuals or agencies for purposes other than those of a particular research study. However, what some define as a secondary source, others define as a tertiary source. For example, if a magazine writer wrote about the speech Nelson Mandela delivered when he was inaugurated President of South Africa in 1990, it will be a secondary source.

The information is not original, but an analysis of the speech. If a government department has conducted a survey of, say, family food expenditures, then, a food manufacturer might use this data in the organization's evaluations of the total potential market for a new product. Similarly, statistics prepared by a pharmaceutical company on the production of a particular drug will prove useful to a host of people and organizations, including those marketing the drug. For secondary sources, often the best are those that have been published most recently.

If you use a secondary source that was published decades ago, it is important to know what subsequent scholars have written on the topic and what criticism they have made about the earlier work or its approach to the topic. The definition of a secondary source may vary depending upon the discipline or context. Most often how a source is used determines whether it is a primary or secondary source. For the purposes of a historical research project, secondary sources are generally scholarly books and articles. Also included in this category would be reference sources such as encyclopedias.

Other examples of secondary sources are:

- Bibliographies
- Biographical works;
- Commentaries;
- Criticisms;
- Dictionaries;
- Histories;
- Journal articles;
- Magazine and newspaper articles;
- Monographs, other than fiction and autobiography;
- Textbooks; and
- Websites.

TERTIARY SOURCES

Definition

Tertiary sources consist of information which is a distillation and collection of primary and secondary sources. Generally, tertiary sources are not considered to be acceptable material on which to base academic research. Tertiary sources are usually not credited to a particular author. They are intended only to provide an overview of what the topic includes, its basic terminology, and often references for further reading.

Some reference materials and textbooks are considered tertiary sources when their chief purpose is to list, summarize or simply repackage ideas or other information. Examples of tertiary sources include dictionaries and encyclopedias, *Wikipedia* and similar user-contributed online 'encyclopedias' and reference materials, as well as various digests and schoolbooks.

In a nutshell, tertiary sources are:

- Works which list primary and secondary resources in a specific subject area.
- Works which index, organize and compile citations to, and show secondary sources can be used.
- Materials in which the information from secondary sources has been "digested"-reformatted and condensed, to put it into a convenient, easy-to-read form.
- Sources which are once removed in time from secondary sources.

Table. General Classification of Selected Primary, Secondary and Tertiary Sources of Information

Primary Sources	Secondary Sources	Tertiary Sources
• Autobiographies • Correspondence: e-mail, letters • Descriptions of travel • Diaries, • Eyewitnesses • Oral histories • Literary works • Interviews • Personal narratives • First-hand newspaper and magazine • Legal cases, treaties • Statistics, surveys, opinion polls, • Scientific data, transcripts • Journal articles • Records of organizations literature reviews, and government agencies • Original works of literature, art or music • Cartoons, postcards, posters • Map, paintings, photographs, films	• Biographies, Encyclopedias, dictionaries, handbooks • Textbooks and monographs on a topic • Literary criticism and interpretation • History and historical criticism • Political analyses • Reviews of law accounts of events • Essays on morals and ethics • Analyses of social policy • Study and teaching material • Articles, such as • Commentaries, research articles in all subject disciplines • Criticism of works of literature, art and music	• Chronologies • Classifications • Dictionaries • Encyclopedias • Directories • Guidebooks and manuals • Population registers statistics • Abstracts • Indexes • Bibliographies • Manuals/Guide and legislation books

DIFFERENCE BETWEEN PRIMARY, SECONDARY AND TERTIARY SOURCES OF INFORMATION

Primary sources of information are original manuscripts, documents or records used in preparing a published or unpublished work. For example, an article in a peer reviewed journal that discussed the development of a new vaccine for the prevention of HIV infection will be considered a primary source. Secondary sources are published or unpublished works that rely on primary source.

A commentary by a magazine reporter based on the peer reviewed journal article on the newly invented vaccine for HIV prevention, would be a secondary source. Tertiary sources are published or unpublished works that are based on secondary sources. Tertiary sources are index to primary sources. Science Citation Index would be considered a tertiary source. It is sometimes difficult to differentiate between primary, secondary and tertiary sources.

The following publication details of the information adapted from University of Wisconsin libraries can be helpful in determining whether a material is primary, secondary or tertiary source:

- *Timing of the Event Recorded*: If the article was composed close to the time of the event recorded, chances are it is primary material. For instance, a letter written by a soldier during the Second World War is primary material, as is an article written in the newspaper or a soldier's letter home during the Liberian Civil War. However, an article written analysing the results of the battle during the Liberian Civil War is secondary material.
- *Rhetorical Aim of the Written Item*: Often, an item that is written with a persuasive, or analytical aim is secondary material. These materials have digested and interpreted the event, rather than reported on it.
- *Context of the Researching Scholar*: Primary materials for a critic studying the literature of the Civil War are different from primary materials for a historian studying Civil War prisons. The critic's primary materials are the poems, stories, and films of the era. The research scientist's primary materials would be the diaries and writings of the prisoners.

FORMATS OF INFORMATION SOURCES

Information is available and accessible in two main formats namely, print and non-print and these include published and unpublished sources.

PRINT MATERIALS (PUBLISHED SOURCES)

Information could be in print format and these include: all printed books, periodicals, maps, bibliographies, indexes and abstracts, photographs, government documents, technical reports, etc. Books are the most common type of printed materials. *The Oxford Advanced Learner's Dictionary* defines a book as 'a set of printed pages that are fastened inside a cover so that you can turn them and read them. A book is described by some people as a written work or composition that has been published, printed on pages bound together while others say it's just the content, separate from its container. Books are categorized into two, namely: fiction and non-fiction. Fiction contains information that are not true and all the scenes and characters are made up by the author. Non-fiction books deals with information that is true, about real things, people, events and places.

NON-PRINT MATERIALS

In addition to printed materials, information is also produced in other formats (non-print) including audio, audiovisual, multimedia, microform and electronic books, journals, images, texts/records from the Internet.

AUDIO-VISUAL AND MULTIMEDIA

In the past decades, much of the information created by members of a given society is produced in audio, audio-visual and multimedia formats. Example of audio information is music recorded on CDs and books on audio or video tapes. Video information includes VCR tapes of TV shows, movies and documentaries. Other examples are information on CD-ROMs, DVDs, Flash drives and Web documents etc.

MICROFORM

The American Heritage Dictionary defines microform as an arrangement of images reduced in size, as on microfilm or microfiche. Microforms are any form, either films or paper, containing micro reproductions of documents for transmission, storage, reading, and printing. Microform images are commonly reduced about 25 times from the original document size, (miniaturized or compressed images) which cannot be read without special display devices (the reader). Archival materials are frequently placed in microform format because this medium is very stable and economical for storage of information for extended periods of time. There are two major types, namely: Microfilm and Microfiche.

MICROFILM

Microfilm is a roll of transparent film used to store micro-scopic images of documents. A microfilm reader is required to read the images in the microfilm. Documents are recorded in microfilm because of the risk of damage to a fragile original or to save storage space. Microfilm when properly processed and stored within special envelopes and placed in a climate-controlled room, has a life expectancy of approximately 500 years. Most libraries have a collection of microfilm stored in their archives.

MICROFICHE

Microfiche Is a small sheet of transparent photographic film usually 4 inches by 6 inches containing printed information in a size too small to be seen by the naked eye and needs a special device to read the images. The major advantages of microfiche include storage in a small space, stability of the format, and not needing knowledge to read it. As long as a microfiche machine is available to magnify the print to a readable size, anyone who can read the language can read the information on microfiche. When kept in a temperature-controlled environment, it can last for approximately 500 years; it is a good medium for saving and preserving cultural documents.

UNPUBLISHED SOURCES — INDIGENOUS KNOWLEDGE (IK)

In local communities in Africa, there is a rich body of information or knowledge which has been handed down by word of mouth from generation to generation. This is known as indigenous knowledge. It is neither written nor published but provides people in the community with strategies for survival. Indigenous knowledge is the sum total of knowledge and skills which people in a particular geographical area possess that enables them to get the most out of their natural environment. This information/knowledge is not systematically documented. It is oral in nature, usually transmitted through personal communication; it is culture-specific and often generated within communities for local level decision-making in agriculture, healthcare, food preparation, education, natural resources management and other activities. Examples of areas where indigenous knowledge has been very useful include, among others, African traditional medicine, conflict resolution and culture-dance steps and traditional attire.

WHERE TO FIND INFORMATION SOURCES

Places to begin looking for information are:

- Human sources;
- Archives;
- Libraries; and
- Internet.

HUMAN SOURCES (COLLEAGUES/PEERS)

Communication with peers and colleagues are a good way of obtaining vital information. For example, doctors have been found to rely on their colleagues for information in order to solve a patient's problems. The value of informal sources of information especially colleagues and peers cannot be overstressed.

The good side of it is that human sources (colleagues/peers) are readily available to provide needed information at the right time. If the right person is contacted, quality and up-to-date information will be obtained. The downside of using human sources is that there may be some element of bias in the information provided, or some people will say things from their own point of view or exaggerate it.

ARCHIVES

Archives are places where records of all types and formats are kept and made accessible for research and other purposes. They are a good place to find primary sources, both unpublished materials and those that have been published for their parent institution's members or constituencies. Personal and institutional records of all types can be found in archives, as well as media, ephemera, oral histories, and even artifacts. The term *archives*can also refer to the records themselves. The materials housed in the archives are unique, usually one of a kind items. Archives store, preserve and make accessible records of enduring value that have not been produced in great quantities for the general public for research and understanding. Archival materials are rare and irreplaceable and therefore they are not loaned out to users.

LIBRARY

When you think about libraries, the first things that come to mind are probably printed materials such as books, journals and magazines. Libraries also provide access to resources such as fulltext journal and magazine articles, periodical indexes, and online encyclopedias. Libraries collect quality information in a wide variety of formats. Academic libraries purchase these sources for their "community" of students, faculty, and staff. Unlike archives, libraries have mass produced items such as books, government reports, CDs, DVDs, magazines and journals. The exceptions are rare books, manuscripts, map and other special collections. These resources are different from most of the information that is freely available to you over the Web because they have been reviewed and recommended by the library with input from the faculty members.

Like archives, libraries have primary source materials in many forms: historical newspapers, published letters, diaries, and government reports are just a few of the types of primary sources that can be found in libraries. In addition, some libraries are similar to archives in that they specialize in information materials such as rare books and unpublished manuscripts.

WHY GO TO A LIBRARY FOR INFORMATION

The main purpose of libraries, particularly those situated in University campuses, is to collect a large quantity of scholarly materials from different time periods and on diverse topics to make research easier for members of the community they serve (staff and students in the case of a university.) Library resources are free for use by members of the community. Libraries purchase materials that are normally too expensive for library patrons. Library materials, unlike those found on the Internet, go through a review process. Librarians select books, magazines, journals databases and even Websites for use by their patrons. This selection process enables the library to collect resources considered to be reliable, relevant and valuable. In addition, library resources are organized by subjects thus making them easy to find. For easy access, each item of library material has a call number that indicates where it is located on the stack/shelf. Libraries have collections with in-depth information that has been published over time. Both current and out of print books and magazines are stocked in libraries most of which are in print formats. With the advent of the electronic age, some of these are now accessible through digital libraries collections on the Web. Libraries have trained staff called librarians who serve as a bridge between users and information sources. They assist users in sorting through the maze of information in their library collections. Librarians answer reference questions and also help patrons to learn how to use new information tools. If you need help with accessing information, contact your librarian.

SEARCHING THE LIBRARY CATALOGUE

For example, you can search the library catalogue of a University such as the University of Maryland or University of Zimbabwe to find primary, secondary and tertiary sources of information.

Table. Sample Catalogue Searches.

Primary	Diaries Nigerian Civil War
Secondary	Biography Nigerian Civil War
Tertiary	Encyclopedia Nigerian Civil War

When seeking information for academic purposes, it is advisable to start your search from the library and save yourself time and effort, as well as obtain relevant and quality information. You can then search the Internet if you need more information. Also, if you do not have the skills to search the Internet for relevant information, the librarians are there to assist you.

THE INTERNET

Definition of the Internet and the World Wide Web

The Internet is a global system of networked computers that allow user-to-user communication and transfer of data files from one computer to another on the network. It is a worldwide system of computer networks – a network of networks in which users at any one computer can, if they have permission, get information from any other computer (and sometimes talk directly to users at other computers) on the network. On the other hand, the World Wide Web (WWW) provides the technology needed to navigate the Internet is vast sea of resources. The WWW is a path-way of accessing information over the Internet via Uniform Resource Locator (URL) or web address.

Types of Information on the Internet

In the distant past humans sought to record information for future reference using clay tablets, papyrus, parchment and paper. However; the development of the printing press in the 16th Century forever changed the communication process. Currently the introduction of computers and the Internet has sky rocketed the amount of information now available to students, researchers, scientist, healthcare workers, policy makers, and faculty among others. Unlike the libraries, some of the information available on the Web is not peer-reviewed or referred as no one individual or group dictates what information should be published or how it should be presented. This freedom to post items allows individuals to publish their opinions, ideas and creative works on the Internet. As a result, the Internet has some information that may be interesting but cannot be referenced and used for academic purposes because no authority takes responsibility for it. Unlike libraries where librarians help users in accessing information, the Web is primarily a do-it-yourself endeavor.

The Internet contains all kinds of information sources including, among others:

- Bibliographic information such as library catalogs.
- Multimedia-Audio, video and graphical sources of information.
- Reference sources such as Encyclopedias, Dictio-naries, Handbooks, and others.
- Journals, Newspapers, Magazines and Databases.
- Subject related gateways.
- Reports/Grey literature.
- Movies and videos.

INFORMATION SOURCES IN THE LIBRARY/INTERNET

The Internet has become a big library for all kinds of information. Some information sources are available online free of charge while others are fee-based. Examples include online books, databases, journals and reference resources. Some of these are free on the Internet while others are based on subscription or purchase. MEDLINE/PubMed is a good example of a free online database while EMBASE is based on subscription.

The various categories of information sources that could be accessed through the Web:

- Reference;
- Monographs;
- Periodicals;
- Indexes and abstracts;
- Drug information; and
- Databases.

REFERENCE SOURCES

These are authoritative works that provide specific answers or information. As you go through school, you will need to use reference sources to find information about topics, locate facts, and answer questions. There are many types of reference sources, including atlases, dictionaries, encyclopedias, thesauri, directories, almanacs, manuals, biographies, and handbooks, among others. Each type is available either in print, on CD-ROMs and the Internet. Reference information sources can be general or subject specific. For example, The Encyclopedia *Britannica* is general while *The Encyclopedia of Stem-Cell* Research, *The Encyclopedia of Pain,* and *The Gale Encyclopedia of Medicine* are subject encyclopedias. Other reference sources such as dictionaries, atlases, directories also have both general and subject categories.

Fig. A Set of Encyclopedia Britannicagale Encyclopedia of Medicine.

MONOGRAPHS

A monograph is a scholarly piece of writing in form of an essay or book on a specific, often limited subject. It is a book that stands on its own rather than being part of a series. National Research Council (NRC), a monograph is a specialized scientific book. Monographs are written by specialists for the benefit of other specialists and demand the highest standards of scholarship. Most monographic manuscripts are critically reviewed and edited resulting in books that are expected to have a reasonably long shelf life. Monographs serve as an important means for conveying basic background information, such as a narrative description of a disease, path-physiology, diagnostic techniques and common therapeutic regimes etc. This trend remains true today, whether the monograph is in the print or electronic format.

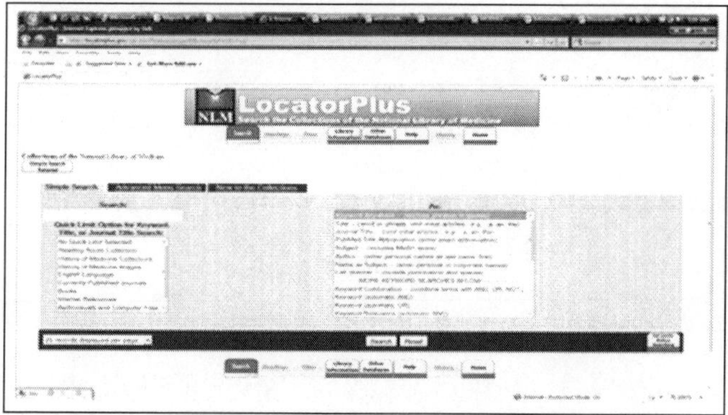

Monographs can be located using bibliographies that list references of books with detailed bibliographic information (author, title, year of publication, publisher and date of publication). Bibliographies serve as tools for verification, location and selection of monographs. Today, many print sources for monographs are now in electronic formats. To locate monographs in a library collection requires using the library catalogue and most libraries now have Online Public Access Catalogue (OPAC). A good example is the National Library of Medicine LOCATOR plus.

PERIODICALS

Periodicals are publications such as journals, newspapers, or magazines published on a regular basis-daily, weekly, bi-weekly, monthly, bimonthly, quarterly, yearly, etc. The information in periodicals covers a wide variety of topics and is very uptodate. Periodicals are available in both print and electronic formats. Common examples of periodicals include popular magazines (or general interest magazines), professional and trade magazines, scholarly journals, newsletters, and newspapers. The two basic types of periodicals are: popular (or general interest magazines), and scholarly.

POPULAR

Popular magazines are periodicals of non-specialist nature. The published articles are usually written by staff writers, and chosen by the editor of the publication. Magazine articles are usually shorter, written in non-technical language, and designed for the general population. Articles in popular magazines are reviewed by one or two members of staff of the organization where they are published. Popular magazines have a glossy appearance, contains many photographs and advertisements.

Examples of popular magazines are:

- O, The Oprah Magazine.
- Readers Digest.
- People.
- Time Magazine.

TRADE MAGAZINES

These are magazines that present information about a profession or a particular trade. They are written for members of a specific business, industry or organization. Trade magazines cover industry trends, new products or techniques, and organizational news written by staff or contributing authors. Good examples of trade magazines are: *The Economist, APA Monitor* and *Computer World.*

SCHOLARLY JOURNALS

Journals are written by experts or specialists in a particular field/discipline and geared towards other scholars. The purpose of scholarly publications is to report research or advance knowledge. The articles are usually longer and may contain charts, graphs, statistics, etc., as well as extensive bibliographies. The articles usually involve extensive research and in-depth studies. The writing style is more complex and the language may be technical. Examples of this type of periodical are academic journals and professional journals. Academic journals are written by members of an academic community and are reviewed by their peers while professional journals are written by member of a professional body including librarians, lawyers, doctors and nurses.

Examples of academic journals are:

- *British Medical Journal.*
- *New England Journal of Medicine.*
- *African Journal of Medicine and Medical Sciences.*
- *East African Medical Journal.*
- *African Health Sciences.*

Examples of professional/academic journals include:

- *Journal of the American Medical Association.*
- *Journal of the Medical Library Association.*
- *African Journal of Library, Archival and Information Science.*

Access to journals either in print or electronic formats is based on subscription, however; fulltext articles of some electronic journals can be accessed free on the Internet. Also, more than 7000 electronic journals are available to students, researchers, scientists, healthcare workers, and policy makers in Africa through the Health Internetwork Access to Research Initiative (HINARI). Using this resource requires institutional registration and login with the User Identification and Password.

NEWSPAPERS

Newspaper articles are short and written in non-technical language. They provide first-hand account of an event and so are primary sources. Newspapers come in different forms and are designed for the general public and are business in nature. Newspaper articles are usually short and written in an easy to understand language by staff reporters and reviewed by staff within the organization. Newspapers are also good sources for secondary information. However, not all information in newspapers is reliable. Newspapers are published daily, weekly or monthly. Example of newspapers include: *The New York Times, The Guardian,* and *Nigerian Tribune* etc.

INDEXES AND ABSTRACTS

Abstracts and indexes provide citations to papers dealing with specific topics in a field of knowledge. Indexes provide the essential bibliographic information needed to identify an article or other publications and usually include information about the author of the work, the source journal or other publication, volume, issue, and pagination. Abstracting tools include the same key elements but also a summary of the work usually written by the author or sometimes generated by the reviewer where an author did not submit one. Most indexing and abstracting services allow access to their content through subject and author indexes. However, each tool differs on how data is presented and the nature by which access is organized.

Examples of abstracts and indexes include:

- *Index Medicus.*
- *International Pharmaceutical Abstracts.*
- *Index to Dental Literature.*
- *Science Citation Index.*
- *Current Contents: Clinical Practice.*
- *Psychological Abstracts.*
- *Cumulative Index to Nursing and Allied Health Literature* (CINAHL).

Most of the popular databases searched by librarians and library users originated from printbased abstracting and indexing services. For example, the Index Medicus resulted in MEDLINE now accessible online through PubMed.

DRUG INFORMATION SOURCES

Butros and McGuinness, drug information sources cover the fields of pharmacology, pharmacy and toxicology. There are as many drug information sources as there are various specialties.

DATABASES

These are systematically organized collections of information covering different subject matters or specializing in one given subject or topic.

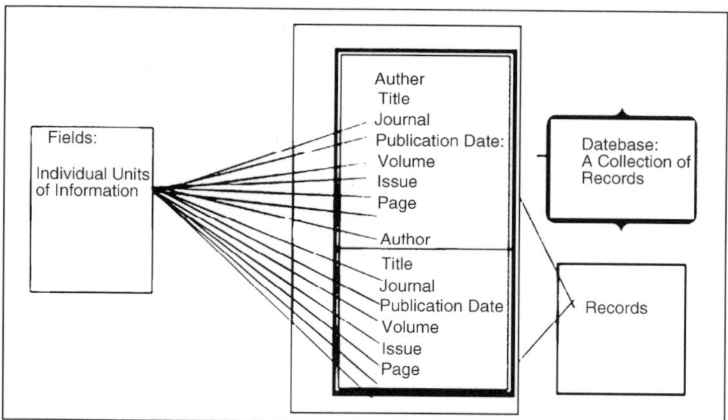

Fig. Components of a Biblographic Database

They may be arranged in a table of contents, alphabetically, in numerical order, in an index or in subject categories. A database is made up of records. Each item in the database has one record. Records consist of smaller units of information called fields. Common bibliographic database fields are: author, publication title, article title, subject or keywords, publication date, volume, issue and page number. For example, in the MEDLINE/PubMed database, each journal citation has one record. The record consists of the following fields: author, article title, journal title, date of publication, volume, issue, page number, PubMed ID, and abstract. A digital database (8.3) is a computer programme that organizes, describes, and indexes information. It permits the user to search for specific types of information, depending upon the selected search parameters.

INVISIBLE OR DEEP WEB

The "invisible Web" is what you cannot find using search engines and what you see in almost all subject directories. They are gold mines of information you need to search directly. These includes all of the licensed article, magazine, reference, news archives, and other research resources that libraries and some industries buy for those authorized to use them. There is lots of helpful information locked away in databases that can never be indexed by search engines. The services that let you search this "invisible Web" or "deep Web include: Invisi-bleweb.com, Lycos Invisible Catalogue, Direct search and WebData.

Examples of searchable databases containing invisible web pages valuable in academic research are:

- ipl2.
- Infomine.
- Online Bibliographic Databases:
  - African Index Medicus (AIM);
  - MEDLINE/PubMed;
  - Cumulative Index to Nursing and Allied Health Literature (CINAHL);
  - Web of Knowledge;
  - Scopus; and
  - EMBASE.

African Index Medicus (AIM)

African Index Medicus (AIM) is a collaborative effort between the World Health Organization (WHO) and the Association for Health Information and Libraries in Africa (AHILA). AIM gives access to information published or related to Africa and also encourages local publishing. A total of 140 journals published in Africa are indexed in AIM as of October 1, 2010. This database provides access to mainly abstracts and a few full-text articles published in African journals.

MEDLINE/PubMed

MEDLINE is the premier bibliographic database of the National Library of Medicine, Bethesda, Maryland, USA. It covers the field of medicine, nursing dentistry, veterinary medicine, the healthcare systems, the preclinical sciences and other areas related to the life sciences and is updated daily. MEDLINE records contain bibliographic citations from over 5,000 print and electronic biomedical journals published across the globe. It has over 12 million citations of which approximately 76 per cent include abstracts.

Cumulative Index to Nursing and Allied Health Literature (CINAHL)

Cumulative Index to Nursing and Allied Health Literature (CINAHL) CINAHL gives access to citations and abstracts for nursing and allied health information. It includes citations from over 2000 journals and abstracts are available for over 1200 titles with full text of over 7,000 records available in the database. This database also provides some coverage of biomedicine, alternative/ complementary medicine and consumer health information. CINAHL is based on subscription. However, it could be accessed free of charge through HINARI by institutions in Africa.

Web of Science

Web or science Provides access to the Science Citation Index Expanded and Social Science Citation Index. It covers science and provides technical journals in biochemistry, biology, genetics, biomedicine, genetics, microbiology, nuclear science with abstracts. It covers more than 8,000 journals. It offers current and retrospective bibliographic information, author abstracts and cited references and allows users to conduct broad-based comprehensive searches that uncover all the relevant information they need. It provides cited reference searching, the unique ISI search and retrieval feature that lets users track the literature forward, backward and through the database. It is updated weekly. Web of Knowledge (PubMed) is accessible free of charge via HINARI.

Scopus

Scopus is an interdisciplinary bibliographic database that indexes the content of more than 15,000 peer-reviewed journals from more than 4000 international publishers. It covers subjects such as the physical sciences, engineering, earth and environmental sciences, life and health sciences, social sciences, psychology, business, and management. Scopus content includes MEDLINE and EMBASE citations. Also, Scopus covers 1,000 Open Access Journals, 500 Conference Proceedings, Over 600 Trade Publications and over 125 Book titles. In addition, Scopus covers 386 million quality Web sources including 21 million patents.

Embase

Provides content to biomedical (clinical and experimental) information with extensive coverage of drug research, pharmacology, pharmacy, and toxicology, public health and mental health topics with abstracts back to 1974 and it is updated daily with pharmacological information. The database indexes more than 7000 journals, has over 18 million records. It has more than the 11 million EMBASE records from 1974 to date and seven million for unique MEDLINE records from 1966 to the present.

EVIDENCE-BASED MEDICINE (EBM) RESOURCES/DATABASES

Evidence-Based Medicine is about using information from the medical literature in making informed decision about patient care.

Many EBM databases are now accessible online including, among others:

- Clinical Queries.
- Cochrane Library.
- Clinical Evidence.
- DynaMed.
- Best Evidence.

In this module, Clinical Queries and the Cochrane Library will be discussed

Clinical Queries

This is accessible through PubMed and covers three main areas namely:

- *Clinical Study Category Query*: This filters citations to a specific clinical study category and scope.
- *Systematic Reviews:* These filter citations for systematic reviews, meta-analyses, reviews of clinical trials, evidence-based medicine, consensus development conferences, and guidelines..
- *Medical Genetics:* Filter citations to topics in medical genetics.

The Cochrane Library

The Cochrane Library is a collection of databases, published on CD-ROM and the Internet and updated quarterly, containing the Cochrane Database of Systematic Reviews, the Cochrane Central Register of Controlled Trials, the Database of Abstracts of Reviews of Effects, the Cochrane Methodology Register, the HTA Database, NHSEED, and information about

The Cochrane Collaboration. The Cochrane Library has about 4,000 reviews meant for use by health care workers to enable them to make informed decisions with respect to patient care. Reviews are unique because they are both produced by, and are relevant to everyone interested in the effects of health care. Based on the best available evidence, healthcare providers can decide if they should fund production of a particular drug. Practitioners can find out if an intervention is effective in a specific clinical context.

Patients and other healthcare consumers can assess the potential risks and benefits of their treatment:

- Systematic reviews seek to collate all evidence that fits pre-specified eligibility criteria in order to address a specific research question.
- They aim to minimize bias by using explicit, syste-matic methods.
- The Cochrane Collaboration prepares, maintains and promotes

systematic reviews to inform healthcare decisions (Cochrane reviews).

- Cochrane reviews are published in the *Cochrane Database of Systematic Reviews* in *The Cochrane Library.*

CONSUMER HEALTH INFORMATION RESOURCES/DATABASES

- MEDLINEPlus.
- National Institute of Health (NIH) Senior Health.
- New York Online Access to Health (NOAH).
- HealthyRoadsMedia.
- Toxtown.
- Toxnet.
- Household products database.

Medline Plus

Medline Plus is a product of the National Library of Medicine (NLM). Medline Plus offers information on selected, organized links to online consumer health information on hundreds of topics about diseases, conditions, and wellness issues in language you can understand. Medline Plus offers reliable, up-to-date health information, anytime, anywhere for free. You can use Medline Plus to learn about the latest treatments, look up information on a drug or supplement, find out the meanings of words, or view medical videos or illustrations. You can also get links to the latest medical research on your topic or learn about clinical trials on a disease or condition. It also includes tutorials. Also featured are an online encyclopedia, medical dictio-nary, audio-visual resources, and extensive links to Spanish-language health information. Medline Plus is the premier consumer health site. It should be any consumer health information seeker's first stop, and can fill the vast majority of information needs. The homepage is very well-organized; everything is accessible from there. When searching, multiple search terms automatically combined with "And". Search engine will detect misspelled words and suggest alternatives.

NIH Senior Health

This is a website for the elderly, developed by the National Institute on Aging and the National Library of Medicine. Senior-friendly features include the ability to adjust font size and contrast, an audio option that reads text on the page aloud, and videos. Seniors with low vision, and anyone with low literacy needs, although most topics are senior-specific (*i.e.* Exercise for Older Adults). A short list of topics is easy to browse. No search option is included. Audio text reading function is very literal and function is spotty: may repeat phrases several times and/or skip words or sentences.

NOAH: New York Online Access to Health

A collaborative effort of New York librarians, NOAH provides access to selected, organized links to online consumer health information. It has a wide range of topics and extensive Spanish-language content. Non-Spanish-speaking users can navigate organized topic pages in English, and then click on "en espanol" link at bottom of page to access available Spanish language links for that topic. It is well-organized and easy to browse; browsing is often more efficient than using the search engine.

Healthy Roads Media

A collaborative effort of many different public health agencies, social services organizations, and librarians, HealthyRoadsMedia collects, creates and provides free online access to multilingual health information overviews on various topics in a variety of formats: audio, audiovisual, and written. Health topics provided in English and eight other languages: Arabic, Bosnian, Hmong, Khmer, Russian, Somali, Spanish, and Vietnamese. It is best for patients with lower literacy English and/or need for information in a language other than English. Focus is on prevention and wellness, and safety. Not all topics are available in all languages.

Household Products Database

This database links over 10,000 consumer brands to health effects from Material Safety Data Sheets (MSDS) provided by manufacturers and allows scientists and consumers to research products based on chemical ingredients. Household product database was developed by the Specialized Information Services Division at the National Library of Medicine, National Institutes of Health, Bethesda, Maryland, USA.

The database is designed to help answer the following typical questions:

- What are the chemical ingredients and their percentage in specific brands?
- Which products contain specific chemical ingredients?
- Who manufactures a specific brand? How do I contact this manufacturer?
- What are the acute and chronic effects of chemical ingredients in a specific brand?
- What other information is available about chemicals in the toxicology-related databases of the National Library of Medicine?

Tox Town

Tox Town: is designed to give you information on:

- Everyday locations where you might find toxic chemicals.
- Non-technical descriptions of chemicals.
- Links to selected, authoritative chemical information on the Internet.
- How the environment can impact human health.
- Internet resources on environmental health topics.

Tox Town uses colour, graphics, sounds and animation to add interest to learning about connections between chemicals, the environment, and the public's health. Tox Town's target audience is students above elementary-school level, educators, and the general public. It is a companion to the extensive information in the TOXNET collection of databases that are typically used by toxicologists and health professionals.

Toxnet

Toxnet is a database on toxicology, hazardous chemicals, environmental health, toxic releases and other information resources from the Toxicology and Environmental Health Information Programme. Developed by the U.S National Library of Medicine.

INTERNET PORTALS, DIGITAL ARCHIVES AND INSTITUTIONAL REPOSITORIES

- Health Internetwork Access to Research Initiative (HINARI) African Journals Online (AJOL).
- PubMed Central (PMC).
- *Bioline International (BI):* Through this site you can search through free and open access medical journals.
- *Biomed Central*: Open Access (OA) journal publisher that allow readers free access to published full text journal articles while authors pay fees to get published.
- *Scientific Online Library (SciELO):* An AO publisher that gives access to full text articles.
- *Directory of Open Access Journals (DOAJ):* Gives you free access to online journals related to your subject area.
- Loughborough University's Institutional Repository.
- *Google Scholar:* While regular Google can be a helpful tool, sometimes you just need scholarly results, and that's just what this tool does, paring down results to the most reliable and academic sources.

INFORMATION SOURCES ON SOCIAL NETWORKING APPLICATIONS

In recent years social networking applications popularly known as Web 2.0 are now being used as a means of communication, especially in sharing and dissemination of information. Libraries are also using this media to reach out to their clients.

Common Web 2.0 applications that have become sources of information include:

- Facebook;
- Blogs;
- Twitter;
- MySpace;
- YouTube; and
- RSS.

7

Vital Resources and Technical Services in Libraries

THE CONCEPTUAL FRAMEWORK

The conceptual framework rests on a synthesis of cognitive learning theories about scientific reasoning and concepts. Many theories discuss learning and define the characteristic steps of learning: component display, information- processing theory, modes of learning, and mental models.

From the perspective of cognitive processes that make up a scientific reasoning skill set, these theories show general agreement that scientific reasoning is closely related to problem solving and that it involves both inductive and deductive reasoning.

A spatial representation theory of reasoning suggests that people do better when visualizing things, and therefore successful scientific reasoning includes observation and visualization skills. Ziman in his discussion of scientific research and knowledge provides a summary of many important aspects of science, such as patterns of fact, differentiating facts into categories, skills of observation, accuracy, relevancy, explanation, description, generality, and extensive reliance on and use of instrumentation, measurement, and models. From these theories and research studies, it is possible to derive an operational definition of the selective skills and critical steps in learning that are an integral part of the scientific reasoning process.

We define scientific reasoning as inductive and deductive thinking. Inductive thinking includes concept development, which is composed of concept acquisition, concept formation, and concept mapping. Deductive thinking includes hypothesis development, which comprises discovery, observation, model building, and evaluation/proof formulation based on empirical evidence.

This definition can be correlated with educational objectives when teaching, and with learning outcomes while or after being exposed to learning activities such as lectures and laboratories. For example, training in concept mapping has been shown to facilitate acquisition of text information.

Therefore, in measurable terms of cognitive processes, scientific reasoning comprises:

- Concept acquisition
- Concept formation and analysis
- Concept mapping
- Instantiation
- Generalization and categorization
- Problem formulation
- Hypothesis generation
- Explanation
- Prediction
- Evaluation

This is neither a comprehensive, definitive, nor sequential list of scientific reasoning skills. It provides the theoretical framework for our design and prototype development of learning spaces. In this framework, concepts emerge as the foundational units for facilitating science learning. For a similar approach based on concepts. There are a number of definitions of the word "concept" in the learning sciences.

These definitions have been contributed by psychologists, educators, philosophers, linguists, and cognitive scientists and include the following:

- A concept is an idea or thought, more precisely the abstraction that represents or signifies the unifying principle of various distinct particulars.
- Concepts represent the fundamental elements of all concept areas. In formal content situations, concepts are classes of objects, symbols, and events that are grouped together in some fashion by shared characteristics.
- Most concepts are structured mental representations that encode a set of necessary and sufficient conditions for their application, if possible, in sensory or perceptual terms.

These definitions show that concepts are not studied in an isolated manner; rather, they are studied in their associations or relationships with other concepts. An important component of instructional design is the analysis of the concepts to be learned.

Two basic types of analysis are:

- Content task analysis, which focuses on defining the critical characteristics of the concepts and the relationship of those characteristics according to superordinate and subordinate organizations, and
- Contextual analysis, which focuses on the memory and organization of the concepts.

Both types of concept analysis imply the specification of relationships among concepts. These relationships can be restated in the terminology of librarians: analysing characteristics and superordinate and subordinate organizations of concepts, students define generic-specific and object-property types of relationships. During contextual analysis, students determine other types of relationships between concepts, which librarians know as associative relationships. Associations can also be defined between objects and processes, objects and events, tools and methods, etc. Related to concepts, but not quite the same from the standpoint of educators, are the words "subject," "topic," and "class."

The subject is a field of knowledge or established area of instruction, for example, the subject of mathematics. Subjects are often associated with disciplines. Teachers, scholars, and other workers tend to specialize in the study or use of a particular body of knowledge—or we could say subject/ discipline. Subjects involve not merely their particular subject matter, but a particular kind of activity related to it. Topics, on the other hand, are subjects that invite treatment by a number of disciplines. The topic may involve a number of concepts from different subjects, or it may be led or dominated by a single subject. The topic web is a schematic, annotated way of planning the topic, showing how a variety of ideas, activities, subject areas, or skills are related to the core idea. Class is a group, set, or kind of things sharing common attributes. It is frequently associated with the set: a number of things of the same kind that belong or are used together. Theoretically, a discipline determines its subject, identifies topics, breaks them down into classes and concepts, determines relationships, and teaches them via a number of activities. Physical geography is the domain used here to investigate how concepts are organized in classroom teaching and learning.

THE DISCIPLINE OF PHYSICAL GEOGRAPHY

Document analysis was used to examine the organization of content in one textbook as well as traditional classroom lectures supplemented by Microsoft PowerPoint presentations. We chose materials from introductory freshman and sophomore courses in physical geography. Informal interviews with two teaching faculty supplemented the formal document analyses. Curriculum materials used include Christopherson. Document analysis is a method of research that is used to study historical documents, usually primary source materials.

This method can be used to investigate details like document type, date, creator, as well as answer questions like why was the document written and what can be inferred about the document creator and other pertinent subject matters. Education staff at the National Archives and Historical Administration have created and made publicly available via their Web site a number of document analysis worksheets for different types of documents, such as maps, text, etc. Lectures and textbooks have been the primary tools of Western education for some time now. Lecture materials are unusual in that they can be considered as both primary and secondary source materials. Textbooks are clearly secondary source materials. Good lectures summarize, synthesize, and present a vast amount of material in a bite-sized chunk. Textbooks provide explanation, corroboration, and pointers to more materials on the subject. Both types of materials were examined in order to identify key aspects of their organizational structure. A limitation of these analyses is the lack of observation of real learning activities, evaluation, and user studies of physical geography learning in students. However, we feel that such studies, while useful, should be preceded by a clear understanding of the nature of the discipline as perceived and presented by its expert teachers. We found that organization by concepts is the preferred method for presenting learning material. Concepts are the building blocks in the educational process. Instructors teaching concepts also defined the terminology and explained the relationships among concepts.

Thus, in geography teaching, a variety of resources for particular natural processes or phenomena are presented as terms selected and defined by the instructor; and relationships within and external to other processes, phenomena, tools, methods, classifications, theories, and states are explained, explored, and studied. One of the key aspects of geography learning at the undergraduate level is vocabulary—terminological lists, lists of standard terms, and their definitions. Additionally, many geographic terms and concepts represent details of natural phenomena and require pictorial explanation. For example, alluvial fans and geologic folds are explained with text, verbal analogies, images, diagrams, maps, and photographs. Educators create personalized collections of images of natural phenomena, processes, and objects.

These are accompanied by definitions, which sometimes are cross-linked with others, offered as a glossary, and used for presenting new material to students. Scientific classifications are of great importance. The textbook contained about 70 classifications, ranging from objects to phenomena to spatial and temporal divisions such as geologic time periods. Additionally, instructional materials pointed to a number of other classifications of objects and phenomena. For example, there are more than 2,000 coordinate systems alone.

A final aspect of organizing for learning in geography is the attention given to the expression of geographical concepts and their relationships using mathematics— measurements from instruments for specific concepts, equations that specify relationships. Through computation, most of these are ultimately transformed and represented as visualizations such as climographs, hydrographs, hypsographic curves, etc. These visual and mathematical representations are used extensively to promote basic scientific interpretation of complex phenomena and processes, often not possible by mere observation. Real-world phenomena taught in physical geography are presented under disciplinary aspects of geography, geology, physics, biology, chemistry, astronomy, and other science and engineering disciplines. Synthesis of diverse perspectives is considered to be an outcome and strength of geographical knowledge and is consistently highlighted in presentations. This contrasts directly with the widely held view of science as essentially reductionist in nature. But it fits with the study of geography as an applied science, dealing with measurements, forecasting and modeling, and interpretation of natural phenomena.

SIMILARITIES AND DIFFERENCES BETWEEN ORGANIZATION FOR LEARNING AND KNOWLEDGE ORGANIZATION IN LIBRARIES

Summarizing, the two activities of organization for learning and organization for information retrieval in libraries appear to have many similarities. Concepts, relationships, and classifications are also key tools that are used to organize knowledge in libraries. Librarians, like educators, use the same concept-related terminology, specify the same relationships, and are involved in similar processes related to concept analyses. How are library concepts different from concepts used by educators? Are terms, classes, facets, and subjects the same as concepts? How are concepts arranged in library classification schemes? How do librarians analyse concepts? For librarians, a concept is a knowledge unit with similar characteristics.

Often, the term "concept" is used interchangeably with words such as "term," "subject," "subject heading," "topic," and "facet." "Terms" are the main components of thesauruses, while "subjects" or "subject headings" comprise the subject heading lists, like:

- Library of Congress Subject Headings or
- Dewey Decimal Classification.

Unlike terms, which mainly include concepts from a specific domain related to phenomena, subject headings—human constructs—may include different types of concepts, specifically names, time periods, form, and topics.

The main differences between terms and subjects can be described as follows:

- In general, a term denotes a single concept, while a subject heading may consist of composites of terms, although it also may consist of a single concept.
- The guidelines for thesauruses give rules for establishing hierarchical relationships and for assigning associative and hierarchical terms. LCSH also has rules that are used when establishing new headings; however, composite headings are more difficult to relate than terms, and there remain many headings and relationships that were established before the rules were made.

The term "topic" is frequently used interchangeably with the terms "subject" and "subject heading," or "topical subject." Topic represents an aspect of the main subject other than form, place, or period—for example, headings: Libraries, Agriculture. "Subject" is defined as any one of the topics or themes of a work, stated explicitly in the title or text or implicitly in its message. In library cataloguing, books and other items are assigned one or more subject headings that represent their content to assist users in locating information by subject.

In indexes and bibliographic databases, the subject headings assigned to documents are called descriptors. Topics and subjects in library classifications are associated with document aboutness. In library cataloguing, subject analysis has traditionally been carried out on the summarization level that is finding the one overall subject concept that encompasses or can represent what the whole item is about.

Alternatively, the 20 per cent rule is invoked where 20 per cent of the document is about the subject. In library and information science, class is "the first order of structure in a hierarchical classification, at which level major disciplines are represented. A class may incorporate one or more divisions, which in turn may incorporate one or more subdivisions". Examples of classes are the fundamental disciplines or what educators refer to as subjects that are the foundation of the main classification systems: mathematics, physical science, human science, history, art, and so on. Classes are usually divided and arranged according to principles of categorization, such as shared properties and exclusivity. Relationships among concepts are specified to varying degrees by different types of classificatory structures. For example, thesauruses generally specify only three types of semantic relationships. Library classifications are limited in how relationships can be constructed or how many can be specified by many factors, such as the type of scheme and the hospitality of the inherent notation.

In faceted thesauruses or faceted classifications, the relationships are structured with a central idea in mind—for example, object, process, or event. However, most library classifications attempt to preserve the principle of containing relationships.

Containing relationships include:

- Main class or basic subject in relation to all its subdivisions
- Genus in relation to species
- Whole in relation to part
- Class in relation to its members.

The principle of containing relationships does not mean that each item must be more special than the one preceding it. Many items are neither more general nor more special than those adjacent. For example, a book on Mozart in general would precede one on Mozart's operas, etc. Such knowledge organization structures correlate well to topics in education, where concepts from different knowledge domains are related to one topic.

These relationships are often based on contextual analysis, and the relatedness is based on proximity of concepts in the text. For instance, the concept "drainage basin" is highlighted as a heading in a textbook; other concepts like sheetflow, interfluves, gullies. The inclusion relationships principle, drainage basin is a broad term, and sheet flow, interfluves, gullies, and continental divides are narrow terms. Concept, subject, and facet analyses are the processes by which public knowledge structures are used and created. They are familiar activities to librarians, and distinctions between them are often not made. Concept analysis, usually done by indexers, uses an indexing language or thesaurus. Subject analysis as done in library cataloguing is the process of assigning subjects from a controlled vocabulary list to a document. Discourse communities interpret facet analysis in different ways. Classificationists, designers of classification schemes, perform facet analysis when they try to identify the fundamental classes needed or inherent in a subject.

The definition of facet analysis we use in this study is based on the original work of Ranganthan. It is also currently used by the Facet Analysis Theory project to create subject-based portals for the Web. Facet analysis is the "rigourous process of terminological analysis where the vocabulary of a given subject is organized into facets and arrays, resulting in a complex knowledge structure with both semantic and syntactic relationships clearly delineated". These analysis techniques are used to solve the disambiguation problems of semantics, which are well-known problems in information retrieval. When a user searches using a word or phrase, do the records that are retrieved with the same words or phrase really correspond to what the user meant? Classificatory structures take care of semantic problems such as synonyms and homographs in many different ways—for example, thesauruses use qualifiers and parenthetical statements.

They also specify relationships between terms. Semantics therefore refers to the meaning of the term, both its dictionary definition as well as all the associations to it. Definitions are called the "reference" or "denotation," and associations are called "connotation." Definitions are limited and often standardized by community consent and use, but connotations may be infinite since they are determined by personal experience. Thesauruses select associations and include them in three kinds of semantic relationships; indexing languages try to describe many more associations. However, we find that in geography teaching many more associations need to be specified and described for the novice learner. This is one important difference. Another difference is that definitions must also be provided. Given these surface similarities, we decided to find out how, if, and what knowledge organization system could be used to facilitate physical geography science learning.

Our specific questions: How can library classification schemes and thesaurus-type knowledge structures be used for educational purposes? How can differences between organization for learning and for information retrieval be reconciled? There are a number of earth sciences thesauruses that include physical geography. To answer the question of whether a thesaurus can be used for educational purposes, a comparison of concepts in two types of information resources was carried out. Concepts from physical geography texts and the major thesaurus in the geosciences, *GeoRef*, were compared. We also examined the information system *GEOBASE*, a database that indexes materials in physical geography. Physical geography is one of the subjects in geosciences; it may be considered a marginalized knowledge domain because it does not have a major classification scheme or a thesaurus devoted only to it.

We found that documents on physical geography have just a linear list of terms rather than a thesaurus for collection indexing and retrieval. The *GeoRef* thesaurus does contain some terms used in physical geography, but many of them are not included. Our preliminary estimates, 65 per cent of concepts explained in the textbook cannot be found in *GeoRef*. Examples of concepts not found in *GeoRef* are angle of incidence, angle of repose, atomic number, atomic weight, autumnal equinox, available water, average global temperature, azimuth.

To answer the question of how a library classification scheme can be used to support science learning, we examined two widely used classification schemes: Library of Congress Classification and the Dewey Decimal Classification. We found that many physical geography concepts are excluded from these major, albeit general, classification schemes. We speculate that this is so because concepts are neither subjects nor topics. Examples of geography concepts not found in these tools are open and closed systems, law of basin areas, leeward. However, these terms are needed if geographic information resources such as maps and datasets are to be more adequately described for information retrieval in a library catalogue that supports science learning. Some universal classification schemes are employed primarily outside the United States, but many of these are based on subjects and disciplines similar to LCSH and DDC, so geology concepts would be separated from geography, resulting in educational limitations.

Another disadvantage of current universal classification schemes is their use of the principle of containing relationships, not the principle of building relationships around the main idea—object, process, or event—as the guideline for knowledge organization. Thus, they do not represent the concept relationships that reflect the order of things in science. Scientific classifications differ from library classifications and subject thesauruses in many ways. One significant difference is that library classifications are based on the literary warrant and link topics to subtopics. Many scientific classifications belong to disciplines that have widely accepted classifications and categorizations.

Most of the concepts in these disciplines might naturally fit into thesaurus hierarchies based on the is- A relationship, often referred to as broad term - narrow term relationship. The proliferation of special library classifications and thesauruses in many science disciplines shows that many more relationships and deeper subject intension is often needed than provided by general-purpose schemes. Physical geography, however, is a discipline that is somewhat unique. Geographers and geo-morphologists do not have unanimous approaches to classifying real-world phenomena or processes;

rather they have multiple classifications based on various criteria. All are considered equally important for teaching the science of geography.

LIMITATIONS OF EXISTING KNOWLEDGE STRUCTURES

As early as 1944, Swank pleaded for a critical discussion that recognized the interrelationships between classification, library catalogs, indexes, and bibliographies. While in the digital world these tools are certainly merging and can be merged, our analysis shows that other critical interrelationships that need to be considered for the development of digital learning spaces are the ones that integrate knowledge structures and reference sources. This means that we should explore the merging of knowledge structures such as classification schemes and thesauruses with reference works such as encyclopedias and dictionaries. Included in this list are glossaries, gazetteers, and terminology lists.

Reference tools like:

- Xrefer and Atomica
- Thesaurus
- Definition
- Encyclopedia linkages..

We focus only on the limitations of classificatory concepts such as hierarchy, semantic relationships, and order as they are currently implemented or used in knowledge structures. The enhancements needed are also discussed. The thesaurus' hierarchical relationships—generic, instance, and partitive—are not enough to describe the full granularity of how phenomena or processes or objects are analysed in physical geography. To illustrate this point, let us consider types of "atmosphere," specifically, its NTG relationships. Figure shows them listed in alphabetical order.

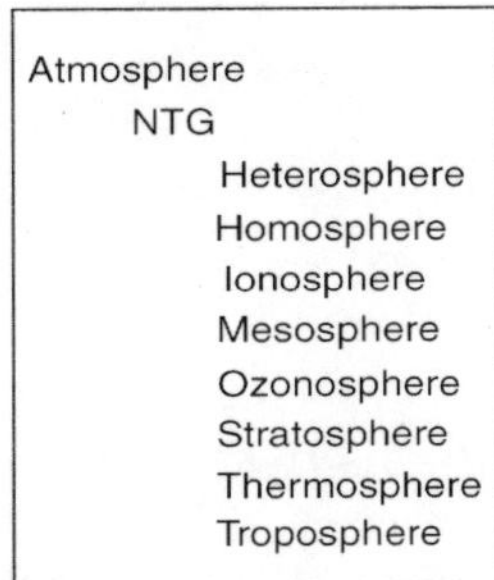

Fig. NTG Relationships for "Atmosphere"

All these concepts represent types of atmosphere. They are all linked to atmosphere with one type of relationship, NTG. However, for a specialist in the field, these concepts differ in their relationship to the concept atmosphere; namely, they are based on different classifications that consider different criteria. Following the faceted thesauruses' practices, such as those in the Art and Architecture Thesaurus, these different classifications can be maintained in different "nodes," which simply mean different sets of subtypes. Nodes themselves are treated as nonindexing terms and are shown in angular brackets in figure.

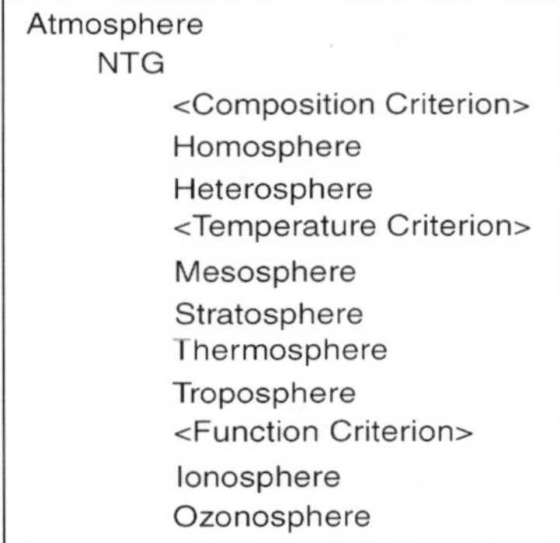

Fig. Nodes for "Atmosphere"

By default, the conventional thesauruses and thesaurus construction software, such as Multi-Tes, arrange narrower concepts in alphabetical order. Such an arrangement is not a satisfactory foundation for building learning spaces in physical geography. In real geography learning, concepts are arranged in a certain order, which is by no means alphabetical, and differs depending on the concept. It may be chronological or based on disciplinary logic. For example, geological time periods are arranged in a chronological order that is based on macro time scales. Other times, arrangements are based on micro time scales. The need for ordering concepts exists in library classification schemes too.

However, general thesauruses usually do not specify a citation or preference order. The exception is faceted thesauruses, such as the A&AT. Our findings suggest that ordering of concepts in sets is desirable for enabling learning. It would also be useful to add multiple ordering of concepts— for example, as the concepts are organized in the textbook.

In the literature, concepts can be repeated as subtypes of one concept under different classifications.

For instance:

- N. Lancaster differentiates the following dune types:
  - Crescentic dunes
  - Linear dunes
  - Star dunes
  - Parabolic dunes
  - Nebkhas
  - Lunettes
- E. D. McKee differentiates:
  - Crescentic dunes

- Linear dunes
- Star dunes
- Other dunes

- L. Aufrere classifies dune in the following way:
  - Longitudinal
  - Oblique
  - Transverse

In these classifications, linear, crescentic, and star dunes appear in two classifications. To incorporate all these classifications into a thesaurus, we would have to list some of the terms as subtypes of sand dunes twice or more. The classifications are taken from Nicholas. Some universal classification schemes are employed primarily outside the United States, but many of these are based on subjects and disciplines, so geology concepts would be separated from geography, resulting in educational limitations. Another peculiarity of concept arrangements in textbooks is that they are not in the alphabetical order usually found in thesauruses. Very often orderings carry additional semantic information—for instance, they show chronological sequence or evolution.

Thesauruses should reflect such scientific orders. These orderings do not necessarily have to be displayed for the users; they can be used only by librarians or in the background. The users will just see the sequence of concepts in a way the phenomena or their types are arranged in nature, or in chronological order or the order in which scientists usually arrange them.

Ranganathan suggested the following possibilities for order in array within a facet in addition to alphabetical order:

- Increasing quantity. Types of polygons could be arranged in this order: triangle, quadrilateral, pentagon, hexagon, heptagon, octagon, nonagon, decagon, hendecagon, dodecagon, etc.
- Later in time. Writers in literature could be arranged according to their date of birth.
- Later in evolution. Living things could be arranged in this way.
- Spatial contiguity
- Increasing complexity. Methods, instruments, machinery could be arranged in this way.
- Canonical order. This means a traditional order, such as arithmetic, algebra, geometry.
- Favoured category or literary warrant. This order could give precedence to the subjects in the array about which most had been published.

Subject intension is depth of the subject, the microtopics. If relationships that support scientific theories, classifications and categorizations, and concepts on a level of even micro-topics are available, they can be used for the construction of concept maps. Concept maps are gaining quick popularity as a favoured instructional material in many disciplines. There are a number of software packages that allow students and instructors to construct concept maps.

However, our experience at ADEPT indicates that many instructors do not have the time to build concept maps and organize their materials using them. Another reason why concepts maps are not widely constructed in science is because it is very difficult to build a concept map from scratch and show the complexity of relationships on one plane, as opposed to multidimensional space. However, instructors are often willing to use concept maps in instruction if they are constructed, maintained, and organized by other responsible entities, such as libraries.

CONVERGENCE

We conclude that a faceted thesaurus based on scientific classifications of disciplinary-specific facets such as objects, processes, phenomena, and methods can provide the foundation for developing digital learning spaces in physical geography. It must be constructed with great care given to the contents, categorization, and quality of the hierarchies. For example, polyhierarchies must specify roles and have more detailed associative relationships. An ALCTS committee has been investigating the area of subject relationships. Hierarchies must also link types and parts of objects to objects, processes to processes, etc.

FACETS

Facets are "clearly defined, mutually exclusive, and collectively exhaustive aspects, properties or characteristics of a class or specific subject".

Our analysis derived similar facets in physical geography that were originally assembled as universals in the context of all disciplines:

- Objects
- Properties, attributes
- Processes and activities
- Instruments
- Theories, principles, classifications
- Applications
- Disciplines

NAMES FOR RELATIONSHIPS

Another desirable enhancement that should not be overlooked is more detailed specification of the associative relationships among concepts. Relational structures—indicated usually by an abbreviation RT for related term or by AS, often used for associative relationships—are neither sufficient nor explicit.

While the task of decoding what is hidden behind the abbreviation would not seem to be complex for the more experienced users of a specific domain, for the novice domain users, in our case, students, it will be difficult to understand the nature of RT relationships without specification. Therefore, for students a short explanation of the associative relationships is necessary.

LABELS FOR NODES

Node labels are organizational devices that are often used to arrange hierarchical displays. Node labels are enclosed within angled brackets.

SUPPORT FOR ORDERS IN ARRAYS OF RELATED CONCEPTS

As discussed previously, concepts in the relationships can be ordered not only alphabetically, but also in chronological, evolutional, canonical, and other sequences. Agreement is needed for how objects should be ordered in geosciences. For instance, in our example with atmospheres, the flexibility of defining sequential orders lets us arrange concepts of atmospheric types in the natural order as is shown in figure.

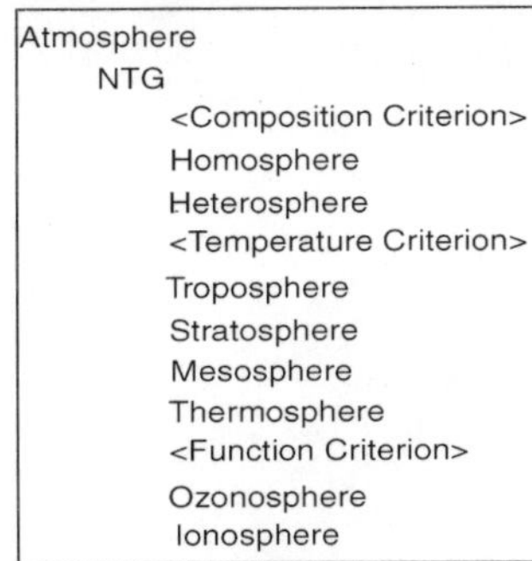

Fig. Natural Order for "Atmosphere"

USING TOPIC MAPS FOR DIGITAL LEARNING SPACES

Many technical and theoretical approaches offer solutions to interlink concepts; semantic nets, ontologies, topic maps, and concept maps are some of them. The use of the ISO Topic Map standard, XTM. Topic maps provide "a standardized notation for interchangeably representing information about the structure of information resources used to define topics, and the relationships between topics". The topic definition in the standard is similar to the librarian's definitions of topics or subjects. However, it is possible to use topic maps for linking concepts and specifying relationships between them. In other words, it is possible to construct information resources such as concept maps based on classificatory knowledge structures, like the faceted thesaurus using the XTM standard. In doing so, no significant distinction between concepts and topics is made.

As examples of topic maps, XTM and faceted thesauruses have many features in common:

- Both link concepts.
- Both treat concepts and relationships separately.
- Both use controlled vocabularies.
- Most relationships in both standards have symmetrical counterparts.
- Both serve as backbones in information systems that allow linking

the information resources to the concepts; the only difference is that topic maps do this internally within the topic map, and thesauruses do this externally—surrogate bibliographic records carry linkages to the concepts in the thesaurus.

- In both standards hierarchies play an important role in information organization. The first step of organizing concepts into classes and subclasses of concepts in topic map construction is similar to the task of defining a genus and species, a primary task in building a thesaurus.
- Classes in topic maps and hierarchies in thesauruses facilitate a systematic approach to cross-referencing concepts from different facets; from these an ontologist will have a clear picture in terms of the categories for characterizing the concepts.

Standard thesaurus relationships can be mapped to topic map terminology as shown in figure.

Thesaurus	Topic Map
BTG-NTG-General Term	<Instance>
USE-Use this Term	<BaseNameString>
UF - Use this Term Instead	<VariantName>
SN - Scope Note	<Scope>
NTG-BTG - Narrower Term	<InstanceOf>

Fig. Thesaurus—Topic Map Relationships Mapping

The advantages of topic maps are that they are in XML format and have a number of software packages—for authoring, navigating, and displaying. These software packages help users and creators visualize the contents of the concept space and display explicitly concepts and relationships among concepts. The visualizations can be shown to users as concept maps. Concepts immediately related to a particular concept can be viewed as a concept map for the particular concept. The relationships in topic maps also have a much richer structure than the relationships in thesauruses.

While thesauruses have only a predefined set of relationships, the XTM standard gives full semantic freedom in the specification of relationships. This is both an advantage and a disadvantage. Since concepts and relationships are important for librarians and educators and may vary based on discipline, different learning spaces can be designed for different domains. Relationships in topic maps have two components: roledefining topic and role. Role-defining topic can be expressed as a verb; for example, written by, has, originates. The idea of including verbs in a concept space is interesting, since most library knowledge organization schemes have always tried to avoid verbs.

In science education, verbs are important information elements and are used quite extensively: modify, move/transport, measure, capture, produce, protect, damage, form, originate, re/distribute, dissipate, accumulate, gravitate, occupy, cover, resist, protect, dissolve, decrease, increase, exist, generate. For the role-defining topics we initially recommend implementing isAssociatedWith, Has-Constitute/Comprise, IsStudiedIn-Studies, Uses-IsUsedBy, IsCausedBy-Causes using XTM. However, a more complex typology of relationships can also be specified. Roles refer to the related concept and explain its category.

For roles, names of basic categories—or facets—such as, processes, methods, tools, properties, objects; or their more detailed subcategories: landforms, landscapes, hydrologic bodies, vegetation, fluvial processes, and other can be applied. Roles are the elements that can make the topic map model especially attractive to educators and novice learners. Figure shows the list of relationships and roles needed for teaching and learning about atmosphere.

Typology of Associative (Related) Relationships for Atmosphere:

- IsStateOf
- IsMethodFor
- IsClassificationFor
- HasClassification
- HasAssociatedMethods
- HasStates
- CanBeMeasuredWith
- IsForMeasuring
- HasProcesses
- IsProcessOf
- HasProperties
- IsPropertyFor
- IsAssociatedWithGeosystem
- IsUsedFor

Due to the complexity of the relationship structure in the XTM standard, the relationships have to be specified in both directions: from concept a to concept b and from concept b to concept a. From this perspective, the thesaurus appears to be a more efficient model; the symmetrical relationships are derived from the relationship between a and b. The weakness of both standards though is that they lack the predefined behaviour of relationships. While in thesaurus the behaviours are described in the NISO standard, no action is taken upon it by the existing software packages.

For instance, knowing classes of concepts and the directionality of relationships, one could impose the constraints that would disallow such entries as Hamlet wrote Shakespeare, or erosion is made of sand. The constraints that would disallow such entries are necessary if we are going to use the help of the scientific community in building the relationships. Additional research of relationship behaviour in concept spaces is highly desirable. The basic idea of topic maps is that all concepts are grouped around one central concept—topic via the inclusive relationship—*instanceOf*—instance. Each relationship can have a reference to a specific role-defining topic. The examples used in the XTM standard indicate that the topics for the relationships can be expressed as verbs. For instance, in creating a topic map about streams we could say: topic streams includes instance—*has*. Further, all related-to-stream concepts that can be linked with the verb has can perform specific roles in the relationship—in this specific case, all the components will have a role—*Part*.

Different types of stream parts can be disambiguated by the more specification of roles:

- Longitudinal Part,
- Cross Sectional Part, and
- Component.

While the topic map standard offers a nice data model, it does not describe the theoretical details of construction for concept spaces: what relationships can be used, or how the relationships should be specified. Such principles must be developed. We believe that the underlying principles that are well suited for topic map construction are the principles of faceted thesauruses. These include strictly defined rules about specification of hierarchical relationships, use of controlled vocabularies, and construction of associative relationships.

As a general organizational principle, we also propose using the "natural order of things" approach, described earlier. This means that as suggested, structure relationships according to the order of things as perceived in science/nature. Streams will be related to streams, parts of streams, stream properties, and other objects related to the streams: *e.g.*, terraces, fluvial processes, and physical, chemical, and biological properties.

When this approach is followed, a subject ontogeny is maintained as well and becomes a part of public knowledge structures. Topic maps can provide the conceptual framework for developing the content domain and scientific reasoning processes of student learning that can be associated with information resources. Because the standard builds a structured semantic network over heterogeneous and topically diverse resources, it allows easy and selective navigation to the requested information as well as easy maintenance.

The interface for topic maps can be either conventional with hyperlinks, or graphical, the so-called hyperbolic browser interface that represents concepts as the nodes in hierarchies. Hyperbolic navigation where the user can rearrange nodes and bring areas into focus with the mouse has been shown to be a better interface for understanding of complex, heterogeneous data sets. Hyperbolic visualizations with Empolis or Ontopia allow users to enter a search term/concept phrase.

The system responds with a concept map for the term/phrase. Each node of this map has other concepts associated with it with specific roles such as *has-parts, isCausedBy-Process,* and so on. Each node can be activated as a live hyperlink to provide entry into other thesaurus maps that extend or narrow the relationships and concepts as appropriate. Each node also has occurrence roles, the information resources associated with each concept.

The use of topic maps for educational purposes may need certain improvements to visualizations, such as:

- Support for multiple ordering
- Display of hierarchical relationships
- More interactive features that allow a user to select and save existing learning spaces. A click on a concept node should display the information about a concept— its scope and variant notes.
- Aggregation of resources by form/type and number of resources
- Visualization limited to one concept with immediate relationships, not the whole body of concepts

Summarizing, we find that classificatory notions, such as hierarchy, concepts, classes, facets, and vocabulary can be used to provide the digital learning spaces needed to support science education in physical geography. To do so, the critical places where the enhancements need to take place in a faceted thesaurus are described: terms to be more rigourously defined and maintained as concepts and facets, scope notes to include nodes that make the relationships explicit, semantic relationships to be extended with other disciplinary classifications and associations, and display of concepts and relationships in multiple orders. Other enhancements needed, such as combining definitions and illustrations with thesaurus terms and better understanding of the behaviour of relationships in concept spaces, have been identified and further investigation is recommended. Development alternatives include concept maps using concept mapping software or ISO topic map authoring. These approaches, specifically XTM, have been compared with existing principles and protocols for thesaurus construction and maintenance, and the advantages and disadvantages have been highlighted.

8

Use and Perception of the DCRB Core Standard

Bibliographic control of rare book collections has always been a time-consuming and specialized process. The materials in special collections are there for particular and compelling reasons. Catalogers of such collections have traditionally identified those special attributes in catalogue records with full-level bibliographic description, extensive notes, and as many access points as are deemed appropriate by both catalogers and curators. The bibliographic standards for cataloguing rare books, with the principles of *Anglo-American Cataloguing Rules*, (AACR2) underlying them, have evolved over a number of years, first in 1981 in *Bibliographic Description of Rare Books* and most recently in *Descriptive Cataloguing of Rare Books* (DCRB), published in 1991. A new edition, with the title *Descriptive Cataloguing of Rare Materials*, is now in preparation by the Association of College and Research Libraries, Rare Books and Manuscripts Section (RBMS), Bibliographic Standards Committee.

The new edition will include rules for the various formats of materials. The documentation for books will be known as DCRM(B). While the current standard of DCRB is written primarily for books printed before 1801, it can be used for post-1800 imprints as well. The Programme for Cooperative Cataloguing (PCC) has defined and approved core standards for many of the bibliographic formats, beginning with the standard for books in the mid-1990s. All the core standards, written for use by the participants in the Bibliographic Records Cooperative (BIBCO) programme, are intended to encourage "faster, better, cheaper" cataloguing. They ensure the same reliability in description, authorized headings, and call numbers as full-level records, but they do not require as many notes or subject headings.

In January 1999, the PCC approved the Core Standard for Rare Books. Called DCRB Core because it is based on the full standard of DCRB, the standard is intended for use in cataloguing books with imprint dates between 1500 and 1800. The text of the standard was written and proposed by the Task Group for Developing a Standard for Core Treatment of Rare Books, a group that was charged with the creation of the core standard by the PCC Standards

Committee and that included several members of the RBMS Bibliographic Standards Committee. The expected use of the DCRB Core standard is for cataloguing books that have been chosen more for their need of accessibility than for their full bibliographic details.

DEFINITION OF THE DCRB CORE STANDARD

Two documents define the core record for rare books: Core Standard for Books and the DCRB Core. The Books Core requires authorized headings, a call number from a standard classification system, full fixed-field data, descriptive fields 245-4XX but fewer notes only one or two subject headings, and as many added entries as the cataloger judges to be appropriate. Significantly, notes for justification of added entries are not required. The frequently occurring bibliographical references note is also not required.

With the requirements of the Books Core as a base, the DCRB Core standard specifies additional or differing elements. Figure presents the DCRB Core elements arranged in MARC tag order, with an indication of how or why the elements should be used. The code "dcrb" in field 040 $e is mandatory because the bibliographic description is based on the full standard of DCRB.

Differing from the Books Core, the DCRB Core does not require a standard call number. Many libraries do classify their rare books, but other libraries use local call numbers. The DCRB Core standard does not require that catalogers who use local call numbers go an extra step and assign a standard call number as well.

040 $e Dcrb	Cataloguing Source: Description Convention Mandatory (Since the Full Standard is DCRB)
050, 082, 086, 090, etc.	Call Number Fields Not Required (Because many Rare Book Collections use Special Call Numbers)
245-4XX	Title, Edition, Imprint, Physical Description, and Series Fields (Following the more Inclusive Descriptive Method and Extent for Recording Biblio-Graphic Details and the Options Prescribed by DCRB)
500	Note Field Mandatory (If Elements on the Title Page have been Transposed in the 245 Field)
510	Citation/References Note Field Mandatory (If One of the Five Citations Specifically Required by DCRB)
655	Index Term – Genre/form Term Not Required but Encouraged

Fig. Elements of the DCRB Core Standard Required in Addition to the Requirements of the Books Core

The title, edition, imprint, physical description, and series areas are all required if appropriate to the item being cataloged, just as they are in the Books Core, but their inclusion follows the descriptive method prescribed by DCRB and may apply the options for shortening the bibliographic record.

The DCRB Core standard specifies two note fields in addition to those required by the Books Core. If the cataloger transposes the elements on the title page in the transcription in the title field of the bibliographic record, the transposition must be acknowledged in a 500 field.

The citation/references note field provides, in standard form, reference to bibliographic sources. In a fulllevel DCRB record, the 510 field may provide justification for information included in the catalogue record. In a DCRB Core record the same reference may lead the user to information that has been omitted from the record, but DCRB Core requires only the five sources listed in DCRB rule 7C14 for post-1500 imprints. The final element of the DCRB Core standard, the index term field that employs genre, form, or physical characteristic terms from standard thesauri, is encouraged but not required. DCRB Core defines the minimum requirements for the bibliographic record. At the discretion of the cataloger, more note fields and more access points may be added to a given record. This flexibility means that a core record may contain more than the minimally required fields without attaining the level of a full record.

Examples of a full-level DCRB bibliographic record and its corresponding DCRB Core record illustrate significant differences between the two standards. A DCRB Core record can be recognized by the encoding level code "4" and "dcrb" in the cataloguing source field 040 $e. The examples used here have the appearance of OCLC records, and the full-level record has been adapted from an existing OCLC record. Other examples illustrating the differences between the two standards can be found on the Web pages of the RBMS Bibliographic Standards Committee.

The difference in the length of the two records is immediately noticeable. The core record has been created by using the options in the full DCRB standard for shortening the bibliographic description in several areas and by omitting fields not required by the core standard. In the publication area, the cataloger has followed the option in rule 4C6 in the full standard to shorten the field. Instead of transcribing all six names of the printers of the book, the cataloger has given the name of the first printer and a bracketed statement that there are five other printers.

The DCRB Core standard does not require any of the thirteen notes used in the full-level record, including the notes that justify the main and added entries. The thirteen note fields in the full-level record have been reduced to one note in the core-level record, the 510 field. While the 510 is not one of the five citations required by the full standard, the cataloger has chosen to include the 510 that gives the reference to the bibliography of Daniel Defoe because the bibliography contains substantially all of the information in the other notes in the full-level record.

Even though this work is a multipart title, the contents note as taken from the title page does not reflect distinct titles of the individual volumes. The contents note, therefore, has been left out of the core record. The DCRB Core record contains only one of the subject headings and one of the added entries used in the full-level record. While the examples are coded as BIBCO records, any library that is not a participating BIBCO member may also create core records. The 042 will be absent from a non-BIBCO record. Creating a core bibliographic record would obviously take much less of the cataloger's time. The time savings and therefore the cost savings may be significant factors for some libraries.

To implement the standard, however, may alter the past practice of describing a book to the fullest to help users find the edition or issue of a title that they are looking for. The DCRB Core standard was written to give catalogers the option and discretion of using a less-than-full standard when collections have been identified as more important for access than for fuller bibliographic details. The flexibility of adding more to the core record and the dependence on the cataloger's judgement in choosing to add more are two key principles of all the core standards. These two characteristics may make use of the DCRB Core, in particular, an attractive alternative to the time-consuming full-level record.

TEXT APPRAISAL

Although a number of articles have been written about the Books Core and other core standards, little has been published about the DCRB Core standard. When the standard was being written, discussion and reports at the RBMS Bibliographic Standards Committee meetings were recorded in the minutes of the committee. The work of the DCRB Task Group was documented in its final report. During the time of the task group's work on the standard, discussion and comments were solicited on the Exlibris list.

All of those exchanges are available in the archives of the list. After the standard was written and approved, discussion concerning issues of its actual implementation and use was not initiated on Exlibris or Autocat, two lists to which many rare book catalogers subscribe. Much of the literature treating the core record describes its development within the context of the history of the PCC, its purpose in encouraging "faster, better, cheaper" cataloguing that can be relied on for quality of description and authorized headings, and its potential contribution to the success of the national programme. There are, however, some studies and reports that investigate particular issues that are relevant to the DCRB Core. Several studies have been done to evaluate the time savings and cost-effectiveness of the core record. Thomas notes that an unpublished study done at Cornell University by Boissonnas found that core records could be created 25 per cent faster than full-level records.

The UCLA/OCLC Core Record Project, conducted from December 1994 to April 1995 with the same group of catalogers creating core- and full-level records, confirmed the assumption that core-level cataloguing is faster than full-level cataloguing and further confirmed that fewer subject headings and added entries are used in the core records. Other libraries' subsequent use of those core records in the OCLC database with little additional editing attested to the reliability of the records. Hyslop discusses an unpublished study of experimental core cataloguing done at the Library of Congress in 1996.

The experiment underscored the efficiency and productivity of cataloguing using the core standard. Cataloguing statistics at Colorado State University over several years indicated that the use of the Books Core to catalogue government publications primarily in the backlog was successful in making a greater number of books accessible more quickly than before the core standard was used. Two recent studies explore the sufficiency of the core record. The first study analyses the access points and notes in the core- and full-level records and finds statistically significant differences in the two levels of records. While the authors indicate the fields that catalogers may want to augment, they acknowledge that catalogers may want to accept basic corelevel requirements unless the need for additional fields outweighs the time savings in the creation of core records.

The second study is a pilot study of library users' opinions about the usefulness of the various elements in the core and full records. Although the study finds the need for further research to confirm the preliminary indications about users' preferences concerning the usefulness of the various access points in the bibliographic records, it does indicate that even though users prefer fulllevel records, they still feel the core record is sufficient for finding the materials they need. In a study conducted by interview of cataloger and cataloguing manager attitudes towards the BIBCO core record, Banush found that both groups of participants, while generally satisfied with the core record, expressed varying opinions about its problems and benefits.

The cataloguing managers expressed more satisfaction with the core record than did the catalogers. Banush notes that this attitude of satisfaction with the core record is in contrast to the reduced percentage of core records actually created by the BIBCO participants during 2000 and early 2001. He also reports that there is a distinction between those accepting core records created by other libraries as copy cataloguing and those creating original core bibliographic records. Even though libraries readily use other libraries' core contributions to the shared cataloguing databases, often without revision, they are more reluctant to create them, preferring instead to create fulllevel records. Cromwell reports that even before the Books Core standard was implemented as part of the BIBCO programme, Stanford University used a similar standard with varying success.

She suggests that the use of the core record cannot achieve the level of cost-effectiveness that is expected without the acceptance and understanding of the catalogers themselves about its purpose and its concomitant emphasis on catalogers' judgement and flexibility. The published and reported studies of the efficiency and cost-effectiveness of creating core records point to an encouraging potential for the application of all the PCC core standards. The research about access points, users' perceptions, and practitioners' opinions tempers the findings of the efficiency of the core record while producing some statistical and qualitative data that encourages further study.

While the DCRB Core standard bears the approval of the PCC to be used by the libraries participating in the BIBCO programme, it may be applied by any library, whether a BIBCO participant or not. In the three years since the approval of the DCRB Core standard by the PCC, however, there has been little evidence that the standard is being widely used. This study investigates the trends in the use of the DCRB Core by means of a survey designed to investigate catalogers' use and perceptions of the standard.

METHOD

To reach catalogers and special collections librarians who would be able to provide information about their experience with the DCRB Core standard, a query was posted to three lists: Autocat, Pcclist, and Exlibris. Although many people subscribe to all three lists, the profile of subscribers is different for each. Autocat is a list of several thousand people worldwide who are interested in cataloguing issues; Pcclist is a list whose subscribers are from participating PCC libraries; and the subscribers to Exlibris are those who have an interest in the field of rare books and special collections.

In November 2001, the query was posted to the three lists, asking three questions:

- If anyone has cataloged using the DCRB Core standard;
- If not, has a decision been made not to use the standard; and
- If either is the case, would the recipient be willing to participate in a longer survey about the use and perceptions of the DCRB Core.

The questions were posed in this way to find catalogers who have given some thought to the use of the core standard, whether or not they actually use it. The intent was not to seek responses from catalogers who do not use the core and have never considered doing so. Within a reasonable amount of time, only 15 libraries had sent responses, and of those, only 4 indicated that they use the DCRB Core standard. Thirteen, however, said they were willing to participate in a survey.

A few respondents to the query to the three lists indicated that they were responding because someone else had forwarded the query to them. Several more focused groups of potential respondents, therefore, were polled by e-mail:

The liaisons at the BIBCO libraries, the members of the RBMS Bibliographic Standards Committee for the past several years, and the heads of cataloguing, heads of special collections or special collections catalogers at member libraries of the Association of Research Libraries (ARL). Using this second method, 135 queries were sent to the three groups. Sixty-five libraries responded and, of those, 30 indicated that they would participate in a survey. By using these two methods, posting to the lists and soliciting individual libraries, 43 libraries were identified that were willing to participate in the survey.

In March 2002, the 43 surveys were distributed to the participants as Word and rich-text-format attachments to e-mail messages. All participants were assured that their names and the names of their institutions would be kept confidential. Thirty-seven surveys were returned. Since most of the solicited libraries are large research institutions, the majority of the returned surveys are from that category of library. The responses to the list postings, however, came from a broader range of libraries. The overall group of respondents therefore has more diverse representation and includes public, private, university, government/national, and special libraries.

The geographic distribution of the respondents includes libraries from the United States, Canada, and the United Kingdom. Fifteen libraries participate in the BIBCO programme of the PCC. Twenty participants are OCLC member libraries, 2 are exclusively RLIN libraries, and 14 contribute catalogue records to both utilities. One library catalogs solely in its own system. Although the initial query was designed to identify willingness to participate in a survey and some responses indicated only yes or no to the three questions, 54 respondents supplied additional comments about the DCRB Core standard or characterized their cataloguing practices or their collections. Of the 54 initial respondents, 24 did not wish to participate further.

In addition, the six libraries that received the survey but did not return it provided some information about their reasons for using or not using the core standard. Their comments will also be included in the following discussion as indicators of perceptions about the DCRB Core standard.

THE SURVEY AND RESULTS

The survey document contained 12 questions, most of which included multiple parts. The first two questions sought information about the type of library, the rare book collection, and the catalogers of the collection. Succeeding questions asked about the original cataloguing policies of the library, whether the DCRB Core standard has been considered, what decision has been made about its use, and whether any DCRB Core cataloguing records have been created. Questions in the next part of the survey suggested reasons for either using or not using the core standard.

Further questions asked how DCRB Core records created by other institutions are handled and whether any studies of users' perceptions have been done. Space for other comments was provided in question 12. While it was expected that the institutional data would vary from the responding libraries, questions 1 and 2 were asked to determine ranges of information to characterize the participants. No clear conclusions can be drawn about the relevance of the type of library, the size of the collection, the number of volumes cataloged or in the backlog, the number of rare book catalogers, or the reporting hierarchy within the institution. Both large and small collections are represented among the responses, ranging between a few hundred rare volumes in a collection to close to or more than one million rare volumes, with dozens to more than 175,000 volumes in the backlog.

The number of original rare book catalogers ranges from.25 full-time equivalents (FTE) to 9 FTE. Only 8 of the 37 libraries have more than 1 FTE rare book cataloger, 11 have less than one FTE, and 2 did not specify a number; the remaining 16 have only a single full-time cataloger. The questions about the size of the collection and the degree to which it is cataloged fully, minimally, or not at all seemed to pose more problems for the respondents than any other questions. Several respondents indicated they would be delayed in returning the questionnaire until they were able to determine the statistical information about their collections. Rare book catalogers report to cataloguing or technical services departments in 19 of the responding libraries, to special collections departments in 12 libraries, and to both departments in 6 libraries. The survey asked about the cataloguing policies of the libraries to determine how many libraries use full-level DCRB or full-level AACR2 for cataloguing pre-1801 books.

The answers were not as straightforward as expected. In responding to how much original cataloguing follows the full DCRB standard, 11 libraries responded that they do all their pre-1801 cataloguing using that standard, and 13 libraries responded that they catalogue none of their books using the standard. When answering the reverse question of how much original cataloguing of pre- 1801 books follows the AACR2 full standard, 14 libraries indicated all and 15 libraries indicated none. One library catalogs none of its books according to either standard, but instead creates bibliographic records that are fuller than either DCRB or AACR2. Among libraries that do not adhere strictly to one standard, 12 libraries answered that they catalogue some of their sixteenth- to eighteenth-century books using the full DCRB standard, and 7 indicated that they use full-level AACR2 for some of their books.

The differences can only be attributed to the complexity with which catalogers of rare material view their work and to exceptions in cataloguing practices. To begin the enquiry about the use of DCRB Core by the responding libraries, four questions were asked: have you considered using the DCRB Core standard, have you decided to use it, have you decided not to use it, and have you actually used it? Eighteen of the 37 libraries have considered using the DCRB Core, 14 have decided not to use it, and 6 have decided they will use it. Six libraries have, in fact, created records using the standard.

The 6 libraries that have decided to use DCRB Core are not the same 6 that actually have used the standard. One library said that the decision has been made to use the standard, but implementation has been hindered by staffing difficulties. Another library has applied the core standard without having made the policy decision that it expects to make in the near future.

Two other libraries expressed their intention to use the standard in the future, one as soon as appropriate collections have been identified. Depending on the answer to the question of use of the DCRB Core, respondents were asked to indicate why and how they use the standard or why they do not. In each case, a list of reasons was given for potential responses with additional space for other comments. In the discussion that follows, the responses of those libraries that use the DCRB Core standard will precede the responses of those libraries that do not use the standard.

Each of the 6 libraries that use the DCRB Core did not answer all the questions; and since the number is small, only the positive responses will be noted. One library uses the DCRB Core standard to catalogue all of its sixteenth- to eighteenth- century books. Four use DCRB Core for some of their cataloguing; 1 among them uses the standard as the default, but enhances the record if there is a compelling reason. The sixth library uses the DCRB Core to catalogue its rare books even though none are pre-1801 imprints. Three of the 6 libraries use the DCRB Core for particular reasons: for a specific collection or when lack of expertise or want of a significant reference work would make it impossible to catalogue at the full level.

All 6 have applied the standard at cataloger discretion. and 2 of the 6 also have applied it at curator discretion. In response to why and how they use the DCRB Core standard, four libraries answered that they use it to save time, three to increase production, four to gain faster control over their backlog, and three because it is more costeffective. In addition, one librarian whose institution does not hold any pre-1801 imprints replied that they use the DCRB Core because it is "better to capture the uniqueness of what we own in the archival and special collections department," and another respondent noted that they upgrade to the level of the DCRB Core standard some of the brief records for early imprints that can be found in the OCLC database.

Only 1 library uses the standard as it is written, "since it is written to be flexible"; 2 other libraries sometimes use it as written. Four libraries add more fields than the standard requires. The additional fields include: notes for contents, immediate source of acquisition, and ownership and custodial history; genre, form, or physical characteristic terms; added titles; and local information required by the library's online system or cataloguing policies. Five of the libraries encourage cataloger's discretion to determine whether to include additional fields and what the fields should be.

The 6 libraries indicated the percentage of bibliographic records created using the DCRB Core standard to be less than 1 per cent, 1 per cent, less than 5 per cent, less than 10 per cent, and 100 per cent, with one library reporting that no statistical records had been kept for DCRB Core records. In actual numbers 4 libraries reported they have created the following numbers of records: 10, 10–15, 18, and ca. 4,400. The fifth and sixth libraries were unable to give figures. The library that catalogs all its sixteenth- to eighteenthcentury books using the DCRB Core standard does not add bibliographic records immediately to OCLC, and there may be a period of time before they appear in the utility's database.

The library that said it starts with the DCRB Core record as the default and enhances as necessary, creates its original catalogue records locally without an 040 field because the generic 040 with the library's holding symbol is added automatically when the records are sent to OCLC. This library has not kept records of the number of DCRB Core records created. Given that these 2 libraries may create a considerable number of DCRB Core records without a way to track them in OCLC and that other libraries, that they have created a minimal number of DCRB Core records, it would be surprising if the national databases have a significant number of DCRB Core records.

The initial responses of the 2 libraries that said they have used the DCRB Core but did not return the survey indicate that they probably have created few catalogue records using the standard. When 1 of the 2 libraries applies the DCRB Core, it does so only for seventeenth- and eighteenth- century books, not for fifteenth- and sixteenth-century books, and it never omits notes justifying added entries.

The other library applies the standard in limited instances because it feels that rare books should be given full-level cataloguing. Since the DCRB Core does not require a standard call number, this second library can contribute BIBCO records for broadsides and pamphlets that it does not classify. Adding these 2 libraries that did not participate in the survey to the 6 that did participate brings the total of known users of the DCRB Core standard to 8.

The 31 libraries that do not use the DCRB Core standard indicated their reasons in response to a ten-part question that suggested 9 possible reasons and asked for others in the tenth part. Each of the reasons was affirmed by some of the libraries.

Table. Thirty-one Survey Respondents'Ranked Choices for Not Using the DCRB Core Standard (from Question 9)

Reasons	Yes	per cent Yes	No	Unanswered
Core is inferior	19	61.3	11	1
Description not accurate enough	15	48.4	14	2
Too few access points	15	48.4	16	–
Requires learning new standard	11	35.5	18	2
Unfamiliarity with standard	8	25.8	22	1
Shortages or changes in staff	6	19.4	24	1
Use would disrupt workflow	5	16.1	24	2
Training is unavailable	5	16.1	25	1
Material not appropriate	4	12.9	27	–
Additional reasons	18	58.1	–	13

That the DCRB Core standard is inferior was the reason cited by most of the libraries, 19, that have not used it in their original cataloguing records for rare books. Fifteen respondents said that the description is not accurate enough and that there are not enough access points with the use of the standard. Eleven stated that they have not used the DCRB Core because it would require learning a new standard, and 8 said they do not use the standard because they are unfamiliar with it. Six respondents reported shortages or changes in staff that have kept them from using the standard.

Five libraries said that training is unavailable, and 5 also indicated that the use of the DCRB Core standard would disrupt the established workflow. Only 4 said they do not have material appropriate to catalogue using the standard. The opinion and perception of nearly two-thirds of the libraries responding that they do not use the DCRB Core standard is that the DCRB Core record is inferior to the full record. Almost half think that the standard does not provide enough access points and that the description is not accurate enough. Clearly these three most prevalent perceptions indicate that the survey respondents have not been willing to give up fuller bibliographic treatment for their rare books.

This opinion of the lesser quality of the DCRB Core record as a reason for non-adoption by most of the respondents is reminiscent of a similar kind of negative perception and resistance to acceptance that were noted for the Books Core by Cromwell in her observation that cataloger's attitude and acceptance are needed for the success of the Books Core. The six other reasons that the respondents affirmed for not using the DCRB Core standard are all operational obstacles within their libraries more than opinions or perceptions. Changes in libraries' current personnel, procedures, or materials issues might create more acceptable conditions for the adoption of the DCRB Core standard. Catalogers could learn the new standard or become familiar with it, changes or shortages in staff could be overcome with time or more money, a new workflow could be established, training could be sought, and appropriate materials might be acquired.

The participants gave a number of other reasons, however, for not undertaking use of the DCRB Core. In response to the possibility that a library may not have appropriate materials for using the core standard, some libraries qualified that reason noting the small quantity of rare books they catalogue. Seven libraries said that they do not catalogue many rare books, that they do so little original cataloguing, especially of rare books, or that they have so few pre-1801 imprints that it is easier to apply the full standard and not worth applying a different standard when they encounter a title that may be eligible for core-level cataloguing.

One librarian replied that the categories of materials that would be candidates for DCRB Core-level cataloguing are generally cataloged to their own minimal-level standard. Administrative or departmental policy to catalogue all books at full-level DCRB was cited by 6 libraries as the reason for not applying the DCRB Core standard. Although 13 libraries answered that they do not use full-level DCRB for cataloguing any of their sixteenth- to eighteenth- century books, 4 specifically reiterated that they use only AACR2 full for cataloguing rare books. Two libraries emphasized their production goals and decisions to apply certain standards as reasons for not taking time to learn a new standard. One librarian thinks "the introduction of a DCRB Core standard runs contrary to the whole intent of DCRB to provide fuller description than AACR2."

Another librarian said that not justifying access points is confusing to users and that if the cataloger starts to add more fields, it would be easier to create full-level records. Two respondents said their reference collections are not comprehensive enough to provide references in a 510 field to allow the abbreviated description of the DCRB Core standard.

Two other libraries indicated that their backlogs are not large enough to need to implement DCRB Core cataloguing. Four librarians each offered one of the following reasons: use of the Core does not increase production, it would create more inconsistencies in the catalogue than are already there from so many changes in standards over the years, there is little time for the catalogers to assimilate the new standard, and catalogers prefer one standard not choices.

These additional reasons and comments express strong opposition to the use of the DCRB Core standard. For the most part, they are internal or operational issues that pose obstacles to the adoption of the standard. Remarks from the 24 libraries that did not wish to participate in the survey provide further insight into why some libraries do not use the DCRB Core. Their reasons are categorized in table.

Table. Categorized Reasons for Not Using DCRB Core from Twenty-four Nonparticipants in Survey

Reasons	No.
Not enough of a collection to make it worthwhile	11
Not informed enough or aware of DCRB Core	6
Cataloger is retiring or have a change of staff	5
Do not use DCRB full	4
Have a shortage of staff	4
Do not use any core standard	3
Policy is to catalogue at full level (including BIBCO records)	3
Other libraries would not be able to enhance records to full level	2
Feels the need to justify added entries	1
Feels limitation in training	1
Feels limitation in knowledge	1
Does not do BIBCO for books	1
Has not cataloged rare books in a while	1
Does not create BIBCO records for rare books	1
Only a few catalogers are trained in DCRB	1
Too little time to discuss issues related to DCRB Core	1
Has a large backlog	1
Uses Books Core	1

Catalogs few original records for rare books	1
Differences between core and full are minor	1
Using core does not save much time	1
Doubts can convince Special	
Collections of value of core records	1
E-resources are becoming priorities	1

Some of the reasons are identical to those of the survey participants:

- The rare book collection is not sufficiently large to warrant learning to catalogue by any standard other than full-level DCRB (11 libraries);
- The library is not familiar with or even aware of DCRB Core (6 libraries);
- There are changes (5 libraries) or shortages (4 libraries) in staff;
- The DCRB full standard is not used (4 libraries);
- The policy is to catalogue at the full level (3 libraries); and
- Training poses a problem (1 library).

In addition to these commonly held reasons for not applying the DCRB Core, 3 libraries indicated that they do not use any of the core standards, and 2 libraries hesitate to use the DCRB Core because it might prohibit a non-BIBCO library from enhancing the core record to a full-level record in OCLC. Each of the following reasons was cited by a single library for not employing the DCRB Core standard: added entries should be justified in a note; knowledge is too limited to apply the standard; BIBCO books records are not created; BIBCO rare books records are not created; rare books have not been cataloged recently; only a few catalogers are trained to use DCRB; too little time is available to discuss DCRB Core and issues related to it; the backlog is large; the Books Core is used instead; too few original records for rare books are created; the differences between core and full level are minor; the core standard does not save much time; the value of DCRB Core records cannot be sold to Special Collections; and, finally, e-resources are becoming more of a cataloguing priority than printed special collections materials.

Common emphases and implications that run through many of these reasons are the little availability of time and the desire for adherence to fuller standards, two characteristics that have long been in competition in technical services processes in libraries. One library, however, intends to use the DCRB Core standard, and two others are considering using it. How well cataloguing copy is viewed and used by other libraries is one way of evaluating the efficacy of a cataloguing standard. Responding to question 10, 9 participants in the survey said their copy catalogers accept DCRB Core records without changing them, although 1 library said there was room for cataloger's judgement and 2 libraries indicated that they might add subject headings or local notes. Nineteen respondents said their copy catalogers edit DCRB Core records locally. In response to the question of whether original catalogers enhance DCRB Core records to full level locally, 29 libraries answered in the affirmative; 5 do not enhance core records to full level locally. At 16 libraries, original catalogers enhance DCRB Core records to full level nationally; at 16 libraries they do not enhance nationally, although 2 libraries said they may do so in the future. Four of the respondents noted that their catalogers have never seen a DCRB Core record; 1 of them would edit if a core record were encountered. Since there is so little evidence for the creation of DCRB Core records, it is surprising that not more libraries commented that they have not seen them in the bibliographic utilities.

Further research in the databases of the bibliographic utilities is needed to confirm that the DCRB Core standard has as yet found little acceptance and use among rare book catalogers and curators. The final question on the survey asked if any use studies of DCRB Core records have been conducted. Not surprisingly, none of the respondents has done such a survey. In their additional comments, however, three librarians said they think the purported time savings of core cataloguing records are not worth the cost to the users in locating materials they need. These opinions are greatly supported by many special collections departments' preferences for using the DCRB full standard.

WRAPPING UP

Clearly, the preponderance of the evidence indicates that most libraries surveyed have not used the DCRB Core standard and prefer to catalogue their rare books using a full standard, whether DCRB or AACR2. The DCRB Core standard was not written as a replacement for full-level cataloguing for all rare books. The standard states that the expectation is that materials cataloged using the DCRB Core will be chosen more for their accessibility than for full bibliographic treatment. Eight libraries have identified appropriate collections to catalogue using the DCRB Core standard.

Among the responses received both in the initial query and in the survey itself, six additional libraries indicated that although they do not now use the DCRB Core standard in their cataloguing, they are expecting to do so in the future or seriously want to consider using it. The total of fourteen libraries that either do use the DCRB Core or almost assuredly will use it in the future indicates the beginning of acknowledgement of the value of the standard and a more positive attitude among some catalogers towards the standard. A recent survey of the special collections departments of the ARL libraries finds that large portions of the collections are uncataloged.

Although formats other than books form the bulk of the uncataloged collections, an average of 15 per cent of the book collections have no access through any form of bibliographic description, and 49 per cent have access only through a card catalogue. Many non-ARL libraries may also have large proportions of their special collections in uncataloged backlogs. According to the minutes of recent meetings of the ARL Task Force on Special Collections, one primary issue under discussion is the question of providing increased access to those backlogged materials through bibliographic control.

Many of the books in backlogs may have existing bibliographic records in OCLC and RLIN that can be used by copy catalogers. For those books that do not already have catalogue records in the bibliographic utilities, however, the application of the DCRB Core standard in creating original bibliographic records has potential. To begin a project to catalogue backlogged material using the DCRB Core standard, a primary task for special collections librarians is to identify specific collections that will be appropriate for DCRB Corelevel cataloguing. One library among the survey respondents is considering cataloguing its early French pamphlets using the DCRB Core. Other pamphlet collections or subject collections, such as political or religious tracts, may be candidates for DCRB Core cataloguing.

One librarian said that using a cataloguing template for materials issued by the same publisher would make DCRB Core cataloguing even more efficient. Several libraries indicated that they are looking for appropriate collections. One respondent noted that sometimes the DCRB Core standard is applied to enhance a brief cataloguing record to bring it up to a higher level without the necessity of enhancing to the full level. In addition to identifying collections that are candidates for DCRB Core cataloguing, libraries will need to encourage cataloger's judgement to help overcome the resistance to using core standards. Because the flexibility of the core standard permits a wide range of additional elements in the core record, the cataloger is not limited to the bare minimum requirements. Not every book in a backlog will be a candidate for core-level cataloguing, but identifying the proper collections and undertaking DCRB Core-level cataloguing projects can help increase accessibility to those materials that users do not know exist in rare book collections.

9

Managing Administrative Metadata

A growing need exists for metadata management of administrative issues related to electronic resources. Some of these issues include license restrictions, authentication means, technical contacts, and statistics availability. *Integrated library systems* (ILS) do not easily accommodate such metadata, and paper files maintained by serials librarians have proven inadequate both in accessibility and organization. Making e-resource metadata quickly available to interlibrary loan and reference staffs is facilitated by an online gateway of the ERTS model.

IN THE BEGINNING

Discussions about the state of Tri-College e-resources were held in 2001. The focus of these discussions, which were sponsored by a Mellon Foundation grant, was ensuring consistent access to e-journals throughout the consortium. This original charge was broadened later that year and resulted in development of the ERTS system. The authors comprise the founding members of the ERTS Team. We held a number of brainstorming sessions to identify the results each library hoped to achieve with ERTS.

Particularly due to our consortium status, numerous discussions were necessary so as not to overlook any one library's specific needs. Some of the goals for ERTS included:

- Immediate access to license information for all e-resources purchased by the Tri-College Consortium libraries
- Various statistical reports not easily available, if at all, through our integrated library system
- Notification services that alert staff when e-resources are about to expire

We began identifying data elements based on these needs.

The suggested fields, and the information we expected to place within them, fit into four categories:

- *Licensors:* Entities from whom we license e-resources
- *Items:* Individual e-resource titles
- *Purchases:* Acquisitions data concerning e-resources

- *Vendors:* Entities from whom we purchase e-resources

After consulting established element sets, particularly those maintained by the University of Washington and Johns Hopkins University, it was comforting to see that our direction was quite similar.

SCOPE

ERTS exists in large part because of limitations inherent within integrated library systems. That said, the ERTS Team was wary of duplicating information already held in our local catalogue. Thus we sought to restrict ERTS's scope to those data either unavailable, or not easily retrievable, through our ILS. Since the predominant mission of ERTS is to track license information, few freely available electronic resources are entered. Only in cases where a certain aspect of a freely available e-resource requires tracking, such as how the consortium has decided to catalogue it, is it entered in ERTS. In cases of volatile aggregators, only a collectionlevel record is maintained.

Resources we have decided to exclude from ERTS generally fall into these categories:

- Extending less than a year's guarantee of access
- Delivering incomplete holdings
- Not providing ready title-level access

LICENSE INFORMATION

As in many institutions, electronic resources are heavily used in our libraries. As a result, serials and acquisitions personnel field numerous questions from public services staff regarding license restrictions. The paper files we maintained before ERTS were not an adequate medium for promulgating license-related information. Ellen Finnie Duranceau's efforts with license tracking at MIT were influential at pointing the way towards a networked file for staff use. Apart from the license terms related to legal responsibilities, ERTS stores elements that directly address what library services we can provide and what our patrons can do with a given resource.

Some of these data include:

- *ILL Allowability:* We have buttons for yes, no, n/a, and unknown. There is also a free text box to allow for further details. Our ILL staffs need to know this information, and occasionally reference librarians are asked about such restrictions.
- *Number of Simultaneous Users:* Because certain resources carry this restriction, this element helps public services staff troubleshoot the cause of a user not being allowed access. Documenting simultaneous user limits in ERTS provides a check that may help public services staff before assuming a more involved access problem is the culprit.
- *Print Restrictions:* Some resources limit the number of pages printed per session, and others even prohibit printing. This element prevents

the expenditure of valuable time trying to diagnose an apparent printing problem.

- *Reserve Restrictions:* Staff responsible for electronic reserves need to know if such mounting is restricted in any way. An example of such a restriction is having a strict time frame for the duration of the e-reserve link. As with print restrictions, the licensor may obligate us to inform users of such restrictions or other license terms.
- *SDI Availability:* This element indicates the availability of a service allowing patrons to register for e-mail notification when new content becomes available. Often, such content is in the form of journal issues or tables of contents.
- *Archival Guarantee:* As we exchange print subscriptions for electronic equivalents, access to this information has become a great concern, especially since it is often hard to tease out of veiled licensing language.
- *Negotiation Contact:* This element stores the name of the licensor's negotiation representative. This information is useful when we wish to alter the language in our license.
- *General Comments:* This catch-all field is used to capture license data not covered in the fields, such as a note concerning license revision dates.

CATALOGUING INFORMATION

Cataloguing electronic resources in the Tri-College setting poses complications beyond the natural challenges inherent with this ever-changing media. When the Tri-Colleges first purchased electronic resources, a commitment was made to provide individual bibliographic records in our local catalogue for each title. During this time, many journal publishers provided online access to their content, often free with the print subscriptions. As aggregators and large publisher collections became available, the challenge to provide title and subject access grew into an even more formidable task, as described expertly by Calhoun and Kara. In order to continue providing individual title access in this environment, the Tri-Colleges employed several methods of cataloguing, including a locally derived batch method, along with the more standard copy cataloguing via cooperative resources like OCLC.

Further adding to this quandary, the consortium libraries share a catalogue. Although the libraries purchase many online resources collectively, there are numerous eresources unique to a single library. Maintaining consistent cataloguing standards across three separate technical services units is a challenge. ERTS supports sharing of these standards by centralizing cataloguing information for the Tri-Colleges. Initially, the cataloguing elements in ERTS were linked to the licensor database.

This architecture posed three problems, however:

- The licensor name is generally not used by cataloguing and reference staff to identify an electronic resource.

- Catalogue librarians describe information about individual and collection titles that is not always consistent across multiple resources offered by the same licensor. For instance, a licensor may place title lists and holdings information for one of its collections on the Web, but not for another. This may affect the way the resources are cataloged. Appending these cataloguing data to title records, rather than licensor records, gives us the flexibility necessary to record differences among collections.
- Several freely available collections for which the Tri- Colleges maintain cataloguing procedures do not warrant a licensor record.

The cataloguing database consists of approximately sixteen fields that are divided into four sections on the cataloguing information page:

- Title;
- Tripod Searching Information;
- Technical Cataloguing Information; and
- Publisher-Related Information.

Title

Cataloguing uses this section, consisting of one element "Title," to identify the individual journal, collection-level, or aggregator title. The Tri-Colleges use the MARC 130 tag for local collocation and retrieval purposes within Tripod. The title field in ERTS replicates the locally derived 130 field. The intention is to facilitate ease of searching for public services staff. If they require more information about an electronic resource, they can then search the title in ERTS.

Tripod Title Searching Information (for Public Services)

This section, designed for use by public services staff, consists of two elements that identify the search keys necessary for retrieval of all titles in a collection or aggregation. The first field contains a URL that invokes an OPAC search in Tripod. The second element contains the Tripod search key and search term. Such a field might look like this: author=Project Muse.

Technical Cataloguing Information

This section centralizes local decisions for Tri-College cataloguing staff. It consists of three elements. The first field notes, whether individual titles within a collection, aggregation, or database, are analysed. The second field indicates what method is used to catalogue analysed titles and where the file used for the locally batch-created records resides. The third field records any MARC fields that are unique to each collection, aggregate, or database. For instance, a cataloger might decide to use a series entry to help collocate related electronic resources. When this is the case, the 4XX field would be recorded in this field. Also, if a 7XX field is recorded for a person or corporate body, it would be accordingly noted in this area.

Publisher-Related Information

This section incorporates URL and note fields. The URL field directs catalogers to a title list, usually located on the licensor's Web site, that is used in our batch load procedures. A brief note about the update pattern and frequency of these titles lists is also located here. The final element in this section is a note about whom to contact at the vendor for service updates. Overall, the cataloguing database is a modest component of ERTS. Yet it provides the Tri-College's cataloguing community an invaluable tool. ERTS circumvents the need to record cataloguing decisions on paper files or "in our heads," making for a stronger, more fluid approach to cataloguing electronic materials throughout the consortium.

PURCHASE INFORMATION

Although much purchase information is available in our local catalogue, we felt it would be useful to be able to view a title's cost over a five-year period, as well as to easily distinguish any one-time fees. Additionally, we wanted to have the ability to generate reports that would tell us how much we were spending on different categories of electronic titles.

Each purchase event is captured in ERTS by entering the following data:

- *Library:* This is the purchasing library or in some cases may be the consortium as a whole.
- *Licensor:* Selected from a drop-down list of licensors; this is usually the publisher/creator of the title.
- *Vendor:* Also selected from a drop-down list; this is from whom we purchase the title. For cases in which one of the libraries acts as purchasing agent for the other two, that library would be recorded as the vendor.
- *Purchase Type:* We have a need to distinguish among titles that are paid as electronic only, titles that carry an added cost over the cost of the print subscription, and titles that offer free online access as a consequence of a print subscription.
- *One-time Charges:* We wanted to record this information separately so that it could be distinguished from annual costs. Price, paid date, expiration date, and ILS order number are also entered.

Generally, much discussion surrounds the initial decision to purchase a particular resource. The decision to renew a resource, however, is often made with less thought and in a very short time frame. It is most often the case that the need to make the renewal decision is prompted by a renewal form or invoice from a vendor and is sometimes received after the previous subscription has expired.

We often do not take the time to ask ourselves important questions such as: How often was this resource used? Has the licensor provided good service in the case of technical problems? Can we justify the cost? Instead, we often rely on the gut feeling of our bibliographers. While their sense of the usefulness of the resource may be valid, we want to be able to provide more data and more time for them to make the renewal decision. Therefore, we have added an e-mail-alerting component to ERTS which uses the expiration date in the purchase record and notifies selected staff sixty days prior to the expiration of a title. This is a strategy we learned from the HERMES system implemented at Johns Hopkins University. We believe this gives us sufficient time to analyse usage statistics, cost, and service issues so that we can make informed renewal decisions.

A 'renew' button in the purchase record moves the previous year's purchase data to a new column, retaining the ILS order number and purchase type. ERTS uses the price entered for the new year to calculate the price change from the previous to the current year. A variety of reports can be generated from the purchase data in ERTS. For example, we can create reports totaling electronic acquisitions by purchase type for the fiscal year or for any selected time period, giving us the title, the most recent paid date, and amount of each electronic resource, sorted by type of resource, then by title. A report on the number of records by purchase type and an annual expenditure comparison report can also be generated. Other report types can be created as needed.

TECHNICAL SPECIFICATIONS

ERTS runs on FileMaker Pro, currently version 5.5 desktop software at Haverford's Magill Library. ERTS was developed on a Mac, but currently runs on Windows. Staff use Macintosh and Windows computers to access the database, which performs well on both platforms. Readonly access to ERTS is restricted to the three college campuses by IP address; editing privileges are restricted by passwords.

The staff functions of inputting, editing, and reporting are available in all three campus libraries through FileMaker's sharing system. Search functions for public services staff are available through a Web interface using the FileMaker CDML tags. Through the Web, users on the three campuses can search by licensor name or title and view the license restrictions that apply. Staff can also enter comments about an e-resource's system performance or access difficulties, which can then be made available to them at renewal time.

ERTS consists of six interrelated files or "tables:"

- Licensors—One record is entered for each licensor and used by all three libraries.
- Items—One record is entered for each title and used by all three libraries.
- Purchases— Each library maintains a separate purchase record.
- Vendors—One record is entered for each vendor and used by all three libraries.
- Service comments
- Administration

10

Library Resource Sharing and Networking

INTRODUCTION

In the present era of Information technology, the information needs of the users have been increased so enormously that no single library on its own can meet their information needs. This has necessitated the need for effective linkages and cooperation between libraries and information centers for sharing of available resources and information through networking. The consortia for library can be considered as a major step towards library cooperation in sharing electronic resources. The consortium should take lead role in the development of a national strategy for information provision for research in higher education.

The term resource applies to a thing, person or action to which one resorts to in times of need and sharing indicates allotting, apportioning or contributing something that is owned, to benefit others. Resource sharing, therefore, refers to reciprocity, implying a partnership where each member has something useful to contribute to others and which each is willing and able to make available when needed.

Resource sharing is an empty concept, but for the approach permitting resource sharing to work is that which:

- Entails having resources to share
- Having a willingness to share them, and
- Having a plan for accomplishing resource sharing

Resource Sharing is an integral part of modern library services. In the developed countries, no library services can be thought without sharing of resources. In the past, ₹ was limited to the interlibrary loan system. In the modern age, with the development of science and technology and innovations of techniques and devices, resource sharing has become easier and fruitful due to the availability of databases, information network, and online sharing facilities. Thus, the resourcesharing system helps one library to access to resources of other libraries.

When resource sharing is agreed upon by participating institutions, then the following aspects must be planned:

- Identify and locate major collections, sources and materials
- Assemble, publish and distribute collective information for all participating bodies
- Workout the basis for sharing, reference service, lending service, copying service, access to materials, delivery service, and lists of holdings
- Establish means of sharing ideas, development and problems in the form of a newsletter
- Plan for new developments in the knowledge of what others are doing
- Developing a National Information Policy

The following are the most important benefits of resource sharing to participating institutions:

- Easy access to materials
- Enables co-operating institutions to extend limited resources
- Allow greater staff specialization
- Improve services to users
- Avoids unnecessary duplication
- Reduces the number of places which will need to go for services
- Improves working relationships between cooperating libraries.

Resource sharing refers to a joint use of resources available on a system or a network by user or peripherals. In the language of information management, when we talk about resource sharing we simply mean collective use of information of all types by various end users from a control coordinating unit or from within a network component at a reduced cost with easy accessibility.

Library cooperation and resource-sharing activity can take place in several forms and can happen at many levels, which include:

- Interlibrary loans/reciprocal borrowing privileges
- Exchange or sharing of expertise, resources, and facilities
- Exchange of publications and photocopies and other reprographic services
- Sharing of bibliographic information
- Cooperative acquisition, cooperative cataloguing, and cooperative collection development preparation of union list of holdings
- Cooperative relationship and network development

The implementation of resource sharing is largely depends on library networking. It gives an easy and wider access to information as members have an expanded information-base and service. A network is a form of arrangement or an administrative structure that links a group of individuals or organizations who have agreed to work together and/or share resources. Information networking entails the sharing of resources so that the information needs of both actual and potential users of information—from the local to national level—of all network participants are met. The network enables the participating bodies to facilitate and expand their users' access to literature and information without corresponding investment in purchase, and processing of information is exchanged through the network on a formal basis. The network may be responsible for coordinating, organizing and providing information and literature support at the national and international level.

The main activities and functions of the network are as follows:

Acquisition of materials:

- Joint purchasing of materials
- Assignment of specialization in material acquisition
- Coordinated subscription
- Exchange of duplicate holdings

Technical services:

- Co-operative cataloguing
- Abstracting and indexing services
- Interlibrary loan
- Reciprocal borrowing privileges
- Reference and/or referral services

Publication programme/repackaging information:

- Union catalogue/list of periodicals
- Mutual notification of purchase through lists of new arrivals or acquisition list
- Bibliography development
- Newsletters
- Joint directories of personnel, projects, consultants, resource persons, etc.
- Manuals

Coordination services:

- Clearing house functions
- Retrieval and storage function
- Referral center

Delivery/mailing service:

- Research, training and other special services
  - User interest surveys
  - Joint research projects
  - In-service personnel training
  - Workshops and meetings
  - Translation services

RESOURCE SHARING AND NETWORKS INITIATIVES IN BANGLADESH

In Bangladesh several Resource-sharing and networks initiatives was taken by different organizations in different sectors to launch Resource sharing and networking systems.

Some of these are as follows:

- *National Agricultural Information System (NAIS)*: The Agricultural

Information Centre (AIC) was taken an initiative to develop a network of agricultural institution.

- *Social Science Research Council (SSRC)*: Social Science Research Council, Dhaka was taken an initiative to develop a social science information network in Bangladesh.
- *Health Literature, Library, and Information Service (HeLLIS) Network*: The HeLLIS network was developed by SEARO (WHO), New Delhi, India and National Health Library and Documentation Centre (NHLDOC), Dhaka. All the health libraries of Bangladesh were brought under this network.
- *Development Information Network on South Asia (DEVINSA)*: The DEVINSA network was organized by CSCD (Committee on Studies for Cooperation for Development in South Asia) through the Marga Institute, Colombo, Sri Lanka. All SAARC countries, except Bhutan, were the participants of this network.
- *Information Network on Rural Development (INRD)*: Centre on Integrated Rural Development for Asia and the Pacific (CIRDAP), Dhaka was taken an initiative to develop a regional network on rural development.
- *Women Information Network (WIN)*: Centre on Integrated Rural Development for Asia and the Pacific (CIRDAP), Dhaka was taken another initiative to develop a network on women information.
- *Bangladesh Development Support Information and Communication (BDSIC) Network*: Bangladesh Academy for Rural Development (BARD), Comilla was taken an initiative to launch a network of rural development institutions in Bangladesh
- *National Science and Technology Information Policy (NASTIP)*: Under this policy, a four-tier science and technology information networking system has been recommended.
- *The Association of Management Development Institutes in South Asia (AMDISA) Library Network*: The Association of Management Development Institutes in South Asia was launched a library network on management development. The Headquarter of this network was located at the Administrative Staff College of India, Hyderabad. One institute in each SAARC country was selected as a focal point. The Institute of Business Administration Library, Dhaka University was selected as the National focal point for this network.
- *University Libraries*: Dhaka University Library took an initiative several years' back to develop a network of the university libraries, initially by preparing a union catalogue of the holdings of the university libraries.
- The University Grants Commission of Bangladesh (UGC), in collaboration with the Asia Foundation, took an initiative to compile

a union catalogue of the collections of different universities of Bangladesh and to establish an information network within the universities.

- *Bangladesh National Scientific and Library Information Network (BANSLINK)*: Bangladesh National Scientific and Technical Documentation Centre (BANSDOC) was taken an initiative to build up a Network, known as BANSLINK, to develop a resource-sharing network having dial up connectivity with 15 libraries and information centres of the country.
- *Sustainable Development Network Programme (SDNP)*: SDNP is a UNDP funded programme, which started a union catalogue services in 2002 in their virtual library programme. The SDNP virtual library prepared this union catalogue of 13 libraries, all of which are using CDS/ISIS software for bibliographic record keeping. The SDNP virtual library union catalogue is a webbased Online Public Access Catalogue.

Bangladesh being a developing country cannot effort to waste its resources. To avoid this, an effective resource sharing and networking system is necessary.

At present the following resource sharing and networking systems are working in the country:

- *Population Information Network (POPIN)*: The National Institute of Population Research and Training (NIPORT) has taken an initiative to establish an information networking system in the field of health, population, family planning and maternal and child health in collaboration and cooperation with the government and non-government organizations, autonomous bodies, voluntary organizations, and international organizations.
- National Health Library and Documentation Centre (NHLDOC), (Ministry of Health, Government of Bangladesh) and International Centre for Diarrhoeal Disease Research, Bangladesh (ICDDR,B) signed in 1976 an agreement to facilitate library cooperation through an interlibrary loan system and agreed to cooperate with each other to avoid duplication of journal subscriptions. Subsequently, some other library named, BIDS, BIRDEM, USAID, Dhaka, Aga Khan Community Health Programme, Dhaka, and the Bangladesh Rural Advancement Committee joined this programme by signing interlibrary loan agreements. The system has been working well.
- *United Nations Library Network in Bangladesh (UN L-Net BD)*: In March 2002 United Nations Information Centre (UNIC) Library has taken an initiative to establish the UN Library Network in Bangladesh (UN L-Net BD). Initially the Network consisted of twenty major libraries of different government, NGOs, including the UN agencies in Bangladesh. At present there are 26 members in this network. It

was agreed that UNIC library would act as a focal point and secretariat of the network.

It is not possible for one libraries or information centers to hold the full stock of information resources or to procure all information, which may be in demand by its clientele. Even not a single library or information centers can meet the thrust of knowledge of all the readers from its holdings.

To solve this problem, library cooperation started long ago, such as Inter-library loan, document delivery, library networks etc. At present the more accepted system of resource sharing is library consortia. Consortia approach is one of the many ways of maintaining cooperation and coordination among the libraries and in fact it has emerged as the 'state of the art' in library cooperation in recent years.

The word 'consortia' was originated from the Latin in early 19th century in the sense of partnership. Oxford Advanced Learners Dictionary describes Consortia as 'a group of people, countries, companies, etc. who are working together on a particular project'.

A library Consortia is an association of a group of libraries that agree to share their resources to satisfy the needs of users. Consortia may be formed on a local, regional, national, or international basis; on a functional or format basis; or on a subject basis.

BENEFITS OF CONSORTIA

The benefits of Consortia are many:

- A comprehensive collection is possible
- Building communication among different libraries
- Avoid duplication of core collection specially for core journals
- Scope of electronic archives
- Easy access to resource sharing on Internet by developing common resources databases
- Effective document delivery systems
- Better scope for developing a union catalogue
- Reduce cost of information
- Time saving
- Improved resource sharing
- More professional services to users
- Help to develop a competitive professionalism among LIS professionals

INTERNATIONAL EFFORTS FOR LIBRARY CONSORTIA

The development of library consortia is the outcome of the desire for resource sharing and consortia seem to be getting bigger. The global development of OCLC is prime example. Due to escalating cost of documents, decreasing budgets, inadequate storage area and competent staff, LIS professionals of the world are coming together to form consortia.

There are several International efforts for library consortia are:

- Consortium of University Research Libraries (CURL)
- Consortium of Academic Libraries in Manchester (CALIM)
- Colorado Library Information Network,
- Washington Research Library Consortium (WRLC),
- BIBSYS (Shared University, Research and National Library of Norway)
- Queensland University Libraries Office of Cooperation (QUOLOC)
- China Academic Library and Information System (CALIS), China,
- Takatsu University Library Consortium (YULC), Japan
- Tokyo Western Regional Academic Library Consortium, Japan,
- Yamatesen Ensen Private University Libraries Consortium, Japan
- Korea Resource Sharing Alliance (KORSA), Korea,
- CONsortium on Core Eletronic Resources in Taiwan (CONCERT),
- Ministry of University Affairs (MUA). ThaiLIS.

INDIAN INITIATIVES FOR LIBRARY CONSORTIA

In India at present there are many consortia being run successfully by different organizations. Some of them are as:

- CSIR e-Journal Consortia,
- INDEST (Indian National Digital Library in Science and Technology) Consortia
- FORSA (Forum for Resource Sharing in Astronomy)
- UGC-INFONET
- IIM Library Consortia,
- ICICI Knowledge Park,
- DAE Library Consortium,
- ICMR Library Consortia,
- HELINET (Rajiv Gandhi University of Health Sciences, Karnataka).

BANGLADESH INITIATIVES

The information revolution has brought radical changes to the functions and services in all types of libraries. Many libraries in Bangladesh till today are not in a position to afford to procure all documents and subscribe to core journals in major discipline due to financial constraints. As a result, with the aim of ensuring rapid resource sharing among the major libraries and documentation centers in Bangladesh, many library networking and resources sharing efforts were started to help each other.

The objectives of these consortia are for better resource sharing, to reduce information costs, for speedy delivery of documents, to keep abreast of new developments etc. Much emphasis should be given at the national level in Bangladesh for the development of documentary information resources, because it is considered as vital resources to promote the development of economy, science, technology and culture etc. University Grants Commission of Bangladesh (UGC) and Dr. Javed I. Khan of Kent State University have taken an initiative to develop a digital library system for Bangladesh. A 4-member committee was formed by the UGC to draft a concept paper on forming Consortia in Bangladesh, and the committee has already submitted the report to the UGC for their approval.

CONSIDERATION NEEDED TO FORM CONSORTIA

The following issues need to consider before building the consortia:

- Technology infrastructure
- Resources identification
- Budget and funding
- Pricing issues
- Subscription payment issues
- Access related issues
- Licensing and copyright issues
- Archival issues
- Usages and usability issues
- Coordination among partners
- Availability of efficient staff
- Overcoming political objections
- The egos of individuals and institutions
- Adequate professional training on ICT for the LIS professionals
- Sustainability issues

RECOMMENDATION

In this era of global communication, networks and consortia are highly important. A library consortium in the country is needed to achieve cost effectiveness and bridging of the digital divide. To develop library consortia in Bangladesh we have to overcome many hurdles such as inappropriate ICT infrastructure, inadequate funding, limited trained personnel, technological capability, lack of understanding of the concept of consortia. But anything new comes up with new challenges and opportunity, it is up to the individuals to take up the challenge and accept the opportunity.

So, we can recommend the following suggestions for establishment of library consortia in Bangladesh:

- The Government and LIS Professionals bodies should take initiative to conduct some workshops on Consortia.
- The Government and LIS Professionals bodies should start a forum to bring the librarians/ Information professionals and the publishers/ vendors together for better communication and interactions.
- The Government should also make attempts to provide the necessary ICT infrastructure such as high-speed links and a stable network to access the e-journals.
- Policy makers, both in national and international levels together with

Internet Service Provider (ISP) should have a shared obligation to seek ways to achieve the wide spread use of the internet.

- Bangladesh should have a separate ministry to coordinate the overall development of the library and information system in the country.
- LIS professionals must market their services to the private sector for sponsorship and support.
- The government should encourage and must recognize the role of librarians and information professionals in building an information society for the development of the nation.
- Involvement of management of the parents organization for sustainability

CONCLUSION

Consortia in Bangladesh are still in table talk and there is a need to study the consortia models and guidelines and methodologies. It is recommended that the concept of Consortia can work well among similar organizations having similar situations such as sufficient additional funds available for the libraries of the consortia members and above all the committed mindsets of the library administrators. On the other side the subscription of e-journals are increasing day by day and the library budgets are shrinking, so it is needed for the library professionals to work together and formulate consortia for subscription to e-journals. Bangladeshi LIS professionals should seriously think and take initiative for consortium movement like western countries for maximum utilization of resources at the reduced cost, time and space.

11

Edifice a Protection Programme

You have learned about the factors that cause or accelerate the deterioration of collections, as well as strategies that can be used to prevent or mitigate damage. In this part, you will learn how to pull together these building blocks to create a systematic and well thought out preservation plan for your institution. The preservation planning process has several explicit goals: to determine preservation problems and needs; to identify activities that will solve those problems and meet those needs; to allocate resources to implement preservation activities; and to prepare a detailed plan for carrying out the necessary activities.

The planning process also has the implicit goal of educating staff members and administration about preservation issues. Preservation cuts across existing organizational divisions and affects virtually every aspect of an institution's operations. Thus, creating an environment in which all staff members apply preservation knowledge and skills in their everyday work is very important. This can significantly improve the condition of collections even without large expenditures of funds. To achieve your preservation planning goals, it is best to undertake the planning process by consensus, involving a range of institutional staff, including the institution's senior management (*e.g.*, director, board of trustees). This helps to increase staff understanding of preservation issues and builds support for the inevitable changes the plan will bring.

PRESERVATION PLANNING

Even in the smallest institutions, a preservation programme needs administrative coordination in order to be effective. If individual preservation activities are undertaken in the absence of an overall plan, one or two preservation activities (such as preservation microfilming or rehousing collections) may be well developed, while others (such as monitoring improvement of environmental conditions) are neglected.

The process of development and ongoing review of a preservation plan helps ensure that preservation is considered an integral part of institutional activities, rather than in competition with other activities (such as collection development) for time and resources.

THE PLANNING PROCESS

- *"Planning Provides a Rational Process to Analyse Needs Systematically to Minimize the Problems and Maximize the Opportunities."* —Jutta Reed-Scott, "Planning for Preservation in Libraries," in *Preservation: Issues and Planning*

In her article, Jutta Reed-Scott sets forth the basic components of the preservation planning process:

- Identify and assess preservation needs (through some type of survey)
- Set priorities among preservation needs according to the institution's mission
- Evaluate existing preservation activities
- decide what preservation functions are needed within the institution and how they will be organized
- Allocate resources for preservation
- Write a plan and determine how the plan will be implemented

Identifying and assessing needs is an information-gathering process: what collections does the institution hold and what is their condition? How are collections housed? What are the environmental conditions within the building(s)? Is there a disaster plan? Are collections protected from fire and theft? Are repair, binding, and/or conservation treatment undertaken regularly? How much funding is allocated for preservation? How much staff time?

Once you have discerned your preservation needs, you must consider potential solutions to the problems you have identified. What answers are most appropriate for your particular institution and situation? What existing activities already have a preservation component, and how should existing preservation activities change to meet the needs you have identified?

As part of this process, you will need to assess your institutional mission and goals and the personnel and monetary resources currently available, as well as potential future resources.

Once all the relevant issues have been considered, you should set preservation priorities and pull together a preservation strategy that includes an action plan and timetable. A systematic preservation plan will allow you to respond effectively to preservation needs and take advantage of preservation opportunities that might otherwise have been missed.

PRESERVATION STRATEGIES

Developing a Preservation Strategy

While the basic elements of a preservation programme are fairly straightforward, the emphasis placed on each of these elements will vary according to the institution and situation. The relative importance of each component for your institution will depend on the type, value, and condition of your collections; the importance of specific collections to your institution's mission; the type of access you need to provide (open stacks, closed stacks, offsite storage); and the amount of use the collections receive.

You will need to develop an appropriate preservation strategy for your institution. In general, preservation programme elements that benefit all collections (such as environmental control, security, disaster planning, and proper storage and handling) should be thought of as the basic "umbrella" components of a programme. Other strategies, such as microfilming, library binding, or treatment would be used for individual (or groups of) items as needed.

Strategies for Different Types of Institutions

Preservation needs and responses are specific to a particular institution and each collection within that institution. Some repositories may see their primary responsibility as preserving unique and/or comprehensive collections over the long term, while others may place more emphasis on serving academic teaching and research needs or services to the general public.

In general, institutions with archival or historical collections assume an obligation to preserve those collections over the long term. These institutions will place a strong emphasis on strategies to stabilize the collections as a whole (*e.g.*, holdings maintenance/collections care, environmental control, security, emergency preparedness), with a secondary focus on preservation reformatting (usually microfilming) and/or conservation treatment for the specific collections that require it.

The primary mission of small- to mid-sized public or academic libraries, on the other hand, is to provide access to collections for as long as the materials are needed. These libraries generally have a high level of use and collect basically rather than comprehensively. In these libraries, reference collections and materials related to current courses receive the most use. These institutions will also need to focus on umbrella issues such as storage and handling, environment, security, and disaster planning-but in addition they will undertake library binding, basic book repair, withdrawal of brittle titles that are no longer needed, and replacement of brittle titles with reprints, photocopies or purchased microfilm.

Preservation microfilming and conservation treatment will generally not be a priority, unless the institution also holds historical or other unique collections.

Like smaller academic and public libraries, large research libraries strive to provide users access to collections for as long as the materials are needed.

In addition, they assume responsibility for building and maintaining research collections that are meant to survive over the long term. For these institutions, an even wider range of preservation options will be needed, including umbrella strategies such as environmental control, storage/handling, and disaster planning, as well as preservation reformatting, replacement, library binding, book repair, and conservation treatment.

PROGRAMME MANAGEMENT

Managing a preservation programme involves developing policies, assigning preservation responsibilities to staff members, and documenting preservation activities. Budgeting and identifying funding for preservation activities is also important, but this will be considered separately. Remember that if preventive preservation is to be effective, it must become part of all activities within the organization. Part of your job will be to make your colleagues aware of their roles in the preservation programme. In other words, preservation should not be an "add-on" activity-it must be an integral component of the day-to-day operations and responsibilities in every department, office, and division.

POLICY

The development of written preservation policies and documentation is crucial to the planning process. Written policies provide guidance for carrying out specific activities, help to codify procedures, and ensure that staff members accept them and carry them out.

Overall Preservation Policy

One of the first steps in the planning process must be to develop an overall institutional preservation policy. This document will provide a framework for setting preservation priorities and preparing a detailed preservation plan.

It should reflect the institution's mission and goals and should include:

- A general description of the preservation problems facing the institution
- Definitions/explanations of key preservation concepts and terms
- The general principles and practices that will guide the preservation programme
- A general outline of the preservation programme that includes responsibilities for preservation activities and describes how preservation relates to other functions within the institution (*e.g.*, provision of access, processing of new collections)

Once an overall preservation policy has been developed, more detailed polices will be needed to provide staff with written guidelines for carrying out specific preservation activities as part of everyday collections care efforts. This is particularly important in smaller institutions where there is no separate preservation department.

The policy-development process may also facilitate change within the institution, educating staff and administration about the damaging effects of current practices and procedures. Essentially, the preservation policy articulates the overall goals of the preservation programme. This policy should be revisited periodically, as the institution and circumstances change and as preservation goals are achieved.

Policies for Specific Activities

Preservation should be a part of all activities including, but not limited to:

- Acquisition (use of nondamaging spine labels, etc.)
- Binding (use of archival materials and nondamaging binding techniques that allow the book to open completely, etc.)
- Shelving (storing oversized books flat or spine down, using proper bookends)
- Photocopying (using an "edge" photocopier with an edge platen and being careful not to damage the spines of books)
- Exhibition (supporting collections properly and using nondamaging exhibit techniques, etc.)

Once an overall preservation policy has been developed, strategies will be needed for specific preservation activities, which will provide staff with written guidelines for carrying out these activities as part of everyday collections care efforts. Written policies are best developed over time as preservation activities are systematized.

Following is a list of potential policies and procedures that have a preservation component (all of these may not be needed for every institution):

- Disaster planning and recovery
- Collection acquisitions and processing
- Donor forms and agreements
- Exhibit guidelines
- Rights and reproductions policies
- Book repair policy
- Selection for conservation treatment
- Documenting conservation treatment
- Binding quality check
- Microfilming selection and quality
- Selection for digitization
- Handling materials for digitization
- Food and drinks policy
- Security policy
- Patron access/use policy
- Loan policy
- Environmental monitoring
- Collection storage and rehousing.

In general, clear and well-considered policies that are universally enforced will make preventive preservation measures routine and lengthen the useful life of collections.

ORGANIZATION AND STAFFING

Larger Institutions

There are a number of models for staffing a successful preservation programme at a large institution. The Association of Research Libraries (ARL) 1991 publication *Preservation Programme Models: A Study Project and Report* set out organizational and staffing models for four libraries of varying size, and it is still referenced in the library literature. ARL preservation statistics published annually show that many large research libraries have preservation departments of various sizes, ranging from part-time to full-time preservation administrators, along with library assistants, conservation technicians, and/ or conservators.

Smaller Institutions

Identifying an effective staffing model for a preservation programme in a small or medium-sized institution can be more challenging. In archives, historical societies, public libraries, and small college libraries, it is usually not realistic to have a separate preservation manager. In fact, many small institutions (this is particularly the case in archives) may have only one professional staff member who is responsible for all activities, including preservation. In these situations, preservation management will be a part-time responsibility for one or more staff members. If the institution does not have a full-time preservation manager, it is best for one person on staff to be responsible for acquiring preservation information and making preservation decisions. Even though a number of staff members may carry out preservation activities as part of their regular duties, it is important to have one person responsible for coordinating these activities. In some institutions and situations, however, a committee may be more effective in managing preservation activities. In this case, each member of the committee would oversee a specific area of preservation (*e.g.*, disaster planning, environmental control, housekeeping). If you are responsible for managing preservation in a smaller institution, it is likely that preservation will be only one of many "hats" that you wear. Try not to be discouraged by the scope of the preservation problem. Instead, break tasks down into manageable projects that can be completed in a reasonable amount of time. Your preservation plan will help you to do this and will give you a sense of accomplishment.

Assigning Responsibility

Remember that it is pointless to assign preservation responsibilities if staff members do not have the time to carry them out. Your institution will need to make a commitment to providing staff time for preservation activities, as well as appropriate training. Job descriptions should include preservation activities, and the preservation manager should be at a high enough level within the organization that he or she can effectively work for change.

DOCUMENTATION AND STATISTICS

Ongoing documentation of preservation activities ensures that data is available to support any changes that may be needed. Documentation may involve describing existing preservation procedures, keeping statistics on preservation activities, maintaining records of conservation treatment and other activities, and providing photo documentation.

Documentation of preservation activities is important because it:

- Provides crucial information for new staff in case of reorganization or staff turnover
- Documents current practices so that they can be compared to future practices
- Supports necessary product, equipment, or technology changes
- Provides information that can be used to determine future budgeting and staffing levels

Preservation statistics can be very helpful for planning and budgeting, but you must carefully consider how many to keep, in what categories, and how you will use them.

PROGRAMME FUNDING

Effective preservation requires a dependable budget with active administrative coordination, even if the budget is not large at the beginning. While it is possible to improve conditions to a certain extent through changes in existing procedures, funding will be needed for supplies, training, and equipment if anything more than very basic preservation projects are to be undertaken.

In this part you will learn about budgeting for preservation, identifying outside sources of funding, and writing grants for preservation projects. Keep in mind, however, that although grant funding is an excellent resource for individual preservation projects, it should be used to supplement institutional funding, not to replace it. Institutional commitment to the preservation programme through the allocation of funds for preservation activities is very important.

THE ROLE OF FUNDING IN SETTING PRESERVATION PRIORITIES

Setting preservation priorities involves many cost-related questions. Will you tackle lower-cost preservation options first? How will you plan for higher-cost activities? If your institution needs a preservation survey, will you pay for a professional one or will in-house staff conduct it? If you need to establish an ongoing library binding or book repair programme, how much will it cost, and is your institution willing to bear the charges? Would outsourcing of some preservation activities be cheaper than doing the work in house? How will you fund special projects such as preservation microfilming or conservation treatment? Is outside funding available?

Remember, however, that cost is only one of the factors in setting preservation priorities; you must also consider each activity in the context of the entire preservation programme. Is the activity a critical need? Will it provide a significant benefit for a large number of materials? If it provides a limited benefit, but is also low cost, should it be done anyway? The cost of a preservation activity must also be balanced against the risk of not undertaking the activity; neglecting an activity because of high cost (such as roof repair or installation of fire protection equipment) may have serious negative consequences for all or part of your collection over the long term.

BUDGETING

Budgeting is one of the most challenging aspects of preservation management. You must decide what preservation activities are needed within your institution, how much they will cost, and how you will pay for them. You will also need to decide what work will be carried out in house and what might be outsourced.

Preservation Spending: How Much Is Enough

In an era of declining budgets and staffing, there are never enough resources to address all preservation needs. To determine whether your institution is on the right track in terms of preservation spending, it can be helpful to compare your efforts to those of other institutions.

The Association of Research Libraries (ARL) issues an annual report on preservation statistics in ARL member libraries, which primarily represent libraries that hold two million volumes or more. These reports collect statistics on the organizational structure of library preservation programmes, staffing levels, preservation expenditures, conservation treatment, and preservation reformatting.

ARL statistics gathered over a number of years have shown that research libraries with active preservation programmes spend approximately 5 to 10 per cent of their total budget on preservation (*e.g.*, prevention of deterioration, preparing materials for use, and repairing/copying materials). This statistic does not include costs related to the building and systems that enable the library to maintain a preservation-quality environment. The larger the library, the higher the percentage of total library expenditures that tends to be directed to preservation. While these figures obviously do not apply directly to other types and sizes of institution, they are useful as a general model.

Reallocating Existing Funds

Remember that initiating new preservation activity does not always have to involve allocation of new funds. When planning a preservation programme, review your institution's budget to identify any activities that could be redirected to assist in meeting preservation goals. For example, most archives already purchase folders and storage boxes, and many libraries purchase pamphlet binders or other enclosures. A change in the type of material bought and/or training of staff to use the enclosures properly may greatly improve the overall protection of collections with little or no additional cost. Since reallocation of existing funds may cross departmental lines, it must be undertaken as part of a cooperative preservation planning process that is coordinated with the institution's overall strategic plan.

Cost Analysis

Cost analysis is crucial to effective budgeting for preservation. In order to decide how best to accomplish a particular preservation goal, a preservation manager must be able to analyse a preservation activity and its associated costs.

A cost analysis might be needed in any of the following situations:

- Submitting a budget proposal for a preservation activity within the institution
- Preparing a response to an institutional request for cost reductions
- Developing a cost estimate for a grant proposal
- Comparing the costs of carrying out an activity in house versus using a vendor

The process of carrying out a cost analysis is explained in detail in *The Preservation Manager's Guide to Cost Analysis*. After identifying the product, service, or other activity to be analysed (for example, to determine the costs of producing book boxes in-house), the preservation manager must gather detailed information on the procedures for carrying out the service or activity.

Costs may include supplies and equipment; services; labour; or indirect costs (*e.g.*, overhead). In each of these categories, the cost of each resource needed to complete the activity should be calculated on a per-item basis. Remember to include "hidden" costs (*e.g.*, supply costs may include not just the cost of the items, but shipping costs or custom order fees).

All assumptions made must be documented (for example, if the cost of staff time is not included in a comparative cost analysis because it is the same in both scenarios), and the effectiveness of the cost analysis must be measured by comparison with actual costs or with similar activities at another institution.

FUNDING SOURCES

There are various potential sources of funding for preservation activities; these include internal sources (your parent institution, or possibly fees for services and/or other income-generating projects) and external sources (federal and state grant programmes, as well as local corporations and foundations). For external funding sources, your primary goal should be to develop a network of funders that matches your goals and ideas, and that can provide regular small grants supplemented by periodic larger grants.

Federal Funders

The three major federal sources for preservation funding of paper-based collections are:

- The National Endowment for the Humanities (NEH) Division of Preservation and Access. NEH has a number of grant categories, including Preservation Assistance Grants, Stabilization of Humanities Collections Grants, and Grants to Preserve and Create Access to Humanities Collections. Note that the Preservation Assistance Grants are designed specifically for smaller institutions—they provide funding for preservation surveys; purchase of preservation supplies, equipment, and storage furniture; and other activities.

- The Institute of Museum and Library Services (IMLS). IMLS funds the Conservation Assessment programme and the Conservation Project Support programme (both for historical societies, museums, and state/local governments), as well as the Save America's Treasures programme and National Leadership Grants. IMLS also administers the Library Services and Technology Act (LSTA), through which funds are provided to state libraries, which then make re-grants to individual institutions for various purposes, including preservation.
- The National Historical Publications and Records Commission (NHPRC). NHPRC makes Archival and Records Project Grants to archival institutions to preserve records and make them accessible.

Other potential federal funders include the National Endowment for the Arts (NEA) and the National Science Foundation (NSF).

State Funders

There are numerous state preservation grant programmes around the country; these generally provide funding for preservation planning surveys, and subsequently for implementing survey recommendations. The type and extent of these programmes varies greatly, so it is best to consult your state library or archives to determine whether or not a preservation grant programme exists in your state.

Foundations

Remember that private organizations may also be a source of funding. There are several types of foundations: large general-purpose organizations such as the Ford Foundation or the Mellon Foundation; special-purpose foundations; company-sponsored foundations; community foundations (which usually fund within a specific geographic area); and family foundations (which are often informal and unstaffed).

Many small/local foundations or corporations have specific interests and you may be able to find one that matches your needs. For example, if you are trying to preserve a local history collection, you might consider approaching local businesses or others with an interest in the community. As with federal or state funding, you may have to provide funds to match the grant. Also remember that foundations may help in ways other than providing money directly for preservation activities, including providing funding for printing costs, furniture, or equipment.

GRANTWRITING

The key to writing a successful grant proposal is to understand what needs to be included in each part of the proposal, as well as what the proposal reviewers will be looking for when reading the document.

A grant proposal is a written presentation asking for support of a programme, project, activity, or function that an institution wants to undertake in response to a need. The proposal must articulate this need and provide a plan for carrying out the desired activity. The activity to be funded must have a clear relationship to your institution's mission and purpose. Your written proposal should be clear and realistic and should focus on what you can accomplish.

The general components of a preservation project proposal are as follows:

- *Objectives*: This part includes both your goals (a broad-based statement of the ultimate result of the activity) and objectives (a narrowly defined, measurable, time-specific outcome that your institution expects to accomplish as a result of the grant). Be sure to identify the community being served and to state the results of the project, not the activity itself.
- *Plan of Work*: This is a detailed description of the activities and services to be undertaken to achieve your goals and objectives. It should explain why you chose these methods, and it should enumerate what facilities, personnel, and equipment will be used. It should include a timeline for the process and define tasks and subtasks.
- *Budget*: This provides estimated costs for the activities listed in the plan of work. The forms and guidelines of the funder should be followed; government funders usually require more detail than foundations.
- *Evaluation*:This part describes your plans for evaluating the project to determine whether or not it was successful. You may need to measure whether staff members changed or improved their skills, knowledge, etc., or you may need to measure facts such as items rehoused or treated, materials developed, supplies consumed, etc.
- *Sustainability*: This part indicates how you will maintain the project or programme at the end of the grant period. Will the activities continue? If so, how will they be maintained, and what funding/ resources will you provide?

Helpful Hints for Grant Writing

- There should be one writer, even if there are many contributors.
- Follow the funder's guidelines.
- Do your research and get the facts right-be knowledgeable about the most current preservation practices.

- Be aware of related preservation projects.
- All ideas should flow from one central need.
- Avoid jargon.
- Be compelling, but not overdramatic.
- Get an outside person to edit the proposal and review the budget.
- Be thorough, clear, and concise.

Remember that a good proposal doesn't necessarily result in getting a grant; other factors, such as the number of proposals received or the current priorities of the granting agency, may come into play. Ask the granting agency for feedback, and resubmit if necessary.

EDUCATION AND TRAINING

Preservation education and training of staff and others is necessary to successful preservation efforts. Facilitating preservation awareness for the institution's administrator(s) and/or trustees can be very helpful in encouraging institutional commitment.

Certainly all staff members with preservation responsibilities (*e.g.*, book repair, administering preservation microfilming projects) must be trained in proper preservation techniques. Staff members with management responsibility for preservation activities should also participate in professional activities, which will allow them to keep up with current preservation information and network with peers.

EDUCATING STAFF AND ADMINISTRATORS

One of the most important steps an institution can take is to support the ongoing education and training of staff members with preservation responsibilities. Some preservation projects such as weeding and shelf maintenance do not require a large investment in equipment or supplies, but they do require that staff members have knowledge of preservation principles and proper procedures for care of collections. An investment in training for those who carry out preservation activities will serve to extend the useful life of the collections. The staff member or committee in charge of preservation should coordinate this training.

Staff training and education can be undertaken in-house or through outside workshops, and avenues for raising preservation awareness among administrators may be similar. Administrators and board members or trustees may be interested in attending half- or full-day workshops on general preservation topics. A presentation by the preservation manager at a board of trustees meeting, or a preservation exhibit within the institution, may also be effective at setting the stage for training or raising awareness.

RAISING AWARENESS AND MANAGING CHANGE

While holding training parts and attending workshops is a relatively straightforward activity, you may find that it is much more of a challenge to get staff members and administrators to fully implement and support the preservation programme when it involves changes to the status quo. Staff members may be resistant to changing the way they have always done things, and they may see the change as a threat to their position(s).

How can you make the case for change and handle the transition to new policies and procedures? First, you must be sure that you understand your institutional culture (*i.e.*, how your institution operates). Is the institution's mission formal or implied? Is the organizational structure hierarchical or lateral? Rigid or more flexible? What is the institutional style of communication? Oral or written? Interpersonal or by committee? E-mail or memos? The answers to these questions will help you figure out how to effectively persuade staff and administrators and build consensus.

When introducing new activities or changes to existing preservation activities, try to be aware of how specific staff members may be feeling about the change. Who is having the hardest time with it? Try to acknowledge the difficulty, provide lots of information, and give everyone a part to play in the new arrangement. It is usually a good idea to make the actual change quickly, rather than dragging it out. In managing the change, it may be helpful if you can find out how transitions (*e.g.*, automation, building renovation) have been handled in the past within your institution.

PROFESSIONAL RESOURCES

Ongoing preservation education and professional activities will help you carry out your preservation management duties more effectively. In particular, interaction with other preservation managers can provide encouragement and reinforcement, especially if you are the only person responsible for preservation in your institution. You can update your skills and knowledge (and network with other preservation managers) through workshops, other continuing education programmes, and participation in professional organizations and listserv discussions.

Many workshops are given by regional or state preservation organizations. There are a number of regional organizations throughout the United States that have joined together to form the Regional Alliance for Preservation (RAP). There are a number of regional organizations throughout the United States that have joined together to form the Regional Alliance for Preservation (RAP). Statewide preservation programmes began during the 1980s and 1990s in a number of states throughout the country, based on a number of different models. Many of these have provided grants and workshops, often through the state library or archives. Examples include the New York State Library Programme for the Conservation and Preservation of Library Research Materials and the Massachusetts Board of Library Commissioners preservation advisory services, workshops, and grants. Consult your state library or archives to determine whether or not similar programmes exist in your state.

Both the American Library Association (ALA) and the Society of American Archivists provide resources for preservation professionals:

- ALA's Association for Library Collections and Technical Services division (ALCTS) includes the Preservation and Reformatting Section (PARS). PARS has a number of preservation committees and sponsors workshop and conference programmes. PARS also sponsors two e-mail discussion groups: the Preservation Administrators Discussion List and the Preservation Educators Discussion List.
- The Society of American Archivists (SAA) also has an active preservation part that provides opportunities to get involved with the professional community. SAA also maintains the Archives and Archivists Listserv.

12

Cataloguing Electronic Resources

INTRODUCTION

DEFINITION

AACR defines an electronic resource as material encoded for manipulation by a computerized device. This material may require the use of a peripheral directly connected to a computerized device or a connection to a computer network. Electronic resources that do not require the use of a computer, are not included in this definition.

For cataloguing purposes, electronic resources may be treated in one of two ways depending on whether access is direct (local) or remote (networked):

- Direct–a physical carrier can be described. This carrier, (*e.g.* disc/disk, cassette, cartridge) must be inserted into a computerized device.
- Remote–no physical carrier can be handled. Remote access can only be provided by use of an input-output device.

CONTENT VERSUS CARRIER

Until 1997 electronic resources were coded for carrier and not content. In June 1997 MARBI (the committee that governs MARC changes) revised the definition of code "m" in the fixed field Type. Electronic resources are now cataloged and coded according to their content and not the carrier.

Type code "m" is now used only for the following general classes of electronic resources:

Computer software (including programmes, games, fonts):

- Numeric data
- Computer-oriented multimedia
- Online systems or services

Examples:

- Census data on CD-ROM or the Internet – Type "a" (book)
- Online maps – Type "e" (cartographic materials)
- Maps on floppy disks – Type "e" (cartographic materials)
- Most web pages – Type "a" (book)

- Multimedia encyclopedia on CD-ROM or online –Type "m" (electronic resource)
- Computer games online or on CD-ROM – Type "m" (electronic resource)

GUIDELINES FOR CODING ELECTRONIC RESOURCES IN LEADER/06

DOCUMENTATION

- *MARC 21 Concise Format for Bibliographic Data* defines the codes and conventions that identify data elements in MARC bibliographic records. It is updated on an annual basis.
- OCLC's *Cataloguing Electronic Resources: OCLC-MARC Coding Guidelines* assists catalogers creating biblio-graphic records for electronic resources and includes information on the proper coding of fixed fields, including Leader/06 (Type of record).
- *Guidelines for Distinguishing Cartographic Materials on Computer File Carriers from other Materials on Computer File Carriers* helps catalogers working with carto-graphic electronic resources to distinguish them from other types of electronic resources and to select the correct Leader/06 (Type of record) based on that distinction.
- *Relationship of Fields 006, 007, and 008* explains the general model adopted to indicate how repeti-tions of field 006 (Fixed-length data elements-Additional material characteristics) and a single field 008 (Fixed-length data elements-General information) coexist in bibliographic records, especially in relation to the values in Leader character positions 06 (Type of record) and 07 (Bibliographic level), and clarifies the relationship of field 007 (Physical description fixed field) to fields 006 and 008.
- *Use of fixed fields 006/007/008 and Leader codes in CONSER records* presents guidelines for coding in CONSER records.

PRINCIPLES AND GUIDELINES FOR CODING LEADER/06

An electronic resource is a manifestation of a work that requires the use of a computer for access. Peripheral devices attached to the computer (such as a CD-ROM drive) may also be required. The manifestation's carrier is accessed either directly (*e.g.*, via CD-ROM, etc.) or remotely (*e.g.*, via the Internet). Items that do not require the use of a computer, such as audio CDs or movies on DVD-videodiscs, are excluded from this definition.

The Leader/06 (Type of record) character position in the *MARC 21 Format for Bibliographic Data* contains a one-character alphabetic code that differentiates MARC records created for various types of content and materials. The definition of code "m" (computer file) in Leader/06 was revised in June 1997 as a result of *Proposal No. 97-3R*.

The new definition narrowed the choice of code "m" to the following types of electronic resources:

- Computer software (including programmes, games, fonts)
- Numeric data
- Computer-oriented multimedia
- Online systems or services

Code "m" is defined as follows in the MARC 21 Format for Bibliographic Data:

- *m-ComputerFile:* Code m indicates that the content of the record is for the following classes of electronic resources: computer software (including programmes, games, fonts), numeric data, computer-oriented multi-media, online systems or services. For these classes of materials, if there is a significant aspect that causes it to fall into another Leader/06 category, code for that significant aspect (*e.g.*, vector data that is cartographic is not coded as numeric but as cartographic). Other classes of electronic resources are coded for their most significant aspect (*e.g.* language material, graphic, cartographic material, sound, music, moving image). In case of doubt or if the most significant aspect cannot be determined, consider the item a computer file.

This revised definition stipulates that catalogers code electronic resources for the significant aspects of their content, as opposed to their carrier. The Leader/06 determines which 008 code (Fixed-length data elements-General information) is used and the appropriateness and validity of other fixed data elements in a record.

PRINCIPLES AND GUIDELINES FOR CODING FIELDS 006, 007 AND 008

The 008 field contains character positions that provide coded information about the record as a whole and about special bibliographic aspects of the item cataloged. This field is not repeatable. Field 006 (Fixed-length data elements-Additional material characteristics) permits coding for additional aspects of an electronic resource (including any computer file aspects) if the 007 and 008 fields do not adequately describe it.

Some cataloguing utilities and groups (such as CONSER) require the use of 006 fields under certain conditions. Sample records in this document include 006 fields for those who may wish to use this field. Coding all of these positions involves making a series of decisions.

Consider the following when deciding what code values to select:

- What are the primary characteristics of the content of the resource (as opposed to the physical format or carrier)? Look at the definitions of the various Leader/06 codes. Is the content primarily language material, notated music, cartographic material, a computer file, a musical sound recording, etc.?

- Does the resource match the Leader/06 definition of a computer file? If so, "m" (for computer file) goes in Leader/06, and the 008 field is coded for computer files. Position 008/26 contains the code for the type of computer file described in the record.
- If Leader/06 is coded "a" (language material), is the resource a monograph or a continuing resource? This determines the code in Leader/07 (Bibliographic level), which in turn influences 008 field coding (Books or Continuing resources). For other material types, the Leader/06 code determines 008 coding.
- Does the cataloger wish to add a 006 field to record characteristics that cannot be coded in the 008 field? Some electronic resources might need more than one 006 field. For others, a 006 field may not really add any additional information and could be left out.
- Note that *Proposal No. 97-3R* specifies that a 007 field (Physical description fixed field) for electronic resources is mandatory regardless of the Leader/06 code value when the physical form of the resource is an electronic format in order to provide an explicit indication that the item is in an electronic format.
- Some combinations of 006, 007, and 008 fields may result in a certain amount of redundancy, in the sense that the same information about an electronic resource might appear in more than one of these fields. Catalogers must decide whether the information added as a result of recording additional characteristics of an item justifies the redundancy.

In case of doubt, or if the most significant characteristic cannot be determined, code the resource "m" in the Leader/06 position.

Coding for Different types of Electronic Resources

- Bibliographic database on the Internet
- Collection of databases on the Internet
- Textual continuing resource
- Textual continuing resource with search software
- Textual continuing resource received via e-mail
- Textual document
- Cartographic material
- Still images
- Notated music
- Census in textual form
- Database containing manipulable numeric data
- Computer operating system
- Computer software
- Computer game

- Internet search engine
- Web portal
- System or service on the Internet, such as an E-commerce site
- Web site with significant audio and video content
- Streaming video
- Streaming audio

Notes:

- The sample records are partial records.
- Some of the records have a Leader/07 with a value of "i" (for integrating resource). Bibliographic Level "i" for integrating resources was fully implemented in June 2006.
- Some of the 006 fields in the sample records do not necessarily provide much additional information but were added for illustrative purposes.

Bibliographic Database on the Internet

The record describes collections of bibliographic records retrieved via search software; the presence of such software does not change the content of the resource and does not mean that Leader/06 should be coded "m." The resource is primarily textual bibliographic data, so it is coded as language material. The type of computer file (006/09) is bibliographic data.

- *Example(s):*
  - The Library of Congress' online catalogue of bibliographic data.

Ldr/06	:	a [type of record: language material]
Ldr/07	:	m [bibliographic level: monograph]
007	:	[cr|||||||||||||]
006/00	:	m [form of material: computer files/electronic resources]
006/09	:	e [type of computer file: bibliographic data]

Collection of Databases on the Internet

The record describes the system itself and not the content of individual databases. The type of computer file is online system or service.

- *Example(s):*
  - *MEDLINEplus,* a system of databases and data-banks on the Internet offered by the U.S. National Library of Medicine (NLM) and the National Institutes of Health (NIH).

Ldr/06	:	m [type of record: computer files/ electronic resources]
Ldr/07	:	m [bibliographic level: monograph]
007	:	cr#m|||||||||||
008/26	:	j [type of computer file: online system or service]
245 00	:	$aMEDLINEplus $h [electronic resource]

Textual Continuing Resource

The resource is the equivalent of a print item, but in electronic form. The resource is coded as language material. If a 006 field for computer files/ electronic resources is added, the type of computer file (006/09) depends on the content of the resource.

- *Example(s):*
  - *MEDLINE*, a monthly periodical available in PDF format.

Ldr/06	:	a [type of record: language material]
Ldr/07	:	s [bibliographic level: serial]
006/00	:	m [form of material: computer files/ electronic resources]
006/09	:	d [type of computer file: document]
007	:	cr#c|||||||||| [category of material: electronic resource specific material designation: remote]
008/21	:	# [type of continuing resource: periodical]
008/23	:	s [form of item (continuing resources): electronic]
245 10	:	$a NIH MedlinePlus $h [electronic resource]: $b the magazine.

Textual Continuing Resource with Search Software

The resource is the equivalent of a print item, but in electronic form. Search software is included. The presence of such software and/or the location of the serial on the Internet does not necessarily change the content of the resource and does not mean that Leader/06 should be coded "m." The resource is primarily textual data and is coded as language material. If a 006 field for computer files/ electronic resources is added, the type of computer file (006/09) depends on the content of the resource.

- *Example(s):*
  - *MLA international bibliography*, a database of citations available on CD, cumulated quarterly.

Ldr/06	:	a [type of record: language material]
Ldr/07	:	s [bibliographic level: serial]
006/00	:	m [form of material: computer files/electronic resources]
006/09	:	e [type of computer file: bibliographic data]
007	:	co#ugu|||||||| [category of material: electronic resource specific material designation: optical disc]
008/21	:	p [type of continuing resource: periodical]
008/23	:	s [form of item (continuing resources): electronic]
245 00	:	$a MLA international bibliography $h [electronic resource].

  - *Project Muse*, a service providing Internet access to a collection of over 110 journals from numerous scholarly publishers.

Ldr/06	:	a [type of record: language material]
Ldr/07	:	i [bibliographic level: integrating resource]
006/00	:	m [form of material: computer files/electronic resources]
006/09	:	e [type of computer file: bibliographic data]
007	:	cr|||||||||||| [category of material: electronic resource specific material designation: remote access]
008/2	:	d [type of continuing resource: updating database]
008/23	:	s [form of item (continuing resources): electronic]
245 00	:	$a Project Muse $h [electronic resource]: $b scholarly journals online.

Textual Continuing Resource Received via E-mail

The resource is the equivalent of a print item but is received via e-mail from a news wire service. It is coded as language material. The type of computer file is document.

- *Example(s):*
  - *CNS daily brief,* a daily summary of appellate opinions.

Ldr/06	:	a [type of record: language material]
Ldr/07	:	s [bibliographic level: serial]
006/00	:	m [form of material: computer files/electronic resources]
006/09	:	d [type of computer file: document]
007	:	cr|||||||||||| [category of material: electronic resource specific material designation: remote access]
008/23	:	s [form of item (continuing resources): electronic]
245 00	:	$a CNS daily brief $h [electronic resource].

Textual Document

The resource is the equivalent of a print item, but in electronic form. It is coded as language material. If a 006 field for computer files/electronic resources is added, the type of computer file (006/09) depends on the content of the resource.

- *Example(s):*
  - William Blake's *The book of Urizen,* available on CD-ROM.

Ldr/06	:	a [type of record: language material]
Ldr/07	:	m [bibliographic level: monograph/item]
006/00	:	m [form of material: computer files/electronic resources]
006/09	:	d [type of computer file: document]
007	:	co#ug||||||||| [category of material: electronic resource specific material designation: optical disc]
008/23	:	s [form of item (books): electronic]
245 14	:	$a The book of Urizen $h [electronic resouce]: $b London, ca. 1818/ $c William Blake; commentary by Nicolas Barker.

Cartographic Material in Electronic Form

The resource is non-manuscript cartographic material in electronic form. It is coded as cartographic material. The type of computer file is representational.

- *Example(s):*
  - *Vector map level 0 (VMAP0),* vector-based geo-spatial data issued by the National Imagery and Mapping Agency on optical discs.

Ldr/06	:	e [type of record: cartographic material]
Ldr/07	:	m [bibliographic level: monograph/item]
006/00	:	m [form of material: computer files/electronic resources]
006/09	:	[type of computer file: representational]
007	:	co#cg#ǀǀǀǀǀǀǀǀ [category of material: electronic resource specific material designation: optical disc]
008/29	:	s [form of item (maps): electronic]
245 10	:	$a Vector map level 0 (VMAP0) $h
[electronic resource]		$c National Imagery and Mapping Agency.

Still Images

The resource is an electronic collection of graphic materials, such as drawings or photographic prints. Additional items, such as captions and other explanatory text or manuals, may be present, but the primary content is graphic and the resource is coded as graphic material. The type of computer file is representational.

- *Example(s):*
  - *Corel stock photo library,* a collection of photo-graphs on CD-ROM.

Ldr/06	:	k [type of record: two-dimensional non-projectable graphic]
Ldr/07	:	m [bibliographic level: monograph/item]
006/00	:	m [form of material: computer files/electronic resources]
006/09	:	c [type of computer file: representational]
007	:	co#cg#ǀǀǀǀǀǀǀǀ [category of material: electronic resource specific material designation: optical disc]
008/29	:	s [form of item (visual materials): electronic]
245 04	:	$a The Corel stock photo library $h [electronic resource].

ArtServe, a collection of photographs of art and architec-ture available on the Internet.

Ldr/06	:	k [type of record: two-dimensional nonprojectable graphic]
Ldr/07	:	i [bibliographic level: integrating resource]
006/00	:	m [form of material: computer files/electronic resources]
006/09	:	c [type of computer file: representational]
006/00	:	s [form of material: continuing resource]

006/01 : k [frequency: continuously updated]
006/04 : w [type of continuing resource: updating Web site]
006/06 : s [form of item: electronic]
007 : khbo| [category of material: non-projected graphic] specific material designation: photoprint]
007 : cr|||||||||||| [category of material: electronic resource specific material designation: remote resource]
008/29 : s [form of item (visual materials): electronic]
245 00 : $a ArtServe $h [electronic resource].

Notated Music

The resource is an online collection of sheet music in electronic form. It is coded as notated music. The type of computer file is other.

- *Example(s):*
  - *Historic American sheet music,* a collection of sheet music on the Internet.

Ldr/06 : c [type of record: notated music]
Ldr/07 : m [bibliographic level: monograph/item]
006/00 : m [form of material: computer files/electronic resources]
006/09 : z [type of computer file: other]
007 : cr|||||||||||| [category of material: electronic resource specific material designation: remote resource]
008/23 : s [form of item (music): electronic]
245 00 : $a Historic American sheet music, 1850-1920 $h [electronic:$b selected from the collections of Duke resource] University.

Census in Textual Form

The resource consists largely of numeric data, perhaps in tabular form, but is the electronic equivalent of a print item. It is coded as language material. The type of computer file is document.

- Example(s):
  - *County business patterns (CD-ROM),* an annual series from the US Census Bureau that provides subnational economic data by industry.

Ldr/06 : a [type of record: language material]
Ldr/07 : s [bibliographic level: serial]
006/00 : m [form of material: computer files/electronic resources]
006/09 : d [type of computer file: document]
007 : co#ug||||||||| [category of material: electronic resource specific material designation: optical disc]
008/23 : s [form of item (continuing resources): electronic]
245 00 : $a County business patterns $h [electronic resource].

Database Containing Manipulable Numeric Data

The resource consists largely of numeric data that can be manipulated. It is coded as a computer file. The type of computer file is numeric data.

- *Example(s):*
  - *Census 2000 redistricting data.*

<table>
<tr><td>Ldr/06</td><td>:</td><td>m [type of record: computer file]</td></tr>
<tr><td>Ldr/07</td><td>:</td><td>m [bibliographic level: monograph/item]</td></tr>
<tr><td>007</td><td>:</td><td>co#ug||||||||| [category of material: electronic resource
specific material designation: optical disc]</td></tr>
<tr><td>008/26</td><td>:</td><td>a [type of computer file: numeric data]</td></tr>
<tr><td>245 10</td><td>:</td><td>$a Census 2000 redistricting data (PL 94-171).
$p Summary file$h [electronic resource]</td></tr>
<tr><td></td><td>:</td><td>$b 2000 Census of population and housing.</td></tr>
</table>

Computer Operating System

The resource consists of an ordered set of instructions directing a computer to perform certain operations. It is coded as a computer file in Leader/06 and the type of file is computer programme.

- *Example(s):*
  - *SuSE Linux 10.0,* available on optical disc.

<table>
<tr><td>Ldr/06</td><td>:</td><td>m [type of record: computer file]</td></tr>
<tr><td>Ldr/07</td><td>:</td><td>m [bibliographic level: monograph/item]</td></tr>
<tr><td>007</td><td>:</td><td>co#cgu|||||||| [category of material: electronic resource
specific material designation: optical disc]</td></tr>
<tr><td>008/26</td><td>:</td><td>b [type of computer file: computer programme]</td></tr>
<tr><td>245 00</td><td>:</td><td>$a SuSE Linux 10.0 professional $h [electronic resource].</td></tr>
</table>

Computer Software

The resource consists of an ordered set of instructions directing a computer to perform certain operations. It is coded as a computer file in Leader/06 and the type of file is computer programme.

- Example(s):
  - *Foxit,* a PDF document viewer and printer.

<table>
<tr><td>Ldr/06</td><td>:</td><td>m [type of record: computer file]</td></tr>
<tr><td>Ldr/07</td><td>:</td><td>m [bibliographic level: monograph/item]</td></tr>
<tr><td>007</td><td>:</td><td>cz|||||||||||| [category of material: electronic resource
specific material designation: other]</td></tr>
<tr><td>008/26</td><td>:</td><td>b [type of computer file: computerprogramme]</td></tr>
<tr><td>245 00</td><td>:</td><td>$a Foxit $h [electronic resource].</td></tr>
</table>

Universal currency converter, a continuously-updated software programme on the Internet.

Ldr/06	:	m [type of record: computer file]
Ldr/07	:	i [bibliographic level: integrating resource]
006/00	:	s [form of material: continuing resource]
006/01	:	k [frequency: continuously updated]
006/04	:	w [type of continuing resource: updating Web site]
006/06	:	s [form of item: electronic]
007	:	cr#||||||||||| [category of material:electronic resource specific material designation: remote access]
008/26	:	b [computer programme]
245 04	:	$a The universal currency converter $h [electronic resource].

Computer Game

The resource is a game that allows multi-user play online. The type of file is game.

- *Example(s):*
  - *World of warcraft,* a computer game.

Ldr/06	:	m [type of record: computer file]
Ldr/07	:	m [bibliographic level: monograph/item]
007	:	co#cga|||||||| [category of material: electronic resource specific material designation: optical disc]
008/26	:	g [type of computer file: game]
245 00	:	$a World of warcraft $h [electronic resource].

Internet Search Engine

The bibliographic record below describes the system itself, not the system's content. It is coded as a computer file. The type of file is computer programme. 006 fields may be added to bring out the "seriality" or any additional characteristics of the web site.

- *Example(s):*
  - *Google,* a web search engine that allows users to search the Internet for web sites, news, images and postings in Usenet discussion forums.

Ldr/06	:	m [type of record: computer file]
Ldr/07	:	i [bibliographic level: integrating resource]
006/00	:	s [form of material: continuing resource]
006/01	:	k [frequency: continuously updated]
006/04	:	w [type of continuing resource: updating Web site]
006/06	:	s [form of item: electronic]
007	:	cr|||||||||||| [category of material: electronic resource specific material designation: remote access]
008/26	:	b [type of computer file: computer programme]
245 00	:	$a Google $h [electronic resource].

Web Portal

The bibliographic record describes the system and its content. It is coded as a computer file. The type of file is combination. 006 fields may be added to bring out the "seriality" or any additional characteristics.

- *Example(s):*
  - *Yahoo!*, a web portal organized by subject, that also offers a variety of other features, including news, sports and weather updates, an e-mail service, business and shopping services, as well as a streaming audio and and video service.

Ldr/06	:	m [type of record: computer file]
Ldr/07	:	i [bibliographic level: integrating resource]
006/00	:	s [form of material: continuing resource]
006/01	:	k [frequency: continuously updated]
006/04	:	w [type of continuing resource: updating web site]
006/06	:	s [form of item: electronic]
007	:	cr|||||||||||| [category of material: electronic resource specific material designation: remote access]
008/26	:	m [type of computer file: combination]
245 00	:	$a Yahoo $h [electronic resource].

System or Service on the Internet (Includes E-Commerce Sites)

The resource has system-based user interaction that allows users to purchase various types of products or services. The bibliographic record describes the web site. It is coded as a computer file. The type of file is online system or service. 006 fields may be added to bring out the "seriality" or any additional characteristics of the web site.

- *Example(s):*
  - *Travelocity*, an online travel reservation service that also offers various types of travel pack-ages.

Ldr/06	:	m [type of record: computer file]
Ldr/07	:	i [bibliographic level: integrating resource]
006/00	:	s [form of material: continuing resource]
006/01	:	k [frequency: continuously updated]
006/04	:	w [type of continuing resource: updating web site]
006/06	:	s [form of item: electronic]
007	:	cr|||||||||||| [category of material: electronic resource specific material designation: remote access]
008/26	:	j [type of computer file: online system or service]
245 00	:	$a Travelocity.com $h [electronic resource].

  - *Amazon.com,* an online commerce site with browsing and search access to millions of items available for purchase.

Ldr/06 : i [bibliographic level: integrating resource]
006/00 : s [form of material: continuing resource]
006/01 : k [frequency: continuously updated]
006/04 : w [type of continuing resource: updating web site]
006/06 : s [form of item: electronic]
007 : cr|||||||||||| [category of material: electronic resource specific material designation: remote access]
008/26 : j [type of computer file: online system or service]
245 10 : $a Amazon.com $h [electronic resource].

Web Site with Significant Audio and Video Content

The resource consists of several types of materials, including audio and video. Leader/06 is coded as a computer file. The type of file is combination since there is no one significant aspect. 006 fields may be added to bring out the "seriality" or any additional characteristics.

- *Example(s):*
  - *CNN Web site,* a site that covers news, weather, and other subjects such as sports and enter-tainment. Includes text, still images, video and audio.

Ldr/06 : m [type of record: computer file]
Ldr/07 : i [bibliographic level: integrating resource]
006/00 : s [form of material: continuing resource]
006/01 : k [frequency: continuously updated]
006/04 : w [type of continuing resource: updating web site]
006/06 : s [form of item: electronic]
007 : cr|||||||||||| [category of material: electronic resource specific material designation: remote access]
008/26 : m [type of computer file: combination]
245 00 : $a CNN.com $h [electronic resource].

Streaming Video

The resource is an electronic moving image. It is coded as a projected medium in Leader/06. The type of computer file is combination, as there is audio as well as moving images.

- *Example(s):*
  - *Atoms and molecules,* an educational streaming video.

Ldr/06 : g [type of record: projected medium]
Ldr/07 : m [bibliographic level: monograph/item]
006/00 : m [form of material: computer file]
006/09 : m [type of computer file: combination]
007 : vz#czazzu||||| [category of material: video recording specific material designation: other]

007	:	cr| | | | | | | | | | | | [category of material: electronic resource specific material designation: remote access]
008/29	:	s [form of item (visual materials): electronic]
245 00	:	$a Atoms and molecules $h [electronic resource].

Streaming Audio

The resource is a collection of sound recordings in electronic format. It is coded as either a musical or non-musical sound recording, depending on the content. The type of computer file is sound.

- Example(s):
  - *Fogler Library Listening Center Online,* a collection of sound recordings.

Ldr/06	:	j [type of record: musical sound recording]
Ldr/07	:	c [bibliographic level: collection]
006/00	:	m [form of material: computer file]
006/09	:	h [type of computer file: sound]
007	:	sz|uunnnnnznud [category of material: sound recording specific material designation: other]
007	:	cr| | | | | | | | | | | | [category of material: electronic resource specific material designation: remote access]
008/23	:	s [form of item (music): electronic]
245 00	:	$a Fogler Library Listening Center Online $h [electronic resource]/Fogler Digital Library.

GUIDELINES FOR THE USE OF FIELD 856

Field 856 in the MARC 21 bibliographic, holdings, authority, classification, and community information formats is used for electronic location and access information to an electronic resource.The field may be used in a bibliographic or holdings record for a resource when it or a subset of it is available electronically. In addition, it may be used to locate and access an electronic version of a non-electronic resource described in either the bibliographic record, a portion of the resource described, or a related electronic resource.

Field 856 contains the following elements:

FIELD 856-ELECTRONIC LOCATION AND ACCESS (R)

Indicators:

First Indicator	Access method
#	No information provided
0	E-mail
1	FTP
2	Remote login (Telnet)
3	Dial-up
4	HTTP
7	Method specified in subfield $2

Second Indicator	Relationship
#	No information provided
0	Resource
1	Version of resource
2	Related resource
8	No display constant generated

Subfield Codes:

- *$a:* Host name (R)
- *$b:* Access number (R)
- *$c:* Compression information (R)
- *$d:* Path (R)
- *$f:* Electronic name (R)
- *$h:* Processor of request (NR)
- *$i:* Instruction (R)
- *$j:* Bits per second (NR)
- *$k:* Password (NR)
- *$l:* Logon (NR)
- *$m:* Contact for access assistance (R)
- *$n:* Name of location of host (NR)
- *$o:* Operating system (NR)
- *$p:* Port (NR)
- *$q:* Electronic format type (NR)
- *$r:* Settings (NR)
- *$s:* File size (R)
- *$t:* Terminal emulation (R)
- *$u:* Uniform Resource Identifier (R)
- *$v:* Hours access method available (R)
- *$w:* Record control number (R)
- *$x:* Nonpublic note (R)
- *$y:* Link text (R)
- *$z:* Public note (R)
- *$2:* Access method (NR)
- *$3:* Materials specified (NR)
- *$6:* Linkage (NR)
- *$8:* Field link and sequence number (R)

GENERAL INFORMATION

The data in field 856 may be a Uniform Resource Identifier (URI), which is recorded in subfield $u. The necessary locator information may also be parsed into separate defined subfields. Note that separate subfields for locator data was provided when this field was first established in 1993, but generally, these are seldom used. An access method, or protocol used, is given as a value in the first indicator position (if the access method is e-mail, FTP, remote login (telnet), dial-up, or HTTP) or in subfield $2 (if the access method is anything else). The access method is the first element of a URL. The field may also include a Uniform Resource Name or URN [(*e.g.*, a DOI (Digital Object Identifier) or handle)].

Uniform Resource Identifier

For any access method, a Uniform Resource Identifier (URI) is generally recorded in subfield $u. Separate subfields may be used if it is desirable to display data in a particular way.

The most commonly used data elements in field 856 are as follows:

- 1st indicator = 4 for HTTP (earlier records may use blank)
- Subfield $u = [HTTP URL]
- Subfield $3: data specifying to what the URI refers, if applicable
- Subfield $z (Public note): data relating to the electronic location of the source that is adequate for public display

Required Subfields

A URI in subfield $u is required unless electronic location and access information is parsed into separate subfields, in which case no single subfield is required. When using this technique, the subfields used largely depends on the access method indicated in the first indicator or in subfield $2 (if first indicator = 7).

Encoding Non-MARC Characters

In February 1994, Proposal 93-10 defined additional characters in the MARC character set to both accommodate existing bibliographic needs and to align it with the ASCII and ANSEL character sets. Both the spacing underscore and the spacing tilde were added at the time because of the need in directory and file names for electronic resources. Many systems have implemented these characters.

For systems that have not implemented the spacing underscore and tilde, the following alternative characters may be used:

- Spacing underscore per cent5F
- Spacing tilde per cent7E

Since these characters are valid ASCII strings, the method allows for the functionality supported by Z39.50 clients and Web browsers which permit users to click on links to access resources represented by URLs. When the additions to the MARC 21 character set are implemented to support the encoding of the spacing characters, it will be possible to replace all instances of the per cent xx strings.

Multiple 856 Fields

There are many reasons to include multiple 856 fields in records.

The following are the most common:

- Location data elements vary (the URI in subfield $u or subfields $a, $b, $d, when used)
- Different access methods (*e.g.*, a document available through HTTP and from an FTP server)
- Different parts of the item are electronic, using subfield $3 to indicate the part (*e.g.*, table of contents accessible in one file and an abstract in another)
- Mirror sites (the same resource is made available at two different locations, often to facilitate access, perhaps internationally)
- Different formats/resolutions (*e.g.*, the ASCII version of an electronic journal vs. the Web home page for that journal; a thumbnail vs. archival copy of a digitized photograph)
- Related items, using subfield $3 and second indicator value to specify

Field 856 in Bibliographic or Holdings Records

Since field 856 is valid in both bibliographic and holdings records, institutions may favour recording it in the holdings record. It is intended to be an electronic equivalent to field 852 (Location), which contains information used to identify the holding organization and other detailed information required to locate a physical item in a collection. In early 1999, the Network Development and MARC Standards Office elicited opinions on whether it is desirable to use the field in bibliographic or holdings records. Responses received generally favoured recording the field in the holdings record where practical. However, for a variety of reasons, such as the wider exchange of bibliographic records, many institutions use the bibliographic record despite the benefits of using holdings records.

The following advantages of using holdings records have been expressed:

- Ownership to an electronic resource may vary by institution. Such access information belongs in local holdings.
- The holdings record is a means to bring together various versions.
- Use of a single record approach for the bibliographic item has been implemented widely. This practice makes it clearer to use holdings for the specific versions.
- Having a hot-linked 856 field in holdings forces users to think of it as holdings information, and to separate information about the universal bibliographic item.
- The "universal URL" that is for general access and any general information on access in note fields should be in the bibliographic record. Specific local access URLs should be in holdings (although this may result in unpredictability).
- Bibliographic field 856 might usefully be limited to links that do not apply to the entire bibliographic item (*e.g.*, finding aid, table of content, abstract).

In order to move towards this approach in the future, it will be necessary to persuade vendors to make the following changes to their ILS systems:

- Allow for hot links from holdings records
- Allow for the ability to do link checking from holdings records
- Provide indexing of holdings records
- Allow for the ability to export the fields from holdings, to be exchanged either as separate holdings records or embedded in an exported bibliographic record
- Provide for more logical displays of bibliographic/holdings information where necessary
- Allow for sequencing multiple holdings records

At this point, it is a local decision whether to use the field in bibliographic or holdings records.

SPECIFIC DATA ELEMENTS

First Indicator (Access Method)

The first indicator contains information about the access method to the resource and has values defined for E-mail, FTP, Remote login (Telnet), Dial-up, and HTTP. Access methods without defined values may contain a first indicator value 7 with the method indicated in subfield $2. Older records may contain value 7 and subfield $2 (with content http) if created before value 4 (HTTP) was defined.

The list of indicator values and the values used in subfield $2 is specified in the URL standard (RFC1738) and maintained by the Internet Assigned Numbers Authority (IANA). For those access methods that have an indicator value defined (ftp, telnet, electronic mail), the URI is included in subfield $u with the appropriate indicator value recorded, even though it is redundant with the first element of the URI.

Value # (blank) (No information provided) may be used if only a URN is recorded in subfield $u. If using a URI in subfield $u with one of the access methods that has a value defined in the first indicator, the access method may be repeated in subfield $2. Value 7 and subfield $2 is used for electronic access to host-specific file names (*i.e.*, files stored locally) with the access method, "file." This designation is also a defined URL scheme.

Second Indicator (Relationship)

A second indicator is provided to show the relationship between the information in field 856 and the resource described in the record. This may be used for the generation of a display constant or for ordering multiple 856 fields.

Suggested display constants for the indicator values are:

- # (blank): Electronic resource:
- *0:* Electronic resource:

- *1:* Electronic version:
- *2:* Related electronic resource:
- *8:* [no display constant generated]

Subfield $3 (Materials Specified)

Subfield $3 is used to specify to what portion or aspect of the resource the electronic location and access information applies.

Specific situations may be:

- A portion or subset of the item is electronic
  - *Example:* $3table of contents; $3v. 2-5; $3abstract; $3b&w copy negative
- A related electronic resource is being linked to the record
  - *Example:* $3author's self-portrait

Subfield $q (Electronic Format Type)

Subfield $q was originally defined as File transfer mode to include "binary" or "ascii". It was redefined in June 1997 as Electronic format type to accommodate an Internet Media Type (MIME type), such as text/html. Alternatively, textual information about the electronic format type may also be recorded.

Subfield $u (URI) Repeatability

Subfield $u may be repeated only if both a URN and a URL or more than one URN are recorded. Field 856 is repeated if more than one URL needs to be recorded. Some institutions may wish to record a persistent name (URN) as well as a resolvable HTTP URL in field 856.

Persistent Uniform Resource Locators (PURLs) at OCLC are intended to deal with the problem of changeable URLs. Functionally, a PURL is a URL, but it is intended to point to an intermediate resolution service. Its persistence depends upon the updating of a PURL database when the location of the resource changes. When recorded in field 856, it is intended to allow for persistence so that each record containing the URL need not be updated when the location changes. Since the PURL is supposed to provide persistent access to the resource, it can be argued that there is no reason to retain a URL that might become invalid. However, this is an internal decision, and institutions that use PURLs should use subfield $x (Nonpublic note) for the original URL if they wish to retain it. This is an appropriate subfield, since it may not be desirable to display the URL to the public because it could cause confusion. The CONSER programme has, however, repeated subfield $u to include both the PURL and cooresponding URL in the past.

Subfield $y (Link Text)

Subfield $y contains link text which is used for display in place of the URL in subfield $u. Often URLs are difficult to read and most systems do not display them to the user. Since subfield $y was not approved until June 2000, there have been various practices in terms of systems using data in the field as link text. Some systems have used subfields $3 or $z in the past for this purpose. It is not clear how widespread the use of subfield $y is since its approval.

Subfield $z (Public Note)

Subfield $z may be used for any additional notes about the electronic resource at the specified location. Examples include subscription information or access restrictions. Institutions have used subfield $z in various ways. Some have created a note for display repeating the URL in subfield $u. It would be preferable for systems to display subfield $u rather than have those preparing records to include information redundantly.

URIS IN OTHER FIELDS AND FORMATS

URLs in Fields other than Field 856

Several proposals resulted in the definition of a subfield $u (URI) in other fields.

These fields include:

- 505 (Formatted Contents Note)
- 508 (Creation/Production Credits Note)
- 511 (Participant or Performer Note)
- 514 (Data Quality Note)
- 520 (Summary, Etc.)
- 530 (Additional Physical Form Available Note)
- 538 (System Details Note)
- 555 (Cumulative Index/Finding Aids Note)
- 583 (Action Note)
- 670 (Source Data Found) *in the MARC 21 Format for Authority Data*
- 678 (Biographical or historical data) *in the MARC 21 Format for Authority Data*

As with field 856, subfield $u should be repeated only when both a URL and URN is recorded.

Field 856 in Other Formats

Field 856 is also defined in the authority, classification, and community information formats.

It may be used as follows:

- *Authority Format:* Field 856 was defined in June 1998. Guidelines will be needed from policy making bodies to further describe its use, especially in cooperative projects. The intent of Proposal No. 98-13 (Define Field 856 in the MARC 21 Authorities Format) was to provide electronic access to Web sites for organizations and other supplementary information within an authority record.

- *Classification Format:* Field 856 provides a link from a MARC classification record to a related electro-nic resource. This allows for accessing visual aids from an online database of MARC classification records.
- *Community Information Format:* Field 856 provides a link from a MARC community information record to community information available on the Web, *e.g.,* Web pages for organizations, events, services, etc.

LC USAGE

Field 856 has been used at the Library of Congress as follows. Records for resources that have been digitized (or otherwise made available electronically) as part of the National Digital Library Programme (American Memory) may contain field 856. Generally, the field is added to the record for the original item, rather than a new record created (unless it consists of components that have been gathered together and only exist as an entity in electronic form). In some cases, LC has also recorded a handle, which is a URN. Older records may contain a URN in subfield $g (which is now obsolete).

LC uses local codes in subfield $q to indicate the different categories of a complex object. This is because digital reproductions created by the Library of Congress are not single files and thus, Internet media types recorded in subfield $q are not applicable. For example, the reproduction of a book usually combines page images and text marked up in SGML.

MAJOR CHANGES INCLUDED

The following are major changes made to the August 1999 revision to create these (March 2003 revision) guidelines:

- Added a table of contents, along with making other struc-tural changes to enhance the document's readability.
- Updated the element list to include the changes made to the repeatability of subfield $u. Subfield $g was also deleted because it was made obsolete in 2000.
- Added and revised the repeatability guidelines for field 856 and subfield $u.
- Updated the "Encoding non-MARC characters" section to include implementation information for the spacing underscore and the spacing tilde.
- Added descriptions of subfields $q and $y to the "Specific Data Elements" section.
- Expanded the "URLs in fields other than field 856" section to include

a complete list of bibliographic and authority fields that include subfield $u.

- Expanded and added examples to the "Field 856 in other formats" section.
- Expanded the "LC Usage" section to include updated information about how the Library of Congress uses field 856 in various projects.
- Deleted the "Attachment B: Subfield Use When Not Using $u (URL)" section.
- Updated the examples in the "Examples" section to match current usage of field 856.

13

Cataloguing Electronic Resources: OCLC-MARC Coding Guidelines

This document originally combined and superseded two older sets of OCLC guidelines for dealing with electronic resources: "Cataloguing Electronic Resources: OCLC-MARC Coding Guidelines," by Rich Greene, first published in February 1998; and "OCLC Guidelines on the Choice of Type and BLvl for Electronic Resources," by Jay Weitz, first published in March 1998. This consolidated document was originally prompted by the issuance in June 1999 of "Guidelines for Coding Electronic Resources in Leader/06" by the Library of Congress Network Development and MARC Standards Office.

Like the two superseded OCLC documents, this revised set of guidelines is intended to assist catalogers in creating records for electronic resources in WorldCat, the OCLC Online Union Catalogue. These guidelines pertain to OCLC-MARC tagging (that is, content designation). Cataloguing rules and manuals (such as AACR2) govern the content of records. You should implement these guidelines immediately.

In addition to LC's valuable June 1999 "Guidelines for Coding Electronic Resources in Leader/06", which should be consulted for helpful details, sources for further information include the following documents:

- *CONSER Cataloguing Manual*: Module 31—Remote ccess Electronic Serials (Online Serials)/CONSER.
- *Integrating Resources:* A Cataloguing Manual/Programme for Cooperative Cataloguing.
- Draft Interim Guidelines for Cataloguing Electronic Resources/ Library of Congress.
- Guidelines for Distinguishing Cartographic Materials on Computer File Carriers from Other Materials on Computer File Carriers/Library of Congress.
- Guidelines for the Use of Field 856/Prepared by the Library of Congress, Network Development and MARC Standards Office.

- *ISBD(ER):* International Standard Bibliographic Description for Electronic Resources/recommended by the ISBD(CF) Review Group. (Munchen: K.G. Saur, 1997).
- Use of fixed fields 006/007/008 and Leader codes in CONSER records/ Library of Congress.

All of these documents remain primary sources for guidance in the cataloguing of electronic resources. The recommendations made here are meant to be extensions of these documents, not replacements for them. Note that Nancy Olson's "Cataloguing Internet Resources: A Manual and Practical Guide, 2nd edition," formerly listed here, has been withdrawn because it is out of date.

Remember that these guidelines affect mainly (although not exclusively) the choice of certain fixed field elements, particularly the Type of Record, Bibliographic Level, and Type of File codes. The descriptive rules in AACR2 for cataloguing electronic resources continue to apply, as do most other MARC coding decisions.

DEFINITION OF ELECTRONIC RESOURCE

According to AACR2, 2005 Update, an electronic resource is: "Material (data and/or programme(s)) encoded for manipulation by a computerized device. This material may require the use of a peripheral directly connected to a computerized device (*e.g.*, CD-ROM drive) or a connection to a computer network (*e.g.*, the Internet)." This definition does not include electronic resources that do not require the use of a computer, for example, music compact discs and videodiscs.

"TYPE OF RECORD" CODING (FIXED FIELD "TYPE")

The definition of Leader/06 ("Type of Record") code "m" (Computer file) was revised and greatly narrowed in June 1997 (LC Update No. 3 to *USMARC Format for Bibliographic Data*) to allow for the coding of electronic resources for the significant aspect of the content, rather than their physical form.

Code "m" is now used only for the following general classes of electronic resources:

- Computer software (including programmes, games, fonts)
- Numeric data
- Computer-oriented multimedia
- Online systems or services

For these classes of materials, if there is a significant aspect that causes it to fall into another Leader/06 ("Type of Record") category, code for that significant aspect (for instance, vector data that is cartographic is not coded as numeric but as cartographic). Other classes of electronic resources are coded for their most significant aspect (for instance, language material, graphic, cartographic material, sound, music, moving image). In case of doubt or if the most significant aspect cannot be determined, consider the item a computer file. If the resource is essentially the equivalent of a print item but in electronic form, use the same Type code you would use for the print version.

FIELD 006

In records for electronic resources where the Type Code is not "m," OCLC mandates including the field 006 for the electronic aspects so that the "COM" search qualifier will continue to retrieve these materials. Remember to code the "File" value correctly, usually "d" for textual materials.

"TYPE" AND "FILE" CODING

In keeping with the current definition of Type code "m," OCLC is recommending the following choices of "Type" code and CF 006/09 and CF 008/26 "File" ("Type of Computer File") values for the following categories of electronic resources. Included below are resources accessible directly, such as on CD-ROMs or computer disks, and remotely, such as from Web sites and online files.

In its definitions of certain values for the Computer File 008/26 ("File"), *MARC 21 Format for Bibliographic Data* clarifies coding for electronic resources that include search software. The presence of search software does not alter the basic intent of the resource and does not mean that the resource should be coded as software. If its primary purpose is, for instance, textual or bibliographic, it remains textual or bibliographic and is coded as such.

In the area of online systems and services, consider whether the system itself (for example, a library system providing an interface to several databases), or the content of the several constituent databases, is being cataloged. When cataloguing the system itself, use "Type" code "m" and "File" code "j".

"FORM OF ITEM" CODING

As part of the MARC 21 format changes implemented by OCLC in April 2000, a new code "s" was validated for the "Form of Item" fixed field, 008/23 and 006/06 in the Books, Serials, Mixed Materials, and Scores formats, and 008/29 and 006/12 in the Maps and Visual Materials formats. On 2002 December 1, the code "s" was also implemented in the "Form of Item" fixed field, 008/23 and 006/06 for the Sound Recordings format. When cataloguing an electronic resource that includes a significant aspect in any of these bibliographic formats according to current definitions, use "Form of Item" code "s" in the fixed field "Form" and/or in the "Form element of any 006 fields for that aspect, as appropriate.

FIELD 007

According to LC's Draft Interim Guidelines for Cataloguing Electronic Resources, the computer file 007 is mandatory in any record representing an item whose carrier is a computer file. OCLC endorses this recommendation.

FIELD 856

Please be careful about the correct coding of the field 856 second indicator:

- "Blank" is used when no information is provided about the relationship of the electronic resource to the bibliographic item described in the record (for instance, use "blank" when the subfield $u contains a URI that is no longer accessible but there is another 856 with a currently accessible URI). Display constant: None.
- "0" is used when the electronic location in the field is for the same electronic resource described by the record as a whole. Display constant "Electronic resource:" may be generated.
- "1" is used when the electronic location in the field is for an electronic version of the resource described by the record (for instance, an electronic version when the record is for a nonelectronic version). Note that the Library of Congress uses code "1" in conjunction with subfield $3 to indicate the electronic location of tables of contents. Display constant "Electronic version:" may be generated.
- "2" is used when the electronic location in the field is for an electronic resource that is related to the bibliographic item described by the record. In this case, the item represented by the bibliographic record is not the electronic resource itself. Use subfield $3 to further characterize the relationship between the electronic item identified in field 856 and the item represented by the bibliographic record as a whole. The display constant *Related electronic resource*: may be provided. Limit this use to electronic resources that have a specific bibliographic relationship to the resource described in the body of the record. This would include links to such resources as a finding aid for an archival collection or the Web site of a musical group on a bibliographic record for a sound recording. This would not, however, include Web sites that have merely a general subject relationship to the resource.

LCRI 9.7B, marked "LC Practice," deals with "Remote access electronic resources that are no longer available."

Because of OCLC's indexing needs and its electronic address checking software, however, we suggest leaving URIs in field 856 subfield $u and adding an appropriate subfield $z note under the following circumstances:

- URI no longer works at all, does not redirect to a more current URI.
- 856 4 $u [Dead URI] $z This electronic address not available when searched on [Date].
- URI redirects (either automatically or with a forwar-ding link) to a new URI.
- 856 4 $u [Redirected URI] $z This former electronic address redirects to current address when searched on [Date].

In both of these cases, change the 856 Second Indicator to blank.

Character	Hex Value	Note	
	Spacing Underscore	%5F	Because the spacing underscore may cause problems with MARC output users may prefer to continue entering it with the hex value %5F.
	Spacing tilde	%7E	
	Spacing grave	%60	
	Spacing circumflex	%5E	
	Vertical bar or pipe	%7C	Continue to use the hex value for this character.

In cases where multiple URIs may be appropriate, record them as follows:

- Record a PURL and its corresponding original URL (both of which resolve to the same resource) in separate subfields $u in the same 856 field.
- For most other instances of multiple URIs, record them in separate 856 fields.

When the following characters appear in URIs, you may now use the proper character or substitute the appropriate hex value.

GENERAL MATERIAL DESIGNATION

The General Material Designation (GMD) "[electronic resource]" will now be used for items that are coded as Type "m." Also use the GMD "[electronic resource]" for all records that would include the computer file 006 according to the OCLC guidelines, regardless of the Type Code.

INTEGRATING RESOURCES

According to AACR2, 2005 Update, an integrating resource is: "A bibliographic resource that is added to or changed by means of updates that do not remain discrete and are integrated into the whole. Integrating resources can be finite or continuing. Examples of integrating resources include updating loose-leafs and updating Web sites."

Beginning immediately, follow these guidelines for integrating resources:

- Use the Continuing Resources (formerly Serials) workform when creating records for textual integra-ting resources. Continue to use the 006 field for Continuing Resources (formerly Serials) to create 006 fields for non-textual integrating resources.
- Use Bibliographic Level code "i" (Integrating Resource) when coding a record for an integrating resource. DO NOT use Bibliographic Level code "s" (Serial) or "m" (Monograph) for an integrating resource.
- For an electronic textual integrating resource, the typical Continuing Resource fixed field will be coded as follows:

Type: a	ELvl: ǀ	Srce: d	GPub: _	Ctrl: _	Lang: ǀǀǀ
BLvl: i	Form: s[1]	Conf: 0	Freq: _[2]	MRec: _	Ctry: ǀǀǀ
S/L: 2[3]	Orig: s	EntW: _	Regl: _[2]	Alph: a	
Desc: ǀ	SrTp: _[4]	Cont: ____	DtSt: c[5]	Dates: ǀǀǀǀ,9999	

- [1] *Form:* For electronic integrating resources, continue to use code "s" in Form.
- [2] *Freq and Regl:* If the integrating resource is truly "continuously updated" (for instance, a constantly updating database, a newspaper's Web site that gets updated as news occurs, etc.), use the Frequency Code "k," which means "the item is updated more frequently than daily;" in that case, the correct Regularity code is likely to be "r" for Regular. More commonly, when the resource is updated less frequently than daily and none of the other Frequency codes apply, use "blank" for Frequency and "x" for Regularity.
- [3] *S/L:* In the continuing resources fixed field, use code "2" in Entry Convention (S/L, formerly Successive/Latest Entry) to indicate that the record was formulated using the revised rules for integrated entry.
- [4] *SrTp:* In the element SrTp (Type of Continuing Resource, formerly Type of Serial), use code "d" for updating databases, code "l" for updating loose-leafs, or code "w" for updating Web sites, as appropriate.
- [5] *DtSt:* For integrating resources that are currently published, use code "c" (rather than the former practice of code "m"). For integrating resources that have ceased publication, use code "d" (rather than the former practice of code "m").

• Continue to include a computer file 006 and a computer file 007 field in records for electronic integrating resources. For a textual electronic integrating resource, the typical computer file 006 and 007 fields will be coded as follows:

COM 006:	Type: m	Audn:	File: d	GPub:
COM 007:	c $b r $d c $e n			

URIs and LCRIs 9.7B and 21.3B for Remote Access Electronic Resources

Two Library of Congress Rule Interpretations, 9.7B and 21.3B, offer some guidance about how to deal with remote access electronic integrating resources and the disposition of the resource's Uniform Resource Identifier (URI). When the original URI is no longer accessible, but the resource (or a new iteration thereof) is now accessible at another URI, you may edit the existing record to reflect this. When the original URI is still active but now represents an entirely different resource, rather than a new iteration of the original resource, you may create a new record for the new electronic resource. In cases where you are unable to edit, or prefer not to edit the existing record, you are encouraged to report the necessary changes to OCLC.

SEPARATE RECORDS VERSUS SINGLE RECORD

Creating separate records for an item is preferable when both remote access electronic versions and tangible or direct access (including, but not limited to, print and other nonelectronic) versions exist. You may, however, find a single record approach is better for your local environment. OCLC recommends that you verify the impact of these options with your local system vendor and other partners prior to implementation.

Use of the term "nonelectronic" in the options that follow is meant as shorthand for any tangible resource (including print, videocassette, videodisc, CD-ROM, etc.) and is not meant to exclude, for instance, tangible resources that may have electronic aspects. In that light, elements of the recommendations may need to be adjusted to accommodate such aspects (for example, inclusion of fields 006 and/or 007).

Option 1: Separate Records

Nonelectronic item:

- Select the workform based on the current definition of "Type" and the primary aspect of the item.
- Do not input fields 006 and 007 and do not code "Form of Item" (008/23, 008/29, 006/06, or 006/12, depending on bibliographic format) for the electronic versio
- Note the availability of the electronic version in field 530.
- *Example:* Available also on the Internet.
- Add a 700-730 added entry field for the electronic version when the main entry differs.
- Optionally, link to the electronic record with field 776.
- Optionally, provide the location of any remotely accessible version(s) in field(s) 856. Use second indicator "1" when the address is for a version of the resource other than the one described in the body of the entry, or "2" when the address is for an otherwise related resource.

Electronic Item:

- Select the workform based on the current definition of "Type" and the primary aspect of the item.
- Include field 006 for computer file, if Type is not "m."

- Include field 007 for computer file.
- Code "Form of Item" (008/23, 008/29, 006/06, or 006/12, as appropriate, depending on bibliographic format) for "electronic" (code "s").
- Note the availability of the nonelectronic version in field 530.
- *Example:* Also available in printed form.
- Add a 700-730 added entry field when main entry for the nonelectronic version differs.
- Optionally, link to the nonelectronic version using field 776.
- Provide the location of any remotely accessible version(s) in field(s) 856. Use second indicator "0" when the address is for the resource itself, "1" when the address is for a version of the resource other than the one described in the body of the entry, or "2" when the address is for an otherwise related resource.

Option 2: Single Record with a Reference to the Electronic Item

You may create a record for the nonelectronic version and add an annotation about the existence of and access to the electronic version.

The nonelectronic version is the primary version and the electronic copy is secondary:

- Select the workform based on the current definition of "Type" and the primary aspect of the item.
- Do not input field 006 for the electronic version.
- Do not code "Form of Item"(008/23, 008/29, 006/06, or 006/12, depending on bibliographic format) for the electronic version.
- Optionally, include field 007.
- Note the availability of the electronic version in field 530.
- Add a 740 added entry when the title for the electronic version differs.
- Provide the location of any remotely accessible version in field 856. Use second indicator "1" when the address is for a version of the resource other than the one described in the body of the entry or "2" when the address is for an otherwise related resource.

Additional Separate Versus Single Record Considerations

If you are cataloguing an electronic item, you need not verify the physical existence of the nonelectronic version or whether it has been cataloged. Similarly, when you catalogue a nonelectronic item, you need not verify whether an electronic version exists. In both cases, you need not apply these guidelines, and you may catalogue the item as if no other version exists. Apply the input convention in this document if you have verification that electronic and nonelectronic versions exist, and you want to record the existence of both.

In all cases, you may add references to electronic resources that are related to the item described in the body of the record when those references are thought to add value. The CONSER Cataloguing Manual: Module 31—Remote Access Electronic Serials (Online Serials) permits a single record for a nonelectronic item to include information for the electronic version. OCLC's guidelines are currently compatible with CONSER's.

INTEGRATING RESOURCE OR MONOGRAPH VERSUS SERIAL

The decision to code an electronic resource as a monograph or as a serial is a decision made separately from the Type Code decision. Note that for electronic serials where Type is not "a" or "m", two 006 fields will be necessary, one for the electronic aspects and one for the serial aspects.

Apply the current AACR2 definitions of monograph and serial to electronic resources. Treat as serials (Bibliographic Level: s (or b)) only those continuing resources issued in a succession of discrete parts with no predetermined conclusion. The parts may constitute an issue, or in some cases, an individual article.

Applying the current AACR2R definitions may result in different manifestations receiving different cataloguing treatment. For example, a manifestation in print form, such as an annual directory, is cataloged as a serial whereas it is cataloged as an integrating resource when the directory takes on the form of an electronic file that is continuously updated. LC and CONSER adhere to current definitions, and OCLC recommends its users do the same.

Remotely accessed electronic resources of a dynamic nature that are currently excluded from serial treatment are:

- Databases (including directories, A&I services, etc.)
- Electronic discussion groups (*e.g.*, SERIALST)
- Electronic discussion group digests (*e.g.*, AUTOCAT digest)
- Gopher servers (*e.g.*, LC-MARVEL)
- Online public access catalogues (*e.g.*, OCLC, RLIN)
- Online services (*e.g.*, America Online)
- Web sites (*e.g.*, the CONSER home page)

These electronic resources should be cataloged as integrating resources or monographs, as appropriate.

Electronic Reproductions of Items Previously Published in Print Form

In May 2000, the Library of Congress issued a revised version of LC Rule Interpretation 1.11A. The revision expands LC's "microform exception" to AACR2 to include remotely accessed electronic reproductions of works previously published in printed form (including electronic books). This practice applies only when the reproduction manifestation is represented by its own bibliographic record, separate from any record for the original.

In essence, LCRI 1.11A calls for users to:

- Transcribe the bibliographic data appropriate to the *original* work being reproduced in the following areas: title and statement of responsibility; edition; material (or type of publication) specific details; publication, distribution, etc.; physical description; series.

- If appropriate, give in the title and statement of responsibility area the General Material Designation that is applicable to the format of the reproduction (in the case of electronic reproductions, the GMD "[electronic resource]").
- Give in a single note (533 field) all other details relating to the reproduction and its publication/availability, including format of the reproduction, dates of publication and/or sequential designation of issues reproduced (for serials), place and name of the agency responsible for the reproduction, date of the reproduction, physical description of the reproduction if different from the original, series statement of the reproduction (if applicable), notes relating to the reproduction (if applicable).
- Use a physical description fixed field (007) applicable to the reproduction, and for electronic reproductions, also supply information about the electronic location and access (856 field).

In addition, OCLC users should include the appropriate field 006 and code "Form of Item" for "electronic" (code "s") as outlined earlier in these guidelines.

Optionally, OCLC users may also include a field 539, following field 533, containing data about the reproduction in coded form.

DEALING WITH EXISTING RECORDS

These guidelines, of course, do not resolve all problems. OCLC's Duplicate Detection and Resolution software, for example, cannot always distinguish one version from another. Indexing and identifying a record as a computer file may not be possible if the local system does not index field 006 or field 007. The cataloguing of these electronic resources remains very much in flux, as do the resources themselves. The rules for dealing with them remain a work in progress.

OCLC users are encouraged to submit to the Library of Congress Network Development and MARC Standards Office (ndmso@loc.gov) examples of any electronic resources about which there is ambiguity concerning the coding of Leader/06, CF 008/26, and/or CF 006/09, and any instances not covered by LC's "Guidelines."

OCLC any needed Type and/or BLvl code changes, as well as any other changes to existing WorldCat records, either by phone, paper, or electronically, as appropriate. OCLC would prefer that you not add duplicate records in these instances.

Minimal-Level Upgrade continues to allow changes of BLvl only within the same bibliographic format, except:

- In records with Type Codes "a" or "t," BLvl "a," "c," "d," or "m" can be changed to BLvl "i"

- In records with Type Code "a" and BLvl "b" or "s," the BLvl can be changed to BLvl "i"

WorldCat Database Enrichment currently allows Full Mode users and above to add field 006 and/or 007 to most records through lock and replace. OCLC recognizes that the conversion of existing records for electronic resources is a significant issue for many groups within the OCLC membership. Through Minimal Level Upgrade, Database Enrichment, CONSER, and Enhance, many OCLC members have the ability to fix many of the records in question. OCLC encourages users to report other records that need to be converted, via any of the usual means.

14

Draft Interim Guidelines for Cataloguing Electronic Resources

BACKGROUND

The Library of Congress has become increasingly engaged in the world of those electronic resources requiring the use of a computer. In the early 1980s it began to assign International Standard Serial Numbers (ISSN) to directly accessed serial electronic resources and in 1988 to those that are online. In the early 1990's the Library, through the Cooperative Online Serials (CONSER) Programme, began to address the cataloguing of online serial resources, with an emphasis on those available on the Internet. It began to catalogue monographic computer files in the late 1980's.

In the early 1990's, the Library began the digitization of original materials from its special collections under the aegis of the American Memory programme. In 1996 an informal group of staff members with interests in issues relating to digitization, not only of original materials in special collections, but also including some book materials, met on an irregular basis to begin exploring issues of common interest.

While the group's initial concern was the cataloguing treatment of materials that LC was digitizing from its own collections, it also encountered issues that relate to the bibliographic control of material in special collections, particu-larly "special format" material whose mode of expression is other than that of language material (non-manuscript language material) or whose modes of expression are mixed (*i.e.*, collections of mixed material).

Even so, the issues are not solely the domain of these materials, as the group discovered with some of the collections of language materials (*e.g.*, various pamphlet collections; broadside collections). Cataloguing electronic reproductions of material held by the Library as well as cataloguing other electronic resources, whether electronic manifestations of new or already existing material, raises several issues. One of the most important is the use of one record or two to describe closely related content. Thus a medium that spans both general and special cataloguing requires Library-wide application of a standard set of guidelines to ensure clarity in bibliographic records both for public catalogue users and for effective biblio-graphic control.

It has been the intent of the Cataloguing Policy and Support Office (CPSO) to develop conceptual guidelines for the cataloguing of electronic resources. That effort has been delayed for various reasons, and towards the end of 1996, stimulated by increased activities in the area of digitization, CPSO invited a small group of staff members to develop interim guidelines for cataloguing electronic resources. These guidelines are the result; they have been reviewed within LC by representatives of the units most directly concerned with cataloguing electronic manifestations, particularly by the staff members. Additional consultations were held with Copyright Office staff, and some changes were made to some of the terminology that had originally been proposed to accommodate the copyright perspective.

PURPOSE AND CHARACTER

The purpose is to establish an interim set of guidelines to be used for cataloguing electronic resources in the Library of Congress based on a common conceptual context and a common terminology. The intent of the guidelines is to apply to resources of divergent character produced under varying circumstances and managed by different entities, a set of conventions for bibliographic control that will enable genera-lized, standard practice to the extent judged practicable in a diverse, dynamic environment.

It also endeavours to engage the electronic world on a broader scale by providing a conceptual framework for treating electronic resources. This framework is followed by the establishment and definition of concepts and terms appropriate to electronic resources in an attempt to ensure clear communication based on a common understanding.

The guidelines then include:

- Policies on when to use multiple records and when to use a single record;
- Conventions developed especially for the single-record technique;
- Directions for indicating the existence of other physical formats (530 field);
- Directions related to electronic location (856 field);
- Directions relating to collocating records (710 field) and linking them (76X-78X fields);
- Directions relating to identifying in MUMS those records related to a specific project (985 field; mandatory for American Memory projects).

The overall guidelines try to show how the cataloguing of all electronic resources fits together, but they do not cover the specifics of all resources. This table shows that the specific guidelines are more nearly oriented to electronic reproductions of materials held by the Library, for example, using a single-record approach for delineating these electronic manifestations. This emphasis is driven by the fact that the digitizing efforts of the Library of Congress and the need for their public representation as viable resources compel immediate attention.

In meeting the needs of the Library of Congress in this regard, it remains to be seen whether the guidelines developed for these LC materials will necessarily be applicable elsewhere. The one obvious lacuna in the current document is the absence of guidelines relating to the treatment of Internet resources—particularly with respect to which ones should be represented in the catalogue, under what circumstances, and in what detail. This is because the collection development guidelines for electronic resources are only now beginning to be formulated. Thus the issues related to cataloguing these materials have not been fully confronted.

One question of concern is the impact the nature of the medium itself will have. For tangible non-electronic materials, their very tangibility fixes the intellectual content. This tangibility is common across all items in a particular manifestation, thus allowing the description of one item to apply to all the others in the manifestation. Changes in physical characteristics are used to surmise that there are changes in content, which is the basis of creating a new bibliographic record.

With respect to cataloguing remotely accessed electronic resources, it will be interesting to see what the impact of the accessing mode will be, particularly, with regard to:

- The basis for determining that the content is "fixed," absent tangibility as a basis for doing this;
- The basis for determining that the content has changed, again, absent tangible characteristics for doing this.

On a more mundane level there are issues relating to:

- The disposition of information that is universal and that which is local;
- Determining who we are providing the information for (again universal/local);
- "Custody" (is it relevant?);
- Classification (should we attempt to classify?).

REASONS WHY THE GUIDELINES ARE INTERIM

The Guidelines are interim for the following reasons:

- Some of the copyright and collection development guidelines with respect to remotely accessed electronic resources are only now beginning to be formulated; the universe of material for which bibliographic control is to be applied will have a substantial impact on the resources available for this purpose and will in turn influence the nature of the conventions themselves (the larger the number of materials to be controlled the less labour intensive the conventions to control them can be);

- The dynamic nature of the environment of electronic resources is profoundly affecting the standards upon which current conventions of bibliographic control rest; it is necessary to monitor the changes that are developing in AACR2, in USMARC, and in such international activities as the ISBD (ER): International Standard Bibliographic Description for Electronic Resources and the IFLA study on the Functional Requirements for Bibliographic Records, and make adjustments accordingly;
- Experiments applicable to particular kinds of resources (*e.g.*, serials and CONSER policies; the BEONLINE project for business and economic resources) are under way with evaluation of results and implications for policy guidelines still to be determined;
- System considerations at LC are in a state of flux, particularly with the impending procurement of an Integrated Library System; hypertext links are still not available in the traditional interfaces to MUMS and SCORPIO; once this feature is more widely available, perceptions of which resources should be represented in the catalogue and how data need to be depicted may change.

CONCEPTUAL FRAMEWORK

The Interim Guidelines establish a common context through the use of entities and concepts derived from an entity analysis technique and based on work done heretofore in LC as part of information modelling and in the more recent work that resulted in an IFLA study: Functional Requirements for Bibliographic Records: Final Report. The following entities/concepts, applicable to all forms of material, are taken directly from the aforementioned IFLA study in a condensed but usually directly quoted form. They are stated here because they provide a vocabulary that clarifies conceptually what is currently embodied in a bibliographic record.

- *Work:* A distinct intellectual or artistic creation; a work is an abstract entity
- *Expression:* The intellectual or artistic realization of a work in the form of alpha-numeric, musical, or choreographic notation, sound, image, object, movement, etc., or any combination of such forms; an expression is the specific intellectual or artistic form that a work takes each time it is "realised"; inasmuch as the form of expression is an inherent characteristic of the expression, any change in form (*e.g.*, from alpha-numeric notation to spoken word) results in a new expression; similarly, changes in the intellectual conventions or instruments that are employed to express a work (*e.g.*, translation from one language to another) result in the production of a new expression
- *Manifestation:* The physical embodiment of an expression of a work; as an entity, manifestation represents all the physical objects that bear the same characteristics, in respect to both intellectual content

and physical form; when a work is realised, the resulting expression of the work may be physically embodied on or in a medium such as paper, audio tape, video tape, etc.; the physical embodiment constitutes a manifestation of the work; in some cases there may be only a single physical exemplar produced of that manifestation of the work (*e.g.*, an author's manuscript, a tape recorded for an oral history archive, an original oil painting, etc.); in other cases there are multiple copies produced in order to facilitate public dissemination or distribution

- *Item:* A single exemplar of a manifestation; an item is a concrete entity; it is in many instances a single physical object (*e.g.*, a copy of a one-volume monograph, a single audio cassette, etc.); with respect to intellectual content and physical form, an item exemplifying a manifestation is normally the same as the manifestation itself; however, variations may occur from one item to another, even when the items exemplify the same manifestation, where those variations are the result of actions external to the intent of the producer of the manifestation (*e.g.*, damage occurring after the item was produced, binding performed by a library, etc.)

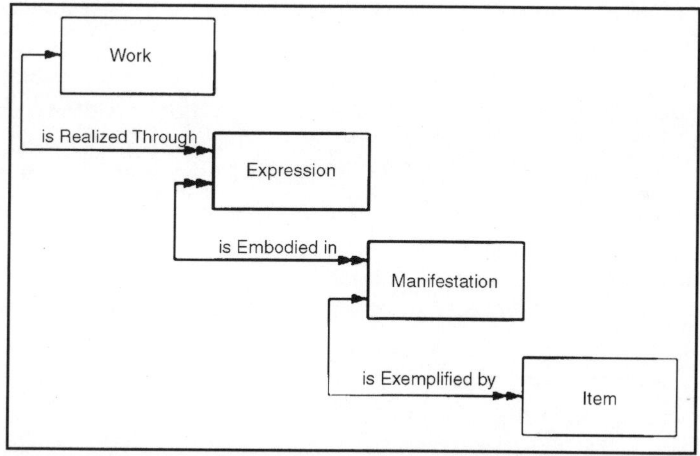

The entities shown in diagram "represent the different aspects of user interests in the products of intellectual or artistic endeavour. The entities defined as work (a distinct intellectual or artistic creation) and expression (the intellectual or artistic realization of a work) reflect intellectual or artistic content. The entities defined as manifestation (the physical embodiment of an expression of a work) and item (a single exemplar of a manifestation), on the other hand reflect physical form. The relationships depicted in the diagram indicate that a work may be realised through one or more than one expression (hence the double arrow on the line that links work to expression). An expression, on the other hand, is the realization of one and only one work (hence the single arrow on the reverse direction of that line linking expression to work). An expression may be embodied in one or more than one manifestation; likewise a manifestation may embody one or more than one expression. A manifestation, in turn, may be exemplified by one or more than one item; but an item may exemplify one and only one manifestation.

BASIC CONCEPTS/TERMS

The Guidelines use the following basic concepts and terms with their associated definition to establish a consistent vocabulary, recognizing that there may not always be full agreement in particular cases. The basic concepts/ terms are presented alphabetically for ease of reference.

Some apply at a general level, others are more nearly related to electronic resources themselves:

- *Accessing Mode:* A concept that characterizes the means of access to an electronic resource; it is applicable at the item level.
  - *Direct Access:* The term used to characterize access to an electronic resource resident in a carrier such as a computer disk or a CD-ROM that a user physically inserts into a computer, typically a microcomputer.
- *Observation:* A tangible resource may also be accessed in an online mode as if remote (*e.g.*, networked CD-ROMS; data copied onto UNIX hosts).
  - *Remote Access:* The term used to characterize access to an electronic resource resident in a carrier that a user cannot physically handle, *i.e.*, a resource accessed, processed, executed, etc. remotely. Frequently this involves connection through a computer network. This type of access is often referred to as "online" access.

Adjunct see under Selected relationships:

- *Aggregates/Components:* Concepts pertinent to the make-up of a work. A work may be an integral unit or it may represent an aggregate of individual works (*e.g.*, a compilation), a set of individual monographs brought together by a common theme or topic (*e.g.*, a series), or a group of private papers organized by an archive as a single collection. A work may also represent an intellectually or artistically discrete component of a larger work, *e.g.*, an article in a journal, a monograph in a series. Entities at the aggregate or component level are seen as the same as entities at the integral unit level.
- *Compilation:* An electronic anthology whose constituent elements have been brought together and selected, coordinated, or arrnaged to form a new work.
- *Delineation:* A technique used in lieu of separately cataloguing a manifestation whereby detailed information about that manifestation is given in the bibliographic record for another manifestation; simply

noting the existence of another manifestation does not constitute what is meant by delineation

Directly accessed electronic resource see under Physicality:

- *Electronic Conference:* A conference held in a virtual mode that takes place within the context of an interactive software environment running on the Internet. Headings for such conferences are treated the same as those for other conferences except headings for electronic conferences do not contain the name of the local place or other location in which the conference was held.
- *Electronic Discussion Group:* The term used to refer to a forum conducted electronically; these services, commonly called newsgroups and listservs, allow a computer user to post messages to, and read messages from, a group of people who have a common interest, usually by means of the Internet, a commercial online service, or electronic mail. For cataloguing purposes, treat such a discussion group as a work entered under title (X30 series of tags).
- *Electronic Resource:* The term used to refer to a manifestation of a work encoded for manipulation by computer. The manifestation resides in a carrier accessed either directly or remotely. It is the term used in the revised ISBD (ER) and serves in lieu of other terms currently in use such as computer file or digital resource. Some electronic resources may require the use of a peripheral device attached to a computer (*e.g.* a CD-ROM player). Note that for these Guidelines this term does not include "electronic" resources that do not require the use of a computer, *e.g.*, music compact discs, videodiscs.

BASE GUIDELINES (GENERAL)

Use the following base guidelines in determining the cataloguing treatment of a particular electronic resource. In general, the cataloguing treatment applied depends upon important factors related to the creation of the electronic resource itself, most importantly whether the resource is a sole manifestation or one of multiple manifestations and the realization of the work as a matter of time, *i.e.*, whether it is judged to be a monograph or a serial.

CONTENT VERSUS CARRIER (ELECTRONIC RESOURCES)

How to characterize records for electronic resources in terms of their primary form of material (the issue of "content versus carrier") has been widely discussed. AACR2 is oriented towards basing cataloguing treatment on carrier. Until 1997 the definition of computer file in USMARC (Leader/06 code"m") also indicated that the record would be coded for carrier. However, as a result of a change approved by MARBI in June 1997, Update No. 3 to the USMARC Bibliographic Format revised the definition of code "m" to allow for computer files to be coded for their most significant aspect.

That definition now reads:

- Code m indicates that the content of the record is for the following classes of electronic resources: computer software (including programmes, games, fonts), numeric data, computer-oriented multimedia, online systems or services. For these classes of materials, if there is a significant aspect that causes it to fall into another Leader/06 category, code for that significant aspect (*e.g.* vector data that is cartographic is not coded as numeric but as cartographic). Other classes of electronic resources are coded for their most significant aspect (*e.g.* language material, graphic, cartographic material, sound, music, moving image). In case of doubt or if the most significant aspect cannot be determined, consider the item a computer file.

In conjunction with this change, field 007 for computer files is now mandatory in any record representing an item whose carrier is a computer file. Directly accessed electronic resources have been treated as computer files at LC as have most of those accessed remotely. Directly accessed electronic resources have been represented in the COMPUTER FILES file, the BOOKS file (those that accompany books), and, with format integration, in the SERIALS file. With respect to cataloguing remotely accessed electronic resources, LC has been most active in cataloguing electronic serials/journals and electronic counterparts or subsets of tangible, original items or collections.

In most cases, the latter do not receive separate catalogue records; instead, they are delineated in records for the original items or collections. The special format divisions are interested in providing an integrated approach to the bibliographic records for the materials of interest to them. Currently, that is done through the disposition of physical files under MUMS, essentially by type of material. Under an ILS it will be a requirement to be able to approach the catalogue in a similar way as at present but it will probably be a logical disposition instead of a physical one.

In the future when the shift in approach from carrier to content is implemented at LC, fundamental changes in the current LC environment will be required. Those electronic resources judged to have a significant aspect other than that of a computer file would now be represented in the file appropriate to what is judged to be the significant aspect. For example, if the significant aspect of a monographic electronic resource is judged to be language material, that resource would be represented in the Books file, not the Computer Files file (use of the GMD "[computer file]" will continue). As of the current writing, not all the details of the impact of this change have been worked out, but it is assumed that staff in the Computer Files/Microforms Team will continue to catalogue those general monographic electronic resources not pertaining to the materials of interest to the special format divisions. However, they will do so by working in the file judged appropriate to the resource being cataloged.

It is further assumed that special format divisions will continue to focus on cataloguing (except for Music, RBSCD) and servicing material acquired for the collections in their custody. The change in approach that emphasizes content will, mean that electronic resources will now be represented throughout the files that constitute the catalogue, not just in the Computer Files file. An issue of potential significant impact relates to those computer-related electronic resources acquired by the special format divisions for their collections.

As of this writing, it is not clear how some of these materials will be treated with respect to:

- Who will catalogue these materials and
- What cataloguing treatment they will receive.

It is assumed that those judged to be cartographic materials will continue to be cataloged by staff in the Geography and Map Division (G&M); those judged to be serials will be cataloged in the Serial Record Division (SRD)). The treatment of other monographic materials is less clear. For example, will a directly accessed electronic resource manifes-ted in multiple copies whose significant aspect is judged to be moving image be cataloged in MBRS under the AMIM rules and, if circumstances warrant, added to the record for another manifestation? This would be in lieu of being cataloged according to the general rules of AACR2 as a manifestation receiving a separate record by staff either in MBRS or in SMCD. The Library of Congress will develop/change workflow and cataloguing policies related to "content vs. carrier" issues and will make them available to the larger cataloguing community.

MONOGRAPH OR SERIAL

Apply the current AACR2 definitions of monograph and serial to electronic resources. Treat digitized texts, individual Web sites, and indeterminate works not issued in separate parts, particularly databases, as monographs. Treat as serials indeterminate works issued in separate, designated parts. The parts may constitute an issue, or in some cases, an individual article.

Applying the current definitions may result in different manifestations receiving different cataloguing treatment. For example, a manifestation in print form, such as an annual directory, is cataloged as a serial whereas it is cataloged as a monograph when the directory takes on the form of an electronic file that is continuously updated. This practice may change, but for the present LC and CONSER adhere to current definitions.

Remotely accessed electronic resources of a dynamic nature that are currently excluded from serial treatment are:

- Databases (including directories, A&I services, etc.)
- Electronic discussion groups (*e.g.*, SERIALST)
- Electronic discussion group digests (*e.g.*, AUTOCAT digest)
- Gopher servers (*e.g.*, LC-MARVEL)

- Online public access catalogues (*e.g.*, OCLC, RLIN)
- Online services (*e.g.*, America Online)
- Web sites (*e.g.*, the CONSER home page)

SINGLE MANIFESTATION

An electronic resource that exists solely in a single manifestation, *e.g.*, a publication that exists solely online, by definition is represented by a single bibliographic record in the same manner as other non-electronic resources that exist in a single manifestation. Currently, those judged to be monographs are cataloged as computer files by the Computer Files/Microforms Team of the Special Materials Cataloguing Division (SMCD) or as cartographic materials by staff in the Geography and Map Division (G&M) or, if judged to be accompanying material, by the general cataloguing divisions. Those judged to be serials are cataloged in the Serial Record Division (SRD). Both monographs and serials are cataloged according to AACR2R, LCRIs, DCM, LCSH, SCM, LCC, USMARC, and supplementary documentation appropriate to each category of material.

MULTIPLE MANIFESTATIONS

An electronic resource that is another manifestation of a work is likely to be one of the following:

- A manifestation that is a counterpart or subset of a published resource (tangible or otherwise, usually directly accessed) or an adjunct to it;
- A directly accessed manifestation that is:
  - A counterpart or subset of a tangible resource (either at the collection level or item level or both);
  - A reproduction in electronic form done by or for the Library of Congress of a resource held by the Library;
- A remotely accessed manifestation that is
  - A counterpart or subset of a tangible resource (either at the collection level or item level or both);
  - A reproduction in electronic form done by or for the Library of Congress of a resource (including material that may have been published) held by the Library.

Materials in categories a) and b) are usually cataloged by staff in the Computer Files/Microforms Team, SMCD (computer files), or in G&M (cartographic materials) or in SRD, depending upon whether the resource is judged to be a monograph or a serial. Materials in category c) are usually delineated by staff in the special format division that has custody of the tangible, non-electronic resource.

Note that a manifestation of conventionally published materials, including directly accessed electronic resources, usually consists of multiple copies. Unique collections usually occur in a single instance, although electronic manifestations of the original collection may be mirrored or copied and therefore exist at several storage locations.

The data elements contained in the USMARC biblio-graphic format are predicated on data elements common to all the copies of a manifestation. Those applicable to a particular copy are generally treated as "local" or as holdings information.

This concept is less appropriate to a unique tangible resource such as an archival collection, although this does not preclude the concept of "copy specific" as applied to a particular item in a collection when the manifestation of the item itself consists of multiple copies.

Single/Multiple Records for Multiple Manifestations (Electronic Resources)

Criteria for Determining Single/Multiple Record Approach

Acquisitions/Initial Bibliographic Control (IBC) Criterion

Determine the processing state of the electronic resource from the perspective of acquisitions or the need for IBC data. The degree of detail required for the management of initial and subsequent acquisitions actions may influence the employment of a single or multiple record approach as may the workflow steps required subsequent to the acquisitions process.

Citation Criterion

A user must be able to get to the manifestation cited in the record the user is observing.

When a single bibliographic record includes one or more citations to multiple manifestations, each citation the user is observing must state clearly and succinctly the content of the manifestation(s) cited:

- For the directly accessed, the format of the manifestation more than likely requires a separate record to fulfil the citation criterion;
- For the remotely accessed, a separate record is less likely to be needed to fulfil the citation criterion unless the content among multiple manifestations varies substantially.

INTERLIBRARY LOAN (ILL) CRITERION

The receiver of a request must know which manifestation is being requested and the initiator of a request must know the manifes-tation(s) available for loan:

- For multiple directly accessed manifestations, multiple bibliographic records make it more clear which manifestation is being requested;
- Employment of a single bibliographic record that represents both tangible and remotely accessed manifestations is unlikely to cause confusion with respect to the manifestation available for loan, since

it is unlikely someone would request the loan of a remotely accessed resource;

- When a single bibliographic record represents both a tangible manifestation (electronic or otherwise) and a remotely accessed one and the Library "holds" only the latter, it is more likely to cause confusion with respect to the manifestation held and whether it s likely to be available for loan.

Bibliographic Details Criterion

When there is more than one manifestation, the significant bibliographic details of each need to be recorded to identify and to access each. When using a single record that includes one or more delineations, it is necessary to find ways to indicate the significant bibliographic details of all the manifestations, not just those for the primary one. In the past the Library of Congress has attempted to provide catalogue records not only for use in the catalogues of the Library of Congress but also of use in the catalogues of other libraries. For economic reasons, the present Guidelines now provide for the use of a single record to represent more than one manifestation in the cases. This necessarily focuses on the needs of the Library of Congress but may pose difficulties on other libraries that may wish to represent such resources in their catalogues.

Multiple Manifestations in a Single Record (Electronic Resources)

Two techniques are available for indicating the existence of an electronic manifestation in a record for another manifestation. Both are in lieu of LC's cataloguing the remotely accessed resource separately.

Delineate Another Manifestation

When using a single record to describe a tangible resource and also to delineate an electronic manifestation, consider the information provided in the delineation of the electronic resource as being in lieu of a separate catalogue record. Use the 530 field (Other Physical Form Available Note) to focus all the information about the electronic resource in one place.

Organize the delineation to include at least:

- An introductory phrase indicating the additional availability of an electronic manifestation;
- The name or title of the electronic manifestation if it varies from that of a tangible counterpart or subset;
- Information about the content of the electronic manifestation when it varies from that of the original, *e.g.,* a subset of the original or additional material;
- General information about access, particularly any restrictions on access or information about availability.

If a finding aid in electronic form is involved and it is the kind that incorporates actual material from the collection such that the finding aid itself becomes a remotely accessed electronic manifestation of the content of the collection or a subset of it, describe this special condition in the delineation.

The data making up a particular delineation are not prone to a structured presentation; therefore, the flexibility of the 530 field was chosen for delineation over the more structured 533 field. Also use of the 530 field avoids any implication that the original is not held, an implication often associated with the use of field 533. When the electronic manifestation bears a title different from that of the tangible resource, provide uncontrolled title access through the title that differs. Do these by means of a 740 field with indicator values set to 0#? This is an exception to the general LC policy of providing title access through a controlled form (730).

Note the Existence of Another Manifestation

The cataloguing rules have long provided for indicating the existence of another manifestation in a note (field 530), usually in a very brief statement. With respect to serials, CONSER's Interim Guidelines for Online Versions allow CONSER institutions either to create separate records or to note the existence of an remotely accessed electronic manifestation on the record for the print (or other) serial. Practically speaking, this policy is quite similar to delineating; however, there is a difference in the intent.

The CONSER guidelines aim to retain the integrity of the print (or other) record in a shared database in which separate records for the remotely accessed electronic manifestation might exist or be created later. Thus, field 007 is not given in such records and 530 notes tend to be less detailed than those given in records for LC's special collections. Field 740 may also be given when the title of the remotely accessed electronic manifestation differs from that of the original. LC applies the CONSER single record option only for one-to-one reproduc-tions of serials and in other cases creates separate records.

Multiple Presentations of the Same Electronic Resource

If an electronic resource is available in multiple presen-tations that may be generated from different underlying digital representations, *e.g.*, images in TIFF or JPEG format, it is not necessary to acknowledge the condition.

Electronic Resources in Bibliographical References

With respect to bibliography notes, interpret the term "bibliographical references" to include all kinds of resources, including electronic resources; do not give any special treatment to, or provide special mention of, the latter.

ELECTRONIC MANIFESATATION–ORIGINAL IN NON–ELECTRONIC FROM–SPECIFIC GUIDELINES

General

This is the condition in which an electronic resource is the digitized counterpart to, subset of, or an adjunct to, a tangible manifestation of a work, and the decision has been made to represent the electronic manifestation in the catalogue. Determine whether it is preferable to do this by a single-or multiple-record approach (the single-record approach requires a record for the original, tangible manifestation; one may already exist or it may need to be created). For remotely accessed manifestations of tangible LC materials, a general reference to the Library of Congress Web site is sufficient, since the specific location is always given in an 856 field.

For uniformity of presentation, use the terminology illustrated in the following examples to the extent practicable:

- 530 ## $a Available also through the Library of Congress Web site under title: America's first look into the camera: daguerreotype portraits and views... This finding aid in electronic form, with reproductions, captions, and subject indexing for each image, was produced in 1995 for the National Digital Library Programme, American Memory collections.
- 530 ## $a Available also through the Library of Congress Web site under title: Colour photographs from the FSA and OWI, ca. 1938-1944. This finding aid in electronic form contains reproductions with full caption information and subject indexing for each image.
- 530 ## $a Available also through the Library of Congress Web site under title: Documents from the Continental Congress and the Constitutional Convention 1774-1789. At least one facsimile image of each broadside is presented along with a narrative introduction.
- 530 ## $a Available also as part of a microfilm with title: Continental Congress and Constitutional convention Collections. Washington, D.C.: Library of Congress Photoduplication Service. 1 microfilm reel; 35 mm.
- 530 ## $a Available also through the Library of Congress Web site in two forms: as facsimile page images and as full text in SGML.
- 530 ## $a Available also through the Library of Congress Web site as a raster image.
- 538 (System Details Note)

15

Understanding the Implications of Educating the Online Catalogue User

An issue which is central to planning for the impleme-ntation of online catalogue systems in libraries of all types, but which received little notice in the literature of the early 1980s on online catalogues, is that of the role of public services staff in the management planning process.'

Because much of the hard work in the early implemen-tation stages was on the technical and technical services side, it was perhaps natural that reference librarians and other public services personnel were not counted among those most responsible for bringing forward the technology in libraries. Now more than midway through a decade of tremendous change in libraries, however, it is clear that the public service aspects of online catalogue implementation are of considerable interest to the field and that reference librarians everywhere are seeking to forge new roles for themselves.

As public services librarians have sought to define their relation-ship to the online catalogue, it has been natural for them to view the relationship in terms of their role vis-à-vis the older card file technology that online technology supplants. The historic relationship cast the public services librarian as "interpreter" of the catalogue, *i.e.*, assisting users to locate items and teaching them how to use the card catalogue by themselves.

It has long been unclear how much such "interpretation" the card catalogue required, though it was long recognized that consistent and clear management of the catalogue on the technical services side relieved the burden considerably on the reference side in this regard. With the bibliographic instruction movement having gained consider-able force and influence on the field within the past fifteen years, the concept of catalogue "interpretation" has come to be understood as man-dating instruction, at least in academic libraries. Do online catalogues require instruction in their use and, if so, how is that instruction best delivered? These questions do not have simple answers, yet from the early online catalogue implementations at the beginning of the decade library managers have taken positions that assumed a rather simple "yes" or "no" to the first question.

To approach answers to the two questions of whether the online catalogue requires instruction and what might be the best means of delivering it, Northwestern University Library undertook a research study, supported by the *Council on Library Resources* (CLR), to test the value of online catalogue user education. In the pages that follow, the research undertaken at Northwestern will be summarized as to the research objectives, the rationale for the study, a description of the methodology and findings, and the study's major conclusions.

Though the research brings new findings to the specific question of how best to provide users with services that will enable them to make best use of an online catalogue, our work also addresses some larger questions:

- What is the role of the reference librarian vis-à-vis a catalogue that is now considered to be self-inter-preting?
- What do our experiences with online catalogue user education lead us to expect in the way of changes in our bibliographic instruction programmes overall?
- What is the future of reference services in an increasingly automated library?

It is hoped that these issues can continue to be seriously addressed as more and more libraries move from an initial "presentation" phase to an ongoing operational phase in online catalogue implementation.

The article begins with an overview of the primary objectives of the "Educating the Online Catalogue User" project. These objectives are described in the context of Northwestern's setting, with a brief description of LUIS (Library User Information Service), the online catalogue component of NOTIS (Northwestern Online Total Integrated System). Following this is a discussion of some of the underlying issues that prompted our interest in online catalogue user education.

The issues that surfaced in establishing broad learning objectives-the framework upon which the model programme was based-are described, and a description of the NOTIS transaction log facility-an important data gathering tool in the research-is provided.

Finally, the article closes by proposing that reference librarians and managers expand the scope of their online catalogue user education efforts to include more than the teaching of a single tool. They should take advantage of the brief historical opportunity presented by the online catalogue to use the novelty it provides as a vehicle for teaching users about other information retrieval systems that are becoming increasingly visible both within and beyond the library environment.

The overall purpose of the "Educating the Online Catalogue User" study was to provide a model for the development and evaluation of an online public access catalogue user education programme that could be employed by other academic libraries with any number of different online catalogues.

The model was developed by collaborative effort among the reference staff at Northwestern and librarians at the University of Wisconsin-Madison and Washington University in St. Louis. Though the project was centred at Northwestern, public services staff at these other institutions provided advice and feedback at several stages of the project in order to keep the research as broadly focused as possible. The experimental stage of the study was conducted exclusively at Northwestern University.

The study had four objectives:

- To develop a set of systematic and formalized instr-uctional objectives for teaching online catalogue use that could be adopted by other academic libraries seeking to develop an online catalogue instruction programme;
- To implement an instructional programme based on those learning objectives at Northwestern University;
- To evaluate the success of this programme through a variety of established evaluative techniques including the use of transaction log data; and
- To assess the viability of transaction log monitoring as a data source for bibliographic instruction evaluation.

It was recognized at the outset that the study's objectives were constrained by the features of the online catalogue to which the researchers had the most complete access. Northwestern University Library uses the LUIS online catalogue, which has a number of features common to many other such systems but also lacks certain features that present significant instructional challenges. LUIS offers title, author, and subject searching but at the time of the study did not provide keyword searching or the ability to use Boolean operators. A number of descriptions of LUISexist in the published literature on online catalogues, and LUIS is now available in over sixty libraries-academic, public, school, and special-in the United States and Canada.

ONLINE CATALOGUE USER EDUCATION ISSUES

The central question that directed this study, "What might be the components of a model programme to instruct users of an online catalogue?" challenges a commonly held view within the field of librarianship and information science. This view is that an effective "user friendly" inter-active computer system-such as an online catalogue-should not require instruction at all. While such a view is not universally held, it is common especially among system developers and others who are steeped in the use of computers in libraries and elsewhere.

A frequently articulated design specification for end user oriented systems is that all system use instruction should be provided as part of its interface-through such things as introductory help screens, user prompts, and labelling conventions-and should be all that even the most naive user needs to know to be able to effectively use that system.

A corollary of this view is that efforts to develop an instructional programme for the online catalogue suggest that the catalogue is not fulfilling its purpose and that its design is flawed. With this logic, any effort to provide instruction in online catalogue use by public services staffs might be viewed as wasted effort at the least, and provide implicit criticism of the designers as well.

Though the project from its inception questioned this view of the incompatibility of "user friendly" online systems and instruction pro-grams, it did not simply embrace the contrary view that formalized instruction must be given to all online catalogue users. Interactive systems for the general public are simply too new and untested for us to assume either of these positions without a period of considerable experimentation and practical examination of what works and what doesn't work for our users. A certain amount of curiosity, fascination, or mystique naturally accompanies technological evolution. At this early stage of online catalogue implementation, learning from the practical experiences of others, as well as from more formal research findings, is essential if we are to move beyond these phases in our programme development. Baker and Nielsen review much of the early literature on the debate about the value of online catalogue user education, pointing out particularly the sampling bias in the widely cited CLR *Online Public Access Catalogue* (OPAC) studies, a bias which caused users who experienced difficulties in using online catalogues to be underrepresented in the findings.

We became interested in creating a model programme for educating online catalogue users for a variety of reasons:

- There was (and is) wide recognition that the perfect online catalogue simply does not (yet) exist.
- There was (and is) a perception by many librarians that the online user interface may not accommodate all user needs at present and may never do so.
- "User friendly" systems are not indeed friendly to all, judging from the experiences of many reference librarians who have worked with users trying to master such systems.
- The pace of change in interface improvements can seem painfully slow once any online catalogue system "works" in the sense that it meets managerial (not necessarily user) criteria for "satisfying."
- A general training programme that conveyed information retrieval concepts might aid users as they moved on to other automated systems both within and beyond the library setting.
- The numerous online catalogue instructional prog-rammes that had been initiated in various settings-particularly in academic libraries-suggested that making an effort for consistency in instructional planning was worthwhile and beneficial.

LEARNING OBJECTIVES

In order for a model online catalogue user education programme to be applicable to a variety of institutions and for the programme to be formally evaluated, it was critical to the Northwestern project that programme learning objectives be stated and generalized beyond those associated with a particular system. The first step in the execution of this research project involved formalizing a set of such objectives which would serve as the basis for teaching the use of an online catalogue. Much of the conceptual work related to this aspect of the project is described by Baker.

In planning the framework of instructional objectives, there was extensive discussion with librarians at each of the participating libraries. These discussions centred on identifying a set of ideal objectives (or goals of instruction) without linking them to features of specific systems or tying them to specific methods of instruction. With the goal of developing a generic instruction programme with generalizable objectives, it was essential to look at online catalogue instruction as it could be applied across many systems. By focusing on such general expectations of online catalogue users, we felt that skills might be more easily transferred across systems.

WHAT TO TEACH: CONCEPTS OR PROCEDURES

In determining an appropriate direction for our online catalogue teaching, two concerns were raised. The first involved what technical aspects of the system's structure should be presented to users; the second questioned the manner in which such aspects should be included in the learning activity. With one of our project objectives being to work towards developing transferability of skills learned about one automated system to skills needed for another, an emphasis on teaching concepts and structure, rather than procedures, was endorsed. In addition to increasing the likelihood for transferability of skills, teaching system structure is useful for conceptualizing the workings of a system. When the way a system works is not transparent to the user, there is little opportunity for self-diagnosis of errors or decision-making for search strategy development.

This instructional approach has been supported by other research in the ways humans interact with computers. Works by Christine Borg-man, Ramsey and Grimes, and others discuss the importance of conceptual models in teaching interactive systems and the resulting mental model the user has available for error diagnosis and problem solving. Such conceptual models are often built around metaphors and often illustrate techniques designed to communicate an overall context for system behaviour to the learner.

Learning occurs whether it is structured in a systematic programme or whether it is coincidental. Coincidental learning of a system through the use of prompts and help screens may actually prove to be an effective means for learning procedures. Focusing an instructional programme around conceptual models does not by any means diminish the necessity for a user to have a functional understanding geared towards learning system-specific searching techniques. These techniques may actually be more easily acquired from instruction embedded in the system once the conceptual model has been learned. One of the most important functions of the user interface for online catalogues has been to provide this task-oriented training. With so many automated systems being used in libraries around the country, transferring skills learned about one sys-tem to another may prove quite difficult. Designing instruction around a conceptual *v.* procedural framework may provide ultimate transfer-ability of learning in the use of online catalogues.

EVALUATING THE MODEL

Because the objectives developed for online catalogue instruction involved acquisition of both cognitive and behavioural learning, it was important to develop an evaluation strategy that addressed objective achievement of a group of representative users at solving both cognitive and behavioural problems. Both pencil-and-paper responses and observation of "hands-on" online catalogue activity were deemed critical to assess the project.

Another issue important to the study was that of cumulative learning. Because the library patron often learns the use of research tools in stages (such as by trial use followed by assistance from a librarian), cumulative learning, or learning that builds on previous learning, frequently occurs.

In the case of learning to use a library catalogue, cumulative learning is especially salient: many users are exposed to repeated instruction in the use of the catalogue in elementary school; many users rely on experience as the most available teacher of library use skills. Bibliographic instruction librarians are aware of the problems inherent in this situation, for they often must help students "unlearn" previously incorrect information concerning the card catalogue.This concern with the effects of cumulative learning led to the development of an experimental design which allowed us to examine and evaluate the effects of two types of bibliographic instruction methods-both individually and combined-taking into account the order of their presentation. The research design protocol called for the creation of two experimental groups (each of which took two tests and participated in two instructional sessions) as well as the use of a control group which only took two tests but received no instruction.

The instructional treatments included a classroom-like presentation on the online catalogue (what Northwestern has dubbed a "LUIS Workshop"), and the reading of a printed brochure designed to convey instructional content. As the tests themselves required participants to use the online catalogue to answer some of the questions, all three groups were exposed to the catalogue and its introductory (tutorial) and "help" screens. The two tests were composed of questions designed to test the same knowledge.

The control group took the first test followed by a "placebo" presentation (a short non-instructional film) and then the second test. The first experimental group, which as suggested, call Group "A," received the classroom instructional session followed by the first test and then read the instructional brochure and took the second test. The second experimental group, which as suggested, call Group "B," read the brochure and took the first test and then received the instructional session and the second test.

SAMPLE SELECTION

A random sample subject population of ninety freshmen students was selected for participation in the study using a sampling technique that insured equal representation by sex and representation by academic major corresponding as much as possible to national norms derived from American Council on Education data.'

Only freshmen who had previously participated in LUIS workshops were excluded from participation. As an incentive for the subjects to commit to participation when they were contacted by telephone, each student was offered a free ticket to a commercial movie theater upon completion of the experiment.'

DATA COLLECTION

The principal means of data collection for the study were a battery of two written tests prepared for the study and transaction data collected by the NOTIS computer as subjects interacted directly with LUIS. The first test consisted of fourteen questions related to background characteristics of the students, forty-five questions tapping knowledge of LUIS-including some which required use of the terminal-and eight attitudinal questions asking how the students liked various features of the catalogue.

Eight catalogue search "practice questions" for which students had to use the terminals were also included. The second test included the same type of questions as the first except for the fourteen initial questions tapping demographic variables. Pretesting of the two tests with twenty randomly selected Northwestern students verified that the tests, though different, were measuring acquisition of the same learning.

Monitoring online catalogue transactions as a means of collecting data was accomplished through utilization of NOTIS software developed initially in connection with the CLR-sponsored OPAC studies of 1980-82 in which Northwestern was a Research Libraries Group participant. The room in which the experiment was conducted was equipped with sixteen online catalogue terminals, each having adjacent to it a copy of the *Library* of *Congress Subject Headings.*

Subjects were instructed to write on their test booklets the identification number of the terminal at which they were searching for the test but were not told that their transactions were being recorded. This protocol device provided a means of unobtrusive measurement of online catalogue use in which transaction data could be associated with user characteristics recorded on the test booklets.

This strategy is especially notable as a monitoring technique as it allows exemption from institutional and federal guide-lines for research on human subjects-due to the educational testing nature of the experiment-and yet is less obtrusive than other monitoring experimental designs in that subjects are led to assume that pencil-and-paper is the sole method of data collection.

ANALYSIS

Following the completion of the data gathering, the 178filled-out tests were first paired by student identification number and subsequently coded for machine processing. Eighty-seven usable pairs of tests were so coded and input for processing using the Statistical Package for the Social Sciences (SPSS). Tabulated responses were scored using a key of correct test items, and raw percentage correct scores were computed.

Analysis was also accomplished in regard to a number of study questions by grouping the raw percentage scores into "high", "middle", and "low" performance groups. This grouping enabled as well the analysis of student performance considered in terms of degree of achievement of five important learning objectives established in conjunction with the model programme developed at Northwestern. A fuller description of the methods used to reduce the data, as well as detailed findings on the effect of demographic variables on perfor-mance, are provided in the authors' final report to the Council on Library Resources on the project."

An indicator of overall test performance for each of the three test groups is the average (mean) test score, again expressed as a percentage of questions answered correctly. Table provides a clear picture of group performance showing the score for each group on both test one and test two. On both tests the performance of the control group was the lowest. Group "A", which received the lecture instruction prior to test one, performed best on test one overall, and their score on test two surprisingly dropped.

Group "B", which read the brochure prior to test one, performed less well on the first test, but, following their receiving the live instruction, performed nearly as well on test two as group two had on test one. Analysis of variance tests with the test one and test two data for the mean score by group revealed that the within-group variation on both scores was less than the variation between groups indicating that the different means for each group are statistically significant.

Table. Average Test Score by Group

	Test 1	Test 2
Control Group	54.66	53.21
Group "A"	77.5	63.3
Group "B"	61.66	76.94
ANOVA Significance <.001		

These average scores represent overall test performance in only a general way and are presented in this manner as a way to look at the cumulative learning issue that was of interest in the study. Because of the length of the instruction period and the opportunity subjects were given to interact with the instructor, the superior performance of group "A" on test one was expected. Why the "A" group's performance dropped on the second test-following their exposure to the brochure-cannot be adequately explained by the analysis presented here, but we may hypothesize that test fatigue may have been an important factor.

Recalling that the "A" group's taking of the second test was nearly ninety minutes into the period set aside for the experiment, and that the intervening period between tests for this group was much shorter than for group "B," it seems highly likely that group "A" was simply tired of responding to questions on the second test. Group "B," while spending as long on the experiment overall as the "A" group, did have a consider-ably longer intervening period between the two tests.

In the matter of evaluating the achievement of specific learning objectives we were less successful. Although we established a means to analyse the result of the evaluative test in a way that treated the achievement of each objective separately, we must acknowledge that a conceptual dilemma exists. As certain objectives dealt more concretely with the learning of definitions and concepts that were easily tested for, while other objectives-concerned as they were with the execution of procedures-were inherently more difficult to test for, we cannot make clear conclusions regarding different levels of attainment on the test.

Different attainment levels may reflect more about the tests themselves than about actual superior performance in online catalogue searching. Because our knowledge of online catalogue users is still so incomplete, instructional evaluation is made difficult especially in respect to validation of the appropriateness of certain cognitive learning tasks for successful performance in searching. There is some danger in evaluation studies of this sort to direct instruction to successful completion of the test rather than to the achievement of skills that the test has been designed to measure.

With these considerations in mind, an analysis of the data showed that the group that had the workshop first scored significantly higher on procedures such as using equipment than the group that had the brochure. One of the most interesting facts is that the control group scored higher than both of these test groups on procedural knowledge. But in interpreting and structuring searches the workshop group did significantly better.

It was followed by the brochure group and then the control group. In terms of concepts, the control group fell far behind the other two test groups with the workshop group in the lead. Among our findings on the analysis of the transaction logging was that subjects who had a workshop presentation made fewer errors than those whose first instructional exposure was to the printed brochure.

What do these findings allow us to say about the cumulative effects of two learning experiences with online catalogue instruction? Because there is no clear pattern in improvement on all the objectives for any of the three groups it is difficult to say. The order of presentation of the two learning experiences-the brochure and the lecture-did not appear to affect group performance on all five learning objectives in the same way; for some objectives a score increase between test one and test two might have been the result of the lecture having been given first, for other objectives it might have been the brochure being presented first. Further work is in order to refine the analysis and sort out what factors may lead to improved test scores.

CONCLUSION

Through a close examination of the process of developing learning objectives, creating a programme to help meet them, and evaluating the outcome of the programme, there are a number of conclusions that we can make. This research has provided some answers to the question which initially motivated the study, "Why teach use of an online catalogue?"

First of all, it is evident that teaching improves user performance on a written test. The development and use of learning objectives has further helped to define specific competencies which may lead to better online catalogue searching. We have further helped define for the field at large those specific competencies that lead to better performance. Another aspect of our response to the "Why teach the online catalogue?" question must be that there are certain concerns that arise with teaching online catalogue use at this time.

Of primary concern is the necessity to train users on some procedural matters on a case-by-case basis leading to possible difficulties in users' assimilating the information? For example, in any online system there will be details and peculiarities about the library's organization and physical layout which may appear in index displays online.

Providing instruction at this level of detail distracts from the overall flow of the presentation and adds only incidental information which the audience is not likely to remember. Perhaps a greater problem that we are confronted with is the fact that such an explanation reveals idiosyncrasy and inconsistency in the sys-tem possibly leading to loss of confidence among users that there is an understandable logic to the system that can be mastered. Such a situation tends to defeat the overall instructional goal.

Inconsistencies are numerous in online catalogues. Explana-tions for these features through printed guides, lectures, online help, or individual assistance may help ease the burden for many users. However, the explanation to a user of one odd feature in one catalogue does not prepare him or her for the next feature or the next catalogue.

As important as making design improvements in online catalogues is at this time it must be recognized that each online catalogue will likely continue to present its own set of instructional problems with which public services librarians must somehow struggle.

There were limitations imposed by the study process itself that point to areas of difficulty in the way library public services staffs perceive the challenge of online catalogue user education and thus approach programme planning. Our experience and training as librarians has led us to view the online catalogue and its use in isolation from other information retrieval developments both within and beyond the scope of libraries."

Focusing only on online catalogue training may result in narrow programme planning. In this research project, we developed a model programme which demonstrated positive results in subjects' performance on tests of online catalogue knowledge. However, there are clear indications that instructional development which embodies objectives for generalized information retrieval may be a more appropriate teaching ideal.

As a new and very important tool, the online catalogue is the focus of a great deal of attention from public services staffs, but this concentration of attention should not necessarily lead to building programmes around the teaching of a single tool alone. Users are, on the whole, pleased with the online catalogue, but for them it is but one tool among many and, more to the point, a means to an end rather than an end in itself.

Our focus in the "Educating the Online Catalogue User" project was to develop a model programme for online catalogue instruction. In seeking a cognitive model or metaphor upon which to base instruction, we used the card catalogue because a number of valuable analogies and comparisons could be made. But as we librarians move further in our own thinking about the direction in which online systems are developing, the card catalogue analogies may become less and less appropriate or relevant.

The advances in computer communications make the acquisition of knowledge about information retrieval, broadly conceived, increasingly valuable for any library user. Many libraries provide public OCLC terminals in addition to an online catalogue of local holdings already in place or planned. Online searching of commercially vended bibliographic files is gradually working its way from behind the reference desk out into the room.

As an outcome of the Linked System Project, one may soon expect to provide the searching of remote files directly within the online catalogue interface now provided users. As these systems are introduced, we need to be aware of the more complex training needs such systems may require: building upon our online catalogue training experience may be a useful way to prepare ourselves, our staffs, and our users. But to do this, our conceptualization of what is most usefully conveyed about the online catalogue must be generalized beyond our traditional notions of catalogue teaching.

The online catalogue towards which the teaching would be directed would serve as an example of a particular implementation of general principles but not the only possible implementation. Bringing in another example-such as a general database management system now commonly available even on the microcomputer-would enrich the instruction. Such a training approach would be more challenging to students and have the great advantage of providing information that would be useful in other contexts.

This approach relegates to a secondary status many of the pieces of helpful information that may make a particular online catalogue easier to use, but we feel a broader view may gain both better acceptance by patrons in general and better trans-ferability to other systems. Overcoming the sense of insecurity that this situation may bring will perhaps be difficult at first, but as risks are taken, the rewards may reinforce the new approach suggested here.

16

Establishment of Library Services: Statement and Project

STATEMENT OF THE PROBLEM

The Emuhaya Constituency Strategic Development Plan 2008-2018, the general trend in education in the constituency has been declining. Among the reasons cited for this negative trend are inadequate learning and teaching resources. Among these inadequate resources are libraries and even the books themselves, where libraries do not exist. Schools and entire community of Emuhaya constituency have a serious shortage of reading materials. Most of the schools in the constituency are day schools with small or no libraries.

Yet the students in these schools are expected to compete with their counterparts in national and provincial schools well endowed with library facilities. Consequently, the performance of students in final exams like KCSE and KCPE has consistently been compromised by the continued lack of adequate information resources in form of books, past examination papers and other pertinent information materials. In addition, even the rest of the community members in the larger parts of the constituency do not have resource centres where they can access information and benefit from the poor of information. This has in turn contributed to the deterioration of the reading culture.

PROJECT SIGNIFICANCE

Establishment of community libraries in the constituency will make tremendous contributions to boosting education and literacy levels in the constituency. First the project will complement school efforts in providing learning materials to school-going generation.

This will address the strain the pupils have to go through to access any useful materials for referral for their studies. By providing an alternative channel for accessing literature for educational and academic work, the libraries will reduce the stress imposed on schools and provide the school going youths and children opportunities to access libraries even if they are day scholars. Secondly, provision of resource materials like newspapers, storybooks and novels and economic-based materials like farming literature and literature on socio-econo-political issues like HIV & AIDS, drug abuse and sexual harassment will be useful to the community. This will boost the knowledge base of the community and reduce levels of ignorance by exposing community to information. Thirdly, the rate of unemployment in Emuhaya constituency is as high as in most parts of the country.

Consequently, idleness resulting from this unemployment drives most youth into crime and immoral behaviour. The libraries will provide an avenue where youths can engage in constructive readership initiatives that will reduce idleness hence improve security. Fourth, community libraries can serve as centres for dissemination of important information from government, NGOs and development partners. By making the library a central repository, dissemination of information from development agencies and government becomes easy to administer and control. Fifth, with the government's effort to establish Information Centres and Digital villages country-wide, the community libraries can offer an ample place to set up an information centre or establish a digital village. Sixth, under the Africana section of the library, the libraries can be excellent points to collect all artifacts and other literatures that preserve the culture of Banyore people.

PROJECT OBJECTIVES

- To provide educational textbooks that can be accessed by secondary and primary school pupils to support their education activities.
- To ensure students who do not have libraries in their home areas have alternative source of information to facilitate studies during holidays or weekends for those in day schools and primary schools.
- Provide materials relevant to the general community – non-school going members- on economic, social and political issues to improve knowledge base and awareness of the people.
- Provide fictional materials for general readership to promote reading culture and control idleness amongst the unemployed youth.
- Keep and provide relevant audio-visual materials on important aspects of socio-economic and political development that can be used for education of the community.
- Provide both in-house and outdoor reader services to students and community in general.
- Ensure availability of relevant information materials-textbooks, general monographs and journals to the users.

IMPLEMENTATION STRATEGIES

LOCATION

The target of the initiative is to have a community library in every sub-location. However for a start, the libraries will be establish in each of the eight locations. This translates to 8 libraries for a start before cascading the project to sub-location level subject to availability of funds. The project will first roll out a pilot project of one library in West Bunyore Location, which is among worst hit locations in terms of inadequacy in education resources. This pilot will then provide insights on how to roll-out and manage subsequent libraries in the constituency.

IMPLEMENTATION APPROACH

It is recommended that for cost effectiveness and ease of security, the libraries be set up at selected secondary or primary schools where library facilities can be constructed. The library once set up in the school will then be open to the community in the location where the school is based, subject to agreed terms with the hosting school. Use of the library facility will be free for individual members. However for institutional registration, an agreeable administrative fee may be levied for sustainability. During implementation, the CDF office and the CLPB shall source for reputable persons or firms to support both technical and professional aspects of the project. Individual consultants or consultant firms in library management could be sought to inject professionalism in the implementation of the project especially on collection development, management and marketing strategies.

RECOMMENDED LIBRARY COLLECTION

- Textbooks-approved by K.*I.E.*
- Higher education and tertiary texts.
- General readership texts and story books.
- Children books-texts and story books.
- Journals and other periodicals.
- Past papers from other schools and KNEC.
- Audio visual materials.
- Artifacts – especially representing the Banyore culture and various Kenyan communities.

SOURCING FOR INFORMATION MATERIALS

- Direct purchase of relevant texts, especially school texts approved by K.*I.E.*
- Donations from Kenya National Library Service.
- Donations from Ministry of Education.
- Donations from NGOs like Children International and Centre for Literacy Development.
- Donation from Private corporate companies and civil society groups.
- Donations from International agencies like CODE and Book Aid International.
- Donations from teaching institutions-universities and polytechnics.

- Donations from individuals within the community.
- Collaborative initiatives from benefiting schools – joint requisitions.

PROJECT MANAGEMENT

ADMINISTRATION

The project shall be managed by a Community Libraries Project Board (CLPB) appointed by the area MP in conjunction with CDF Committee and reporting to the Constituency Development Office. Every library shall have a designate staff employed and remunerated by the Constituency Development office out of the budgetary allocation for the library.

Where a school is hosting the library, the host school will have discretionary powers in regard to overall security and safety of the library and the school may use some of its human capital to support aspects like cleanliness to complete those of designate library manager. The project team shall from time to time seek opinion from professional experts in Library management at Kenya National Library Services and private consultants with regard to management of the community libraries.

FINANCIAL MANAGEMENT

All financial management for the community libraries shall be controlled by the Constituency Development Fund (CDF) office and overseen by the CLPB. This is because the CDF office has necessary personnel, systems and experience in managing community projects. All payments to contractors, consultants and staff shall be made by the CDF office as per the existing systems of payment. All necessary structures, systems and documents for financial expenditure shall be put in place and monitored by the CDF office. The Librarian shall be trained appropriately on financial management aspects, especially where petty cash may have to be utilised.

FUNDING NEEDS

The project will require some funding to:

- Set up the library rooms.
- Set up the library layout, arrange and describe materials, *i.e.,* source for consultant.
- Compensation of Library staff.

BUDGETARY ESTIMATES

The budget indicated here-i-under is the initial costs required to set up one library.

Important Notes to the budget estimates:

- The budget is drawn on assumption that there shall be found an available space at any of the local secondary schools which can be converted into a library.

- Incentives for use of such space for the school shall be waiver of any administrative fees applied to institutional membership for sustainability.
- The costs for wages, security and recurrent costs have been calculated for a period of 2 years.
- The books budget for are initial stock required to start up the library service and that subsequent collections shall be solicited from donations and gifts. Further funding shall be sort for restocking form the CDF kitty.

Description	Quantity	Unit Cost	Total
Books	-	-	1,000,000.00
Renovation of Building	1		1,500,000.00
Furnishing (chairs, tables, shelves, burglar proofing)			800,000.00
Wages for Librarians	2	10,000.00 pm	480,000.00
Security	2	5,000.00 pm	240,000.00
Recurrent Costs – lighting			50,000.00
Miscellaneous			100,000.00
TOTAL			4,170,000.00

Summary

Total costs for 1 library = Kshs. 4,170,000.00

Available funds = nil

Total funding required for eight libraries in the eight locations will be Kshs. 33,36,000.00

PROJECT MONITORING AND EVALUATION

The Constituency Development Office in collaboration with the CLPB shall provide objective monitoring and evaluation of the project to ensure that the project serves the objectives for which it has been setup. This should also be done in line with the Strategic development Plan for the Constituency.

PROJECT SUSTAINABILITY

In order to ensure that the projects are sustained for longer periods, it is anticipated that:

- There shall be continuous efforts by the Constituency Development Office to lobby and solicit more financial and material support.
- All benefiting schools will make subsidised contributions towards sustenance of the libraries.
- The Constituency Development Fund shall make some allocations of the CDF annual budget towards sustaining the libraries as part of its budget on education in the constituency.

- The CLPB shall continue to lobby the surrounding community, in conjunction with the provincial administration, to attract support from the community.

FUTURE PLANS

The libraries would be automated and also be used as digital villages to facilitate diffusion of ICT knowledge in the community and exposure to Internet. The GOK is facilitating availability of sufficient bandwidth which should be harnessed. GOK can easily fund this process through Ministry of Information. The constituency can also source for donors on this plan.

17

Information Retrieval in Digital Libraries: Bringing Search to the Net

INTRODUCTION

The explosion of literature in the form of micro documents on the one hand and the growing number of users demanding more specialised literature/ information on the other hand have led to information scientists to develop an efficient information retrieval systems for the realisation of retrieval suspend on advances in technology and its associated techniques. Database creation of the library resources and the sophistication in indexing techniques has eased the problems of storing and handling of large volumes of data. At the best, it enhanced the retrieval of the items.

Therefore, the focus of the information scientist for the recent past few decades is on the design and development of more powerful information search and retrieval systems.

INFORMATION SYSTEMS

Computer based information system is categorised into:

- Information Storage and Retrieval systems.
- Database Management systems.
- Management Information Systems.
- Decision support systems.

All these systems exhibit similarities to some extent in the area of information processing but differ in their functionalities.

OBJECTIVES OF THE INFORMATION RETRIEVAL SYSTEM

M.L. Pao, "user's input is an important consideration to be incorporated in setting the overall objective of the system for service point of view", as follows:

- Information content of information resources collected.
- Utility of information resources.
- Users.
- Documentary resources.

- Performance resources.
- Economics.

Information retrieval (IR) is the main purpose of any library. The librarian is a nodal point in the IR process and in the traditional library.

INFORMATION SEARCH AND RETRIEVAL IN DIGITAL LIBRARIES

Information search and retrieval of an object from digital library software is a vital feature of the system. The search enables quick retrieval of information. Search services help users to select relevant information from digital library. Digital library's service provides fast access to exact information which is looking for. The success of a search service in digital library relies on the implementation of a powerful retrieval engine and a flexible user interface for metadata support. The Search interface allows users to do "across database" searching without having to modify a query. Search service also covers searching beyond text to multiple media formats, including images, sound and video.

The retrieval formats should be flexible and should provide users to manipulate the search process and results by retrieving search history, adjusting search strategies, editing and sorting search results and choosing preferable delivery formats. Users should also be able to get statistical analysis of the searches they have carried out. Many digital libraries provide different search options to users based on the metadata fields along with the facilities for federated search across a number of digital libraries.

Most digital libraries offer search by Boolean operator, keyword, and phrase and field searches. In the case of information retrieval, evaluation is often focused on the effectiveness of a result set in a specific search. Browsing and searching are two major paradigms for exploring digital libraries. Boolean, proximity and truncation searching are commonly used in digital libraries. They are often provided as separate services. Searching is popular because it is useful when appropriate search keyword are unavailable to users. Table presents the difference between data retrieval and information retrieval.

Table: Data Retrieval vs. Information Retrieval.

	Data Retrieval (DR)	Information Retrieval (IR)
Matching	Exact match	Partial match, best match
Inference	Deduction	Induction
Model	Deterministic	Probabilistic
Classification	Monothetic	Polythetic
Query language	Artificial	Natural
Query specification	Complete	Incomplete
Items wanted	Matching	Relevant
Error response	Sensitive	Insensitive

The use of Information Retrieval is motivated by an information need. This information need can be explicitly or implicitly verbalised. In a 'real world' setting the person seeking information (*i.e.*, the user) formulates such a question and poses it to an expert. The expert calls upon his internal representation of the knowledge space and external documents and formulates answers. From the answers received the user extracts relevant points and gives feedback to the expert. This "conversational loop" can also be found in the use of an Information Retrieval System (IRS).

As the IRS is not capable to understand the information need, thus, an abstraction matching in the IRS is needed. This abstraction is called query. Analogously to the expert, the IRS formulates an answer based upon the internal representation of the knowledge space and external documents. The answer is composed of documents perceived relevant or links to such documents. The user extracts those documents that are indeed relevant.

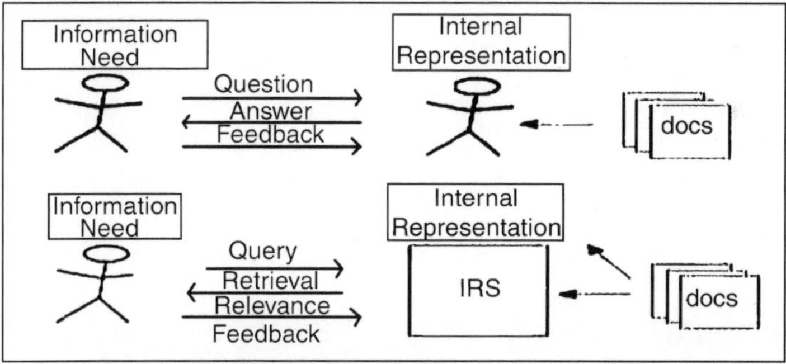

Fig. Conversational Loop.

In some systems relevance feedback can be given. These two forms of the conversational loop are detailed in figure.

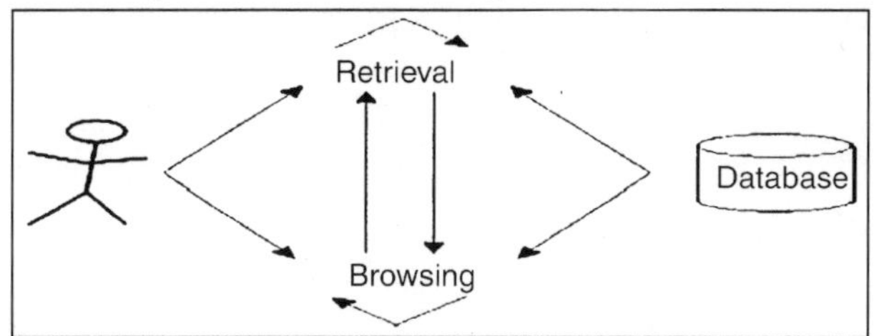

Fig. Interaction with the Retrieval System through Different Tasks.

RETRIEVAL VS. BROWSING

The sequence of action taken to satisfy the information need is called retrieval or searching. Retrieval is used in the case of an explicit information need. The explicit need can be formulated into a query. Searching usually results in lists of results. Sometimes the information need is non-explicit and no query can be formulated. In this case the information need can be satisfied by browsing through the documents of a collection. Browsing is also necessary to find relevant documents from the results of a retrieval process.

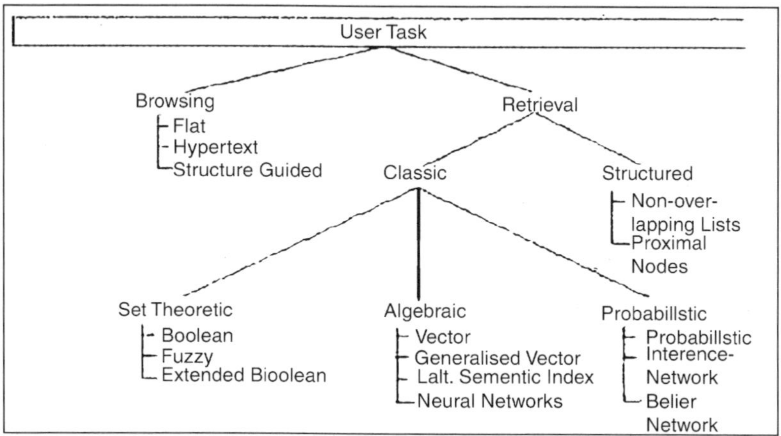

Fig. A Taxonomy of Information Retrieval Models.

Figure illustrates the relation of these two concepts. Both actions are pulling actions interpreting to the user makes request of information interactively. Searching for information in such a manner is called *ad hoc* searching. Alternatively the information may be provided in an automatic and permanent fashion for information by the user. This is called information push and is used in the case of a varying document collection and an unchanging information need.

In the same context as information push, filtering can be applied. Again the document collection is varying while the information need stays the same, but in contrast information push is an active task of the user, while in the case of filtering the information is passively provided by software agents or the like. Browsing can be discerned into flat browsing, structure guided browsing and hypertext browsing. In the case of "flat browsing" the document collection is organised in a flat structure, like a list of search results. The term "structure guided" browsing describes the browsing of collections in structured and hierarchical manner.

The "king" of browsing allowing the highest flexibility is "hypertext browsing". In this case, documents are multiplied connected by hyperlinks. The Information Retrieval Model (IRM) needs introduction to the digital library for describing relevancy in the search results. Such a model describes the fundamental premises forming the basis for a ranking. Over the years, different IRM have been proposed.

The following parts will give an overview of those models which are relevant in the later part of this chapter. In order to build a model, a representation for the documents and its need for the users have to be found. These representations lead to the framework in which they can be modeled. For example, in the vector space model, the framework is composed of a tdimensional vector space and standard linear algebra operations on vectors. In text based IR the information need and the documents are represented with words. In case of the documents these are called index terms. An index term is a word whose semantics matches the document's main themes. These index terms vary in relevance, as the more frequent words in the document collection are less relevant for the retrieval process.

Boolean Model

This simple retrieval model, which was adopted by many early commercial bibliographic systems, is based on set theory and Boolean algebra. The advantages are the intuitiveness of the concept of a set and the precise semantics of Boolean expressions, which form the queries. The major drawback of the model is that the retrieval is based on a binary decision leaving relevancy of the search result.

Moreover it is often not simple to translate an information need into a Boolean expression. In this model, index terms are either considered present or absent in a document, resulting in binary weights. Due to this binary value for relevancy, no partial match to the query is defined. So, if a document includes only one index term it is considered not relevant. As a result, the Boolean model often retrieves very less or too many documents.

Vector Model

The vector model heeds the fact that the use of binary weights is limiting and proposes a framework that allows a partial match. Non- binary term weights are used to compute a degree of similarity. The resulting set of documents retrieved is returned in decreasing order of this degree of similarity.

Though various term weighting techniques exist, only the main idea of the most effective techniques shall be discussed. The basic idea is to separate a document collection into two parts to satisfy the information need. One of the parts is composed of the objects related to the information need while the other is not. To accomplish this separation clustering techniques are utilised. Two sets of features are used to discern sets of related elements from those that are not. The first set of features describes the intra-cluster similarity while the second describes inter-cluster dissimilarity. The improved retrieval performance resulting from the term-weighting scheme is one of the main advantages of the vector model. The second main advantage is the partial matching strategy and the fact that the cosine ranking function sorts the documents according to the degree of similarity to the query. Efficient implementations for the vector model are possible.

Finally, the vector model allows easy relevance feedback. Disadvantages of the vector model include the fact that the term "independency" is not fully given. In fact, real term independency might hurt the retrieval process. Moreover, syntactic information remains unconsidered.

Generalised Vector Space Model

The term "independence" in the classic vector space model is addressed by the generalised vector space model. The independence is interpreted as pair-wise orthogonality among the index term vectors that forms the vector space. Wong *et al.*, proposed an alternate view which leads to the generalised vector space model. In this model, the index term vectors are assumed linearly independent but are not pair wise orthogonal. As such, they are not as like in the classic vector space model where the vectors compose the basis of the space.

They are composed of smaller components derived from the collection. These pair wise orthogonal so called min-term vectors compose the bases of the space. The main advantage of the generalised vector space model is the dependence of the index term. However, this dependence is still a controversial issue. Thus, the advantage of the generalised vector space model in practical situations is not yet proved. The main drawback is the high cost of computation due to the fact that the number of min-terms might be proportional to the number of documents in the collection.

Probabilistic Model

The third of the classic IR models, the probabilistic model, attempts to capture the IR problem within a probabilistic framework. To that end, a set of documents is defined for each user query, which contains only the relevant documents. This set is referred to as the ideal answer set. If the properties of this ideal answer would be known, the documents could be retrieved. The querying process can be described as the process of specifying these initially unknown properties.

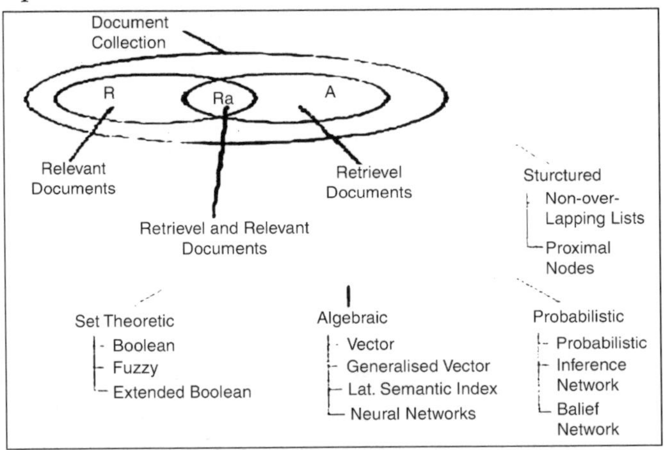

Fig. Precision and Recall for a Given Example Information Request.

The main advantage of the probabilistic model is the ranking by the probability to be relevant. The main disadvantages include the need to guess the initial separation into relevant and non-relevant documents. Moreover, the weights for the index terms are binary. Finally, as in the classic vector space model, the index terms are assumed to be independent. Although experiment exist which show better performance of the probabilistic model when compared to the vector space model, it can be expected that it is outperformed by the latter with general collections.

INFORMATION RETRIEVAL CONCEPTS IN DIGITAL LIBRARIES

Digital libraries rely on effective retrieval methods with easy access to the information. Thus, the success of digital libraries is depends on the quality of retrieval. Research in the IR has traditionally been important in the research pertaining to the digital libraries. One important topic in this context is the search in distributed collections.

As the document collection is managed by different organisational units or even the document collections of different digital libraries are used, the interfaces and functionality of these systems are supposedly inhomogeneous. Gutl part of the difficulties in this context are the variable IR methods and interfaces, like representation and relevance ranking, as well as the scope of the search results.

Another difficulty is the merging of the individual results and the inter-system ranking. The second important topic in this context is the multimedia content in document collection. Baeza-Yates *et al.*, states the need for suiting query languages for different media, like a visual query for image search. In a multimedia environment, the task is even more complex, as the combined search in different media, as Gutl points out.

BROWSING FEATURES

The browsing feature is important for retrieval of neither information that is nor already known in part. Browsing enables people to look through a digital library and discover things that they had no previous knowledge of.

Users should be able to browse digital objects by:

- Author/ Creator/ Contributor.
- Title of the document/ article/ book.
- Issue Date/ Date of Publication.
- Collection.
- Communities.
- Subject browsing.
- Publisher wise browsing.
- Table of contents browsing.
- Multi-dimensional browsing.

SEARCHING FEATURES

Searching in any digital library is one of the important aspects. Hence, it is necessary to know what type of search features are supported by the software.

While, evaluating the software it is necessary to do functional testing of the software, i.e., determining the extent to which a digital library, in whole or in part, is able to perform desired operations.

- Full text searching.
- Boolean (AND, OR, NOT) searching.
- Basic Search.
- Advanced search.
- Truncation/Wild card searching.
- Exact words/phrases searching.
- Proximity searching.
- Stemming search.
- Fuzzy search.
- Phonetic search.
- Case sensitive.
- Case insensitive.
- Boosting the term.
- Range searching.
- Expand search.
- Lateral search.
- Multilingual search.
- Refine search.

QUALITY OF SEARCH RESULTS

Generally IR systems have to cope with a vaguely described information need of the user; the results of an IR process are not exactly matches to this information needs, but are ranked by relevance. The evaluation of the precision of this answer is called information retrieval evaluation. Besides, the performance measures generally important for a software system, like response time, space, and the like, this retrieval performance is the key to an IR system.

Information retrieval evaluation is performed by querying a standardised reference collection. These reference collections consist of a set of documents, a set of example information needs, and corresponding sets of relevant documents.

The relevant documents for example information requests are determined by experts. For a given retrieval strategy, the documents retrieved are compared to the set of relevant documents determined by experts. The similarity between these two sets is quantified by the test collection's evaluation measure and leads to the goodness of the tested retrieval strategy.

RECALL AND PRECISION

Recall and precision are basic evaluation parameters. The drawback of recall and precision is the fact that the examination of all documents of the answer set is assumed. This, however, is contrary to the usual fact that the user is presented only a part of the retrieved documents, ranked by the degree of relevance. Thus, the recall and precision values vary as the user proceeds through his examination of the retrieved documents.

In order to record this development, a precision versus recall curve is plotted. Usually recall and precision values resulting from averaging various queries are used to compare the performance of IR systems. Such average recall versus precision plots trade the advantage of a better overview on the overall retrieval performance for that fact that single mavericks remain undetected. In various situations, such as, to discover the superiority between the single value summary of the recall and precision plots. One possibility is to calculate the Average Precision at Seen Relevant Documents. To that end the precision figures obtained are averaged after each new relevant document which is observed.

CONCLUSION

Digital libraries present still another new environment for information retrieval, presenting new and different challenges and an expanded research agenda. Some of these challenges arise from the nature of the content in digital libraries, others from the nature of the tasks performed and the characteristics of the users of digital libraries. Like the Web, digital libraries incorporate mixed data types. The data may be structured, semi structured, or unstructured; and incorporate text, images, video, and audio information. Information retrieval from this mix of structure and formats is relatively unstudied, since research has usually been based on an assumption of a homogenous collection, and metadata, where available, has been treated as unstructured text.

How do we incorporate evidence from these multiple sources to create an ordered list? Since digital libraries are by definition often distributed or federated systems, another level of complexity is added by the need to make retrieval from multiple sites and multiple collections transparent to the user. Given multiple sites, we need to give priority for search to sites with the highest probability of success.

Searching on multiple sites leads to a data fusion problem as the system must integrate and rank information from different datasets, with different data and metadata. Furthermore the importance and challenges of distributed document collections have been analysed. Though the Web may appear as a distributed digital library at the first glance, there are numerous differences. Information Retrieval system which presents the basic layer applied in conceptualisation processes and discussed the models of the IR system.

18

Expansion of Web-Based Library Services

INTRODUCTION

The Due to the tremendous growth and continuous development of technology, the role of library becomes more responsive in making the users techno-savvy. Technological developments have affected not only the formats and sources of the information, but also how and where to provide library services. Libraries and their resources have partially moved to the virtual world of the Internet. As a result, library users can access the resources from outside the physical library. In an effort to reach users accessing the library via their computers, many libraries and library consortia are extending their services to include virtual reference.

Technology now allows users to submit their queries to the library at any time from any place in the world. Web Based Services, Digital Library Services, Internet Library Services and Electronic Library Services are terms with similar meanings. As more libraries move towards providing services in a digital environment, the improved access to remote library collections is making the use of electronic information resources more realistic and more attractive.

Traditional online services had transformed themselves into internet-based online services using web-based technologies. From traditional online services to today, four generations of information retrieval tools have passed that assist users in searching the World Wide Web.

The first generation of information retrieval tools was designed for use with bibliographic databases. The first generation provided access to references to the end documents rather than to the documents themselves, and indexing and searching were thus applied to document surrogates, such as titles or abstracts. These tools require considerable human efforts to collect, arrange, code, and annotate the various resources.

A primary benefit of the first generation of tools is providing users with easy browsing capabilities. The second generation of tools attempts to collect and index resources as an automated function. Automatic collection and indexing reduces the amount of human effort. The ability to search through massive amounts of information and locate the desired information for the user is the primary benefit of the second generation of tools. The third generation deals with World Wide Web Meta search engines, such as Harvester and Meta crawler.

The fourth generation involves new ideas such as search agent technology currently being developed to search for information on the web. Web-based search engines are as a means of finding relevant pages on the Internet. Different search engines, directory, meta-search engines, gateways, subject portals, electronic journals and on line databases each type could be used in a different way, from simple keyword searching up to peer reviewed web sites.

WHAT IS WEB BASED LIBRARY SERVICE

A digital Library service manages and develops electronic services, the library web sites and library staff. It can be defined broadly as 'an information access service in which users ask questions via electronic means, *e.g.*, e-mail or web forms'.

WHY WEB BASED LIBRARY SERVICE

Library service on the internet requires many of the same qualities as traditional references: accuracy, promptness, courtesy, an understanding of the information need. It provides users with the convenience of accessing information in their own time, saving them traveling cost and time and new options for answering reference questions.

The provision of these services is not constrained by the traditional opening hours but can be offered on a 24-hour, seven-days-a-week basis known as 24/7.

And while there may be a disadvantage in not having a face-to face encounter, there are many advantages to this new medium and the greatest advantage is that many more users can be helped by using electronic library services. Advantages and disadvantages of electronic access over printed form access are showed in table.

Web based services are established due to the following reasons.

- Ensuring the needs of users and the accessible information sources are suitable matched at all times.
- Delivering those information sources to the user in a timely and appropriate fashion.
- Ensuring the information provided is high quality, accurate and appropriate.
- Assisting the user in interpreting the materials, if necessary.
- Promoting user awareness of new services and information sources as they develop.
- Providing users with individualised guidance and support as they build their information search and application skills.

Table. Advantages and Disavantages of Printed from over Electronic Access.

S.N	Advantages of Print Form	Electronic Form
1.	Format is tested and standardised	Format is in the early stages of development
2.	Easy for users to use	Requires some training for users to use
3.	No special equipment needed	Special equipment required (hardware, software, printers, etc.)
4.	Easy to locate (if shelved properly) problems, internet connection	Access is currently unreliable (URL problems, etc.)
5.	Use is limited only to copyright laws licensing	Use is limited by copyright laws and agreements
6.	Archiving is effective and permanent	Archiving is "up in the air"

Table. Advantages and Disadvantages of Printed Form over Electronic Access.

	Disadvantages of Print Form	Electronic Form
1.	Operating costs are considerable (ordering, cataloging, claiming, and binding)	Operating costs are minimal (no cataloging, binding, or claiming)
2.	Requires shelving	No shelving required
3.	Often mutilated, stolen, or misshelved	Cannot be mutilated, stolen, or misshelved
4.	Requires extensive storage space	Saves considerable storage space
5.	Allows only one user at a time	Allows for multiple users with simultaneous access
6.	Slow delivery via "snail mail"	Immediate receipt of issue
7.	Issues are easily lost in the mail or missing	No more missing issues
8	Slow publication	Fast publication

DIFFERENT RESOURCES FOR WEB BASED LIBRARY SERVICES

Today, users may have access a variety of textual information resources. There are different kinds of webbased reference resources and services for accessing information from libraries such as OPAC, Gateways, Portals, Subject Portals, Electronic Journals, Online Databases, Subject Directories and Search Engines. These resources overlap considerably in the type of information they cover, and sometimes it is difficult to distinguish between some of them.

A library should have a good collection of these resources like selected Web links, subscription resources, and library materials in well-organised pages for serving better services to their users. Many libraries and organisations are providing digital reference service through collaborative services. Existing library consortia are adding digital reference to current shared services, and networks of libraries. Some regional library consortia are offering member libraries the opportunity to share reference questions with each other using the Internet and other technologies.

OPAC

OPAS's - On Line Public Access Catalogues, form an important part of many digital library's collections. It allows users to search for the bibliographic records contained within a library's collections. Now days, some OPAC also provide access to electronic resources and databases, in addition to the traditional bibliographic records.

GATEWAYS

A gateway is defined as a facility that allows easier access to network based resources in a given subject area. Gateways provide a simple search facility and a much-enhanced service through a resource database and indexes, which can be searched through a web based interface. Information provided by gateways is catalogued by hand. Gateways cover a wide range of subjects, through some areas, such as music and religious studies, currently lack subject gateways.

Some well-known gateways are as follows:

- Internet Public Library (IPL),
- Bulletin Board for Libraries (BUBL),
- National Information Services and Systems (NISS),

PORTALS

In the library community, portals may be defined as an amalgamation of services to the users where the amalgamation is achieved through seamless integration of existing services by using binding agents such as customisation and authentication services, search protocols such as Z39.50, loan protocols such as ISO10161, and e-commerce. The result is a personalised service which allows the individual to access the rich content of both print-based and electronic systems. Portals are either commercial or free web facilities that offer information services to a specific audience. The facilities include web search to communication to e-mail to news, etc.

There are three kinds of portals; Consumer (or horizontal), Vertical and Enterprise.

1. Consumer portals are aimed at consumer audiences and offer free e-mail, games, chat, etc. Examples are Yahoo!, MSN and AOL.
2. Vertical portals, target a specified audience, such as a particular industry, and offer many of the consumer portal features. Example includes VerticalNet.
3. Enterprise portals on the other hand are similar to consumer portals, but they are offered only to corporations or similar organisations. Examples include Epicentric and Corporate Yahoo! These portals can be best understood as electronic pathfinders for users, pulling

together in one place in a web site selected links to subjects or interest-oriented resources located on the WWW.

SUBJECT PORTALS

Web Search Engines had been developed initially by computer scientists, by borrowing techniques from information retrieval search such as best match searching and relevance ranking. Information professional are increasing bringing their skills to help organise the growing wealth of Internet resources. A good example of their influence is the development of subject-specific web search engines known as subject portals, where evaluation of material covered is a major concern. Two prime UK subject portals are SOSIG Social Science Information Gateway, covering social science resources and OMNI Organising medical networked information covering medical resources. Subject portal sites can be very helpful, but they should be used with care.

Users should bear the following points in their mind:

- The aim of the subject portal is to list and review the most important sites on the web relevant to that subject. The sites are usually constantly peer-reviewed to ensure that the site is relevant and up to date.
- New sites are appearing all the time. Relying on a subject portal site to find everything users require may mean that they miss an important site that has recently appeared and has not yet been reviewed by the producers of the particular subject portal.
- A subject portal is a one stop shop for information on the topic it covers. Users don't have to carry out extensive Internet searches in order to find the information require. They can simply go to the required subject portal site.
- Subject portals save users having to have long lists of bookmarks (saved addresses of web pages), which are often, cumbersome and time consuming to arrange and keep up to date. However, if users do prefer to use bookmarks they can arrange them in an order to suit the way they work and not have an order forced on them by the subject portal.
- A subject portal site is only as good as the reviewers who peer-review the site listed. The reviewers need to have a policy of keeping the portal sites up to date and of constantly reviewing the sites they list, to make sure that they are still relevant and still contain good, timely information.
- A subject portal may be available to everyone who needs to use it to only certain groups of users. A good portal should be publicly available to anyone who needs it.

ELECTRONIC JOURNALS

Electronic journals form a large part of the collection of a library for providing web based services. Today many journals are available electronically - some are full text and some contain only bibliographic information with abstract. Major advantage of electronic journals is that they are constantly updated and easy to access but disadvantage is that breaching of copyright law is very easy. They are available as bitmaps, PostScript, PDF, ASCII, SGML and HTML. Library services may be delivering to users on CDRom, through e-mail or through web. Some international societies and associations have developed their own digital libraries through which users can get access to all their publications. Services are available to the members of society or associations through subscription.

ONLINE DATABASES

These are large collections of machine-readable data that are maintained by commercial agencies and are accessed through communication lines. Many libraries subscribe to them for easy access and use of current information. The disadvantage is that only bibliographic data is presented and not full text. The information cannot be accessed when the system is down for any reason. Examples Ei Compendex, SciFinder Scholar, Web of Science, Current Contents, etc.

SEARCH ENGINES

Search Engines are huge databases of web page files that have been assembled automatically by machines where as the subject directories are human-compiled and maintained. Search engine indexes every page of a web site and subject directories linked only homepages. Search Engine is the popular term for an information retrieval (IR) system. A search engine is computer software that searches a collection of electronic materials to retrieve citations, documents, or information that matches or answers a user's query. The retrieved materials may be text documents, facts that have been extracted from text, images, or sounds. A query is a question phrased so that it can be interpreted properly by search engine. Depending on the type of software, it may be a collection of commands, a statement in either full or partial sentences, one or more keywords, or in the case of non-text searching, an image or sequence of sounds to be matched.

SUBJECT DIRECTORIES

Subject directories differ from search engines in that search engines are populated by robots that finds and index sites whereas humans making editorial decisions that populate subject directories. Subject directories are basically index home pages of sites and can be classified as general, academic, commercial or portal. Among the well known subject directories are the Argus Clearinghouse and Yahoo. Strengths include relevance, effectiveness and relative high quality of content. Weaknesses are that they lack depth in their coverage of the subjects.

NEW WEB BASED LIBRARY SERVICES

VIRTUAL LIBRARY TOURS

Web sites of libraries provides virtual library guide to the physical facilities including collections, services and infrastructure available in the library. The combination of library maps and floor plans, library departments and photographic views are used for the tour. Virtual library tours are also using new technologies such as QuickTime movies etc and are beginning to replace image maps on main campus Web sites.

ASK-A-LIBRARIAN

Ask-A-Librarian services are Internet-based question and answer service that connects users with individuals who possess specialised subject knowledge and skill in conducting precision searches. Most "Ask-a-Librarians" services have a web-based question submission form or an e-mail address or both. Users are invited to submit their queries by using web forms or through e-mail. Once a query is read by a service, it is assigned to an individual expert for answering.

An expert responds to the query with factual information and or a list of information resources. The response is either sent to the user's e-mail account or is posted on the web so that the user can access it after a certain period of time. Many services have informative web sites that include archives of questions and answers and a set of FAQs. Users are usually encouraged to browse archives and FAQs before submitting a question in case sufficient information already exists.

REAL TIME SERVICES

A new and exciting method of digital reference service that libraries are attempting to provide more and more now is live reference. These are real-time, interactive reference services in which the users can talk to a real, live reference librarian at any time, from anywhere in the world. User and librarian can interact using chat technologies, and unlike with e-mail reference the librarian can perform a reference interview of sorts by asking the users to elaborate or clarify if needed before proceeding to answer the question. The librarian can perform Internet searches and push web sites onto the user's browser, and can receive immediate feedback from the users as to whether their question have been answered to satisfaction.

BULLETIN BOARDS

A bulletin board is an electronic communications forum that hosts posted messages and articles connected to a common subject or theme or interest. It allows users to call in and either leaves or retrieves messages. The messages may be directed to all users of the bulletin board or only to particular users. But all messages can be read by all users. Several libraries are using bulletin boards for their web-based library services. The bulletin board system is also used as an interactive interface to invite suggestions on activities and services of a library. It can also be used as an interface to distribute library services.

WEB-BASED USER EDUCATION

Web guides and teaching tools are found everywhere on the Web because they are easily updated, accessed, and printed on demand. The web-based user education provides a high degree of interactivity and flexibility to the users. The library web sites can use web-based user education for imparting training to users in teaching the basic library skills along with glossary of library terms, using Library OPAC, locating books, magazines, biographical data and other library materials, understanding how to navigate the libraries web site and how to select the most relevant database, instructions for searching CD ROM and guidance in locating web-based databases and other electronic resources and instructions on subject searching training, using Boolean operators and searching internet resources through search engines.

WEB FORMS

Library web sites have some web forms for suggestions and comments on the Library Services. Different types of Web Forms are available on web that may be an Indent form for acquiring some publications, interlibrary loan request form for document delivery, Ask-a-Librarian forms, on line reservation form or user survey form, etc.

INDIAN SCENARIO

The Indian libraries also have realised to give web based services to users and they have recognised that working together can accomplish for more than they can do individually. Many Indian libraries in India are not geared up for accessing e-journals due to various reasons including user ignorance, infrastructure and initial funds.

The library and information networks in India were initiated in early eighties. The growth during this period can be linked to some of the policies that Government of India pursued. Some institutions like CSIR, ISRO, DRDO, DAE, ICAR, SIRNET, NICNET, NISSAT, INFLIBNET, MHRD and IIM libraries are actively working continuously to improve the present situation.

They spend annually a huge amount of money towards library acquisition, especially towards journals, e-journals and e-databases. Some initiative include, Indian Institute of Management for accessing bibliographic databases, CSIR laboratories for Science Direct, FORSA for accessing Astronomy and Astrophysics journals, Hyderabad Knowledge park members of J-gate, INFLIBNET (UGC–INFONET) initiative for full text and databases like BIOSIS and CAS and INDEST for a host of full text sources and few bibliographic databases for the benefit of IITs, IISc, NITs and Engineering colleges. In India, library consortia are emerging as one of the important service to users. The Indian consortiums will help the library to provide better services to the users by investing meagre amount. To expand the access for more number of e-journals, e-books and other resources, we have to develop the digital library infrastructure as a platform for e-learning.

THE FUTURE OF WEB BASED SERVICES

Library Web services will continue to spread out, offering more full-text electronic journals and indexes that do not now include full text will begin to do so, or link to external resources. Bibliographic access to full-text periodicals either through cataloging, databases, or vendors will be in improved form. There will be more Web forms for user feedback, and perhaps a virtual librarian who interacts in real time chat or video conferencing. More Document delivery services to distance education or users and Savings on Interlibrary Loan and user convenience are incentives.

Information resources through creative consortia purchasing will be popular. A well-developed user education modules or tutorials, especially to support independent exploration of library and Web resources. Somebody will have to figure out how to keep Word users from saving print documents as XML, without thinking in terms of Web, not print, space. XML will be embraced as a way to control page appearance and behaviour, but it will take a while for people to figure out how to use it well and there will be trends we haven't thought of yet...

WEB PUBLISHING: GETTING STARTED

WEB PUBLISHING

The Oracle's Hyperion® Data Relationship Management Web Publishing module provides an auxiliary means of accessing Data Relationship Management system functionality.

This application provides the following capabilities through a Web browser interface:

- Viewing hierarchies and node properties.
- Running exports.
- Printing hierarchy trees.
- Searching for nodes in a given hierarchy.

Data Relationship Management Web Publishing connects to the Data Relationship Management application server, but operates in a read-only mode. Various requests can be made using HTTP to either retrieve information or execute a command such as running exports or reloading from the database. Figure provides a top-level view of Data Relationship Management Web Publishing in relation to the Data Relationship Management architecture. Web Publishing can be run on its own server or hosted on the Data Relationship Management multi-tier Web Server or the primary application server.

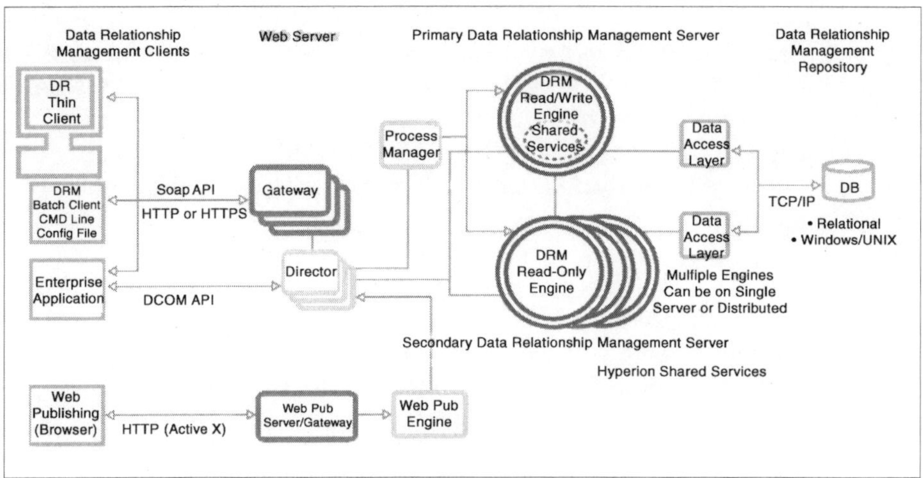

Fig. Data Relationship Management Web Publishing Architecture.

SYSTEM REQUIREMENTS

The following topics describe the Data Relationship Management Web Publishing system requirements for the Web server and the client computers.

Web Server Requirements:

- Windows 2000 Server or Windows Server 2003.
- Internet Information Services (IIS) version 5 or later.
- Microsoft Data Access Components (MDAC) 2.7 or later (required only for MS SQL.)

Client Computer Requirements:

- Windows 2000 or later (ME, 2000, XP, Server 2003)
- Internet Explorer version 5 or later.

INSTALLING, CONFIGURING, AND UNINSTALLING

PRE-INSTALLATION TASKS

The following topics describe tasks that must be performed before you can install and use Data Relationship Management Web Publishing.

System Administrator Tasks

Your Data Relationship Management system administrator must complete the following tasks before you can install and use Data Relationship Management Web Publishing:

- Ensure that the Data Relationship Management system Release 9.3 is currently installed and operational.
- Create a new Data Relationship Management user name specifically for accessing Data Relationship Management Web Publishing (for example: mdm_Web). Assign the desired access rights to the user.

- Since the engine needs access to all paths that might be used for exports, provide a list of these paths to the network administrator. The system preference WebExDir controls the directory root for file storage location on the Web Publishing server.
- Configure the appropriate Data Relationship Management system preferences related to Data Relationship Management Web Publishing.

Network Administrator Tasks

Your network administrator must complete the following tasks before you can install and use Data Relationship Management Web Publishing:

- Create a new network user/application id that the Engine can use to login to the system. This id should have full access rights (including file creation) to any network shares that are designated for Data Relationship Management exports.
- Verify that IE browser policies allow for the use of digitally-signed ActiveX controls. While most Data Relationship Management Web Publishing implementations provide for browser access, some may be used strictly for automating exports. Configuring the browser can be skipped if interactive access is not desired.

General Tasks

In addition to system administrator and network administrator tasks described in the preceding topics, the following tasks must be performed before you can install and use Data Relationship Management Web Publishing:

- You must manually uninstall prior versions of Data Relationship Management Web Publishing before installing Data Relationship Management Web Publishing Release 9.3.
- Ensure that the intended host machine(s) meet or exceed the minimum system requirements defined in this document.
- Ensure that the user performing the installation has administrative rights to the Web server machine.
- Ensure that the Data Relationship Management Web Publishing release package is available.

INSTALLING DATA RELATIONSHIP MANAGEMENT WEB PUBLISHING

To install Data Relationship Management Web Publishing:

- Do one of these tasks:
  - If you have a Data Relationship Management Web Publishing CD or DVD, insert the CD or DVD into your CD or DVD drive.
  - If you downloaded the Data Relationship Management Web Publishing software from the Download Center:

  a. Navigate to the directory where you downloaded the installation programme.

b. Select File > Run or Start > Run and enter Drive:\Folder \mdm_web_pub_server_setup.exe, where *Drive* and *Folder* are the installation programme location.

- Review the Welcome box and click Next.
- Read the license agreement, select I AGREE and click Next.
- From Web Publishing Installation Options, do one of the following:
  - Click Next if the computer where you are installing Data Relationship Management Web Publishing is also a Data Relationship Management Web server.
  - Select Ntier Director if Data Relationship Management Web Publishing is being added to a computer that is not a Data Relationship Management Web server or if it is a standalone server, and click Next.
- Click Next to accept the default installation directory, or click Change to select another directory, and click Next.
- Do one of the following:
  - If you are installing Ntier Director, continue with the next step.
  - If you are not installing Ntier Director, continue with step 8.
- Enter the machine name or IP address of the Data Relationship Management primary application server and click Next.
- From Windows COM+ Logon, enter a user name and password for a user who has rights to perform the following actions and click Next:
  - Edit registry settings
  - Read and write to the local file system
  - Launch processes
  - Run as a service
- Click Install.
- Optional: After installation completes, you can select Launch Data Relationship Management Web Publishing Console.
- Click Finish.

MANUALLY CONFIGURING DATA RELATIONSHIP MANAGEMENT WEB PUBLISHING

Configuration must be completed for the following:

- Data Relationship Management Web Publishing Service
- IIS Virtual Directory/Pool Configuration
- Data Relationship Management Web Publishing Engine
- When installing on a stand-alone server: COM+ Director and Process Manager Proxy Components

Configuring Data Relationship Management Web Publishing Service

To configure the service:

- Select Start > Programmes > Administrative Tools > Services.

- Select the Hyperion Data Relationship Management Web Publishing service.
- Right-click the service and select Properties.
- On the General tab, ensure that Startup Type is set to Automatic.
- On the Log On tab, select This Account.
- Enter a username and password for a Windows administrative user..
- Click OK.
- Close the Services dialog box.

Configuring Internet Information Services

For IIS 5.0:

- Select Start > Programmes > Administrative Tools > Internet Services Manager (or Internet Information Services (IIS) Manager).
- Expand to the default Web site.
- Select the mdm_web virtual directory.
- Right-click and select Properties.
- On the Virtual Directory tab, verify the following:
  - The Local Path is pointing to the Data Relationship Management Web directory.
  - The Read option is selected.
  - Execute Permissions is set to Scripts and Executables.
  - The Application Protection is set to High (Isolated). Selecting this option enables you to unload the mdm_web application without restarting IIS.
- On the Directory Security tab, enable and configure anonymous access.
- Click OK.
- Click OK.
- Close the IIS Manager.

For IIS 6.0 or later:

- Select Start > Programmes > Administrative Tools > Internet Services Manager (or Internet Information Services (IIS) Manager).
- Expand to the default Web site.
- Select the mdm_web virtual directory.
- Right-click and select Properties.
- On the Virtual Directory tab, verify the following:
  - The Local Path is pointing to the Data Relationship Management Web directory.
  - The Read option is selected.
  - Execute Permissions is set to Scripts and Executables.
  - Application Pool is WebPool. This setting enables you to unload the mdm_web application without restarting IIS.
- Click OK.
- Select the Web Service Extensions node and select Active Server Pages from the list of Web Service Extensions on the right.
- Verify that the Status column displays the status Allowed.

- Create a new Web service extension named mdm_web_pub_gateway that points to mdm_web_pub_gateway.dll and is set to Allowed.
- Close the IIS Manager.

Verifying System Access

To verify system access:

- At the prompt, select to install the mdm_web_client ActiveX control: This digitally signed control is safe to install. If you are not prompted to install the component, then it may be necessary to adjust the current browser settings to allow download and installation of ActiveX controls.
- Click OK: The Data Relationship Management Web Client page is displayed. No data (versions or hierarchies) is displayed until the service is started at the end of the installation/configuration/ startup process.

Configuring Data Relationship Management Web Publishing Engine

To configure the Web Publishing Engine:

- Select Start > Administrative Tools > Component Services.
- Expand the Component Services node to the DCOM Config folder.
- In the DCOM Config folder, select the mdm_Web_Pub_Engine object, right-click and select Properties.
- For Windows 2000 only: From a command line prompt, type: dcomcnfg.
  - In the list of applications, select the mdm_Web_Pub_Engine object and click Properties.
  - On the General tab, set Authentication Level to None.
- On the Identity tab, select This User and enter the same user and password that were configured for the Data Relationship Management Web Publishing Service.
- On the Security tab, under Launch and Activation Permissions, select Customise and click Edit.
- Add the user that is configured for IIS anonymous access to the mdm_web virtual directory.
- Allow Local Activation for this user.
- Repeat this process for the Access Permissions section, by selecting Customise > Edit, and adding the same user and enabling the Local Access permission.
- Click OK to close the Properties dialog box.

Configuring Director

If you install on a stand-alone server where Director does not already exist, you must configure the COM+ Director component.

To configure the COM+ Director component:

- Select Start > Programmes > Administrative Tools > Component Services.

- Drill down and select the Director component.
- Right-click and select Properties.
- On the Security tab, verify that Enforce Access Checks for this Application is not selected.
- On the Identity tab, verify that the appropriate user is setup and then close the Properties dialog box.
- Drill down to the Components folder of Director.
- Select all components by pressing CTRL-A, then right-click and select Properties.
- Verify that Enable Object Pooling is selected on the Activation tab and then close the Properties dialog box.
- Close the Component Services window.

Configuring Process Manager

If you install on a stand-alone server where Process Manager does not already exist, you must configure the COM+ Process Manager Proxy component.

To configure the COM+ Process Manager Proxy component:

- Select Start > Programmes > Administrative Tools > Component Services.
- Drill down and select the Process Manager component.
- Right-click the component and select Properties.
- On the Activation tab, verify that the remote server is correct.
- Close the Component Services window.

USING THE DATA RELATIONSHIP MANAGEMENT WEB PUBLISHING CONSOLE

The Data Relationship Management Web Publishing Console is designed to allow configuration, control and monitoring of the Web Publishing system. The Server Monitor Page allows the Web Publishing Service to be controlled (Start, Stop, Restart, Force Shutdown) and displays the current status of the service.

In addition there are three tabs for further information:

- System Status.
- Event Log.
- Web Server.

The System Status tab shows some basic operating system information as well as information on COM+ and DCOM (Out of Process) applications. Currently Web Publishing does not use any COM+ so this section is blank.

The Event Log tab filters the application event log to show events for the Web Publishing module. Clicking on an event in the top panel shows the detail for the event in the lower panel. Events shown are filtered to include only events after the console was started. To see historical events you can check the Show History and click Refresh. Clear resets the filter time to the current date and time.

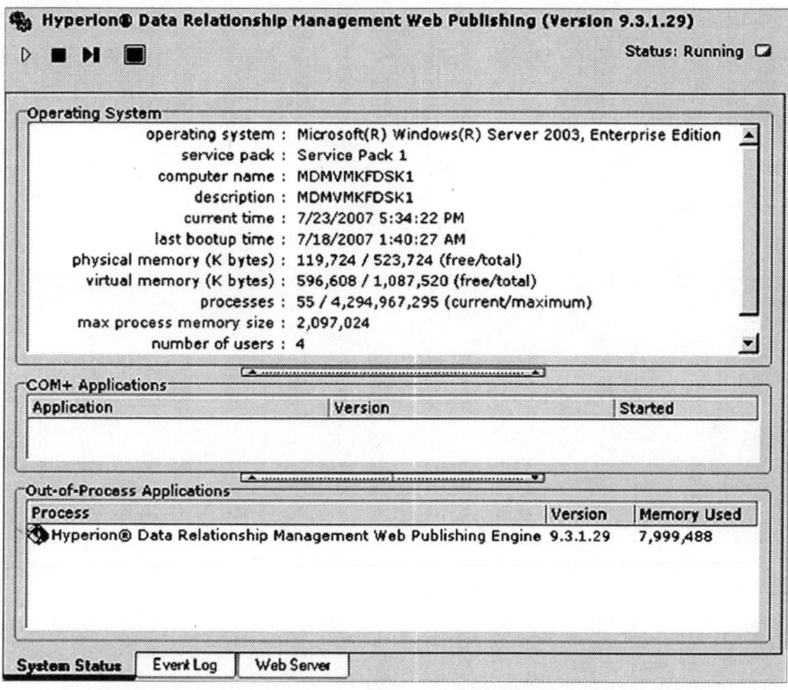

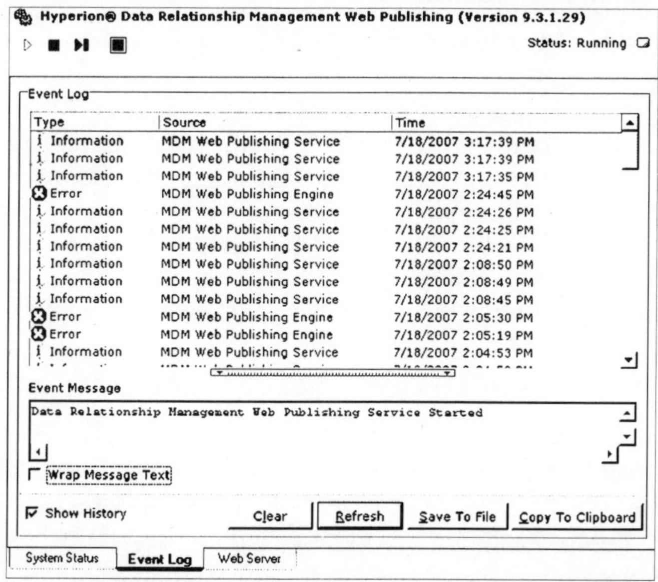

The Web Server tab provides two browser views to validate access to the Web Server system. The first panel displays the test HTML in the mdm_web virtual directory and validates access to the virtual directory for Web Publishing.

The second view tests the Web Publishing Gateway to perform the List Versions command. If the system is up and running, the list of versions available for Web Publishing is displayed. When stopping and starting services such as IIS, you may need to refresh these views. To refresh, right-click on the view and select Refresh.

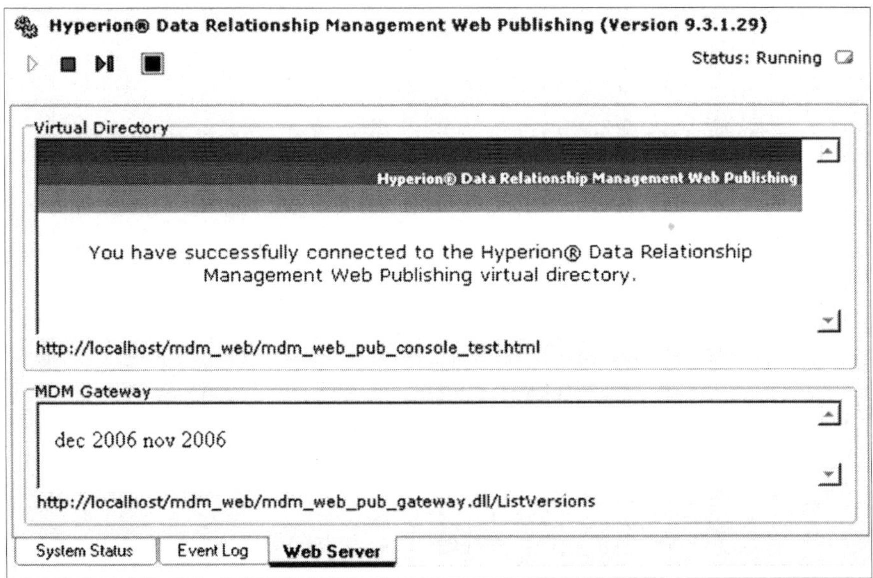

You can set the Data Relationship Management username and password for the Web Publishing module on the Configuration page. This user is the Data Relationship Management user that the Web Publishing engine uses to retrieve the data for display on the Web client. Limiting access to this user allows the Web Publishing to be restricted. It is important that the user specified for Web Publishing be exempt from session timeout. Thus, the system preference IdleTimeExcludeUsers should be set to include the name of the user for Web Publishing. If this user is not excluded from session timeout, then the Web Publishing service needs to be restarted each time the user session expires.

CONFIGURING DATA RELATIONSHIP MANAGEMENT WEB CLIENT

Data Relationship Management Web provides a specific set of frequently-used Data Relationship Management functionality in a Web browser. This document assumes that the user is already familiar with the overall Data Relationship Management system, including its terminology and feature set. The appearance and behaviour of Data Relationship Management Web Publishing can be configured using both System Preferences and embedded parameters.

ELECTRONIC THESES AND DISSERTATIONS FOR INDIAN UNIVERSITIES: A FRAMEWORK

Even though the electronic publishing and writing offer demanding environment in academic scholarship, the theses and dissertations are still written and published in print and archived in shelves in university libraries where the vast majority gather dust, read by perhaps one or two interested researchers who access them in print with lot of difficulty, often for a fee and most are never consulted at all. Digital libraries of electronic theses and dissertations (ETDs) offer an alternative to this waste of valuable academic scholarship and offer researchers and University Libraries in India opportunities to explore the possibilities electronic publishing trend in academic sector. The emergence of UGC Infonet, the aspiring and dream project of University Grants Commission, which also aims at Content Creation by Indian Academic Sector, will definitely boost this idea.

UGC-INFONET

As technology is becoming a driving force in the contemporary education systems, University Grant Commission has launched an ambitious programme to bring about a qualitative change in the academic infrastructure, especially for higher education. Under this initiative UGC is modernising the University Campuses with State-of-the-art campus wide networks and setting up its own nationwide communication network named UGC-Infonet. UGC-Infonet will be a boon to the higher education systems in several ways to facilitate spread of quality education all over the country. This will function as a tool to distribute education material and journals to the remotest of areas and a resource centre for researchers and scholars for tapping the most up-to-date information. As a main feature of UGC Infonet, a data center with large server capacity is being set up, where content of common interest can be maintained. Each University will have the option of hosting their web site, digital content like ETDs and the E-journals subscribed through INFLIBNET Consortia.

THESES AND DISSERTATIONS IN INDIA

Indian universities play a major role in generation and dissemination of knowledge by conducting research works and producing Ph D theses as a unique genre of information sources. Every year, nearly 8000- 10000 Ph Ds are awarding in India. The purpose of the thesis is to provide an experience in scholarship, which will be of enduring value to the student in understanding how new knowledge is acquired and communicated within the chosen field. These works contain valuable content, including focused literature reviews and details on research, which are not generally made available elsewhere.

At present there are some lacunas in publication, control and access theses information in India, and some attempts have been made to address them. At the moment, most unpublished theses are hard to get hold of, as they are filed only in the university library where the student has worked. The Indian thesis literature is beset with many problems like Lack of Systematic acquisition, Lack of Access, Uncertain publication practice, Enormous Growth in the number of theses, etc. In western countries, these problems were addressed already and serious attempts have been made to solve them. In North America, less than 5 per cent of all accepted dissertations and masters' theses are initially conceived of and executed as electronic documents.

BENEFITS OF ETD

- Broader exposure of university research through greater accessibility;
- Opportunities to use new forms of creative scholarship through use of interactive elements, multimedia, hyperlinks, etc.;
- Ability to have a hyperlink to the thesis/dissertation on homepages and electronic CVs;
- Professional development experience for research students as they learn the basic skills of scholarly publishing in an electronic format;
- Conservation of paper, library storage space and of library staff time;
- Theses and dissertations more immediately accessible: publication occurs near point of submission rather than three to four months later; and
- The option to have theses or dissertations accessible to any potential reader every day at any time.

ELECTRONIC THESES AND DISSERTATIONS FOR YOUR UNIVERSITY

Format to Create ETD

PDF stands for *Portable Document Format:* Adobe Systems developed the PDF standard and provides the premiere package for creating and manipulating PDF files, Adobe Acrobat. The process of converting to PDF takes instructions that would ordinarily be sent to a specific printer and prepares them to be viewed or printed on any computer with the free Acrobat Reader installed. Postscript is a standard language developed by Adobe Systems, which is used to send instructions to postscript compatible printers. These instructions describe the contents of all text and graphics to be printed, and where on the page each piece of content is to be printed. Ordinarily, these instructions are transferred to a Postscript printer, which interprets them, creates a printed copy based on the instructions, and then discards the instructions.Other file types for image files can be.gif.jpeg, or.tif; for video files.mov.mpg, or.avi; and for audio files.aif.midi.snd.wav, or as CD-DA, CD-ROM/XA, or MPEG-2.

Facilities Required

Researchers need to create their original thesis using a word processor, such as Microsoft Word or WordPerfect and once it is done, then it can be converted to a PDF file, which will retain the original document format (for the purpose of future editing). Conversion into a PDF file is a straightforward process. Libraries and Campus labs have to be equipped with Windows based computers set up to convert theses and dissertations written in Microsoft Word to Adobe Acrobat format. This application will allow us to convert the word processing document to PDF format as well as create bookmarks. Researchers must submit the document on disk, CD, or Zip drive; the conversion machines are not attached to the network. Library staff can provide assistance with using the software to convert files, but cannot assist with document preparation.

SOFTWARE TO MANAGE ETDS

D-Space is a groundbreaking digital library system that captures, stores, indexes, preserves and redistributes the intellectual output of a university's research faculty in digital formats. The future of Etheses and of archiving and searching in general depends on institutions being able to deliver top quality services, with a high degree of interoperability. This means, among other things, that systems must continue to be developed and they must be able to handle many different types of digital object. It is believed that DSpace will fulfil these requirements to a higher degree and will continue to improve in this way in the future.

As an open source system, DSpace is now freely available to other institutions to run as-is, or to modify and extend as they require to meet local needs. From the outset, HP and MIT designed the system to be run by institutions other than MIT, and to support federation among its adopters, in both the technical and the social sense. INFLIBNET believes that it is our responsibility to lead the charge for a realistic assessment of how we can head off an otherwise inevitable loss of academic resources. Awareness building in Open Archives and Institutional Repositories in Indian academic Institutions will be the main focus of INFLIBNET in coming future. For long-term preservation of our knowledge base and cultures, we have to find out an economical way to save digital content for future generations.

Institutions in India started using variety of open source archiving solutions like Green Stone, E-Print, DSpace etc since 2000. After experimenting all popular solutions, INFLIBNET decided to opt DSpace for its Institutional Repository and archive its publications, conference proceedings, lecture notes, etc. The capability of Dspace to handle multilingual content, even at Metadata level using globally accepted UNICODE standard was the important issue for selecting this solution, especially a country like India with its mullti-lingual dilemma in digital content creation and storage.

It has been installed in test-bed and experimented its capabilities and performance. After all sorts of testing required, Dspace was customised according to our requirements and it was installed on one of the WWW Server on Linux platform. Then we have requested Corporation for National Research Initiatives (CNRI) site for providing *Persistent Identifiers (CNRI Handles)* which promotes interoperability among open archives through Open Archives Initiative Protocol for Metadata Harvesting (OAI-PMH). The Handle System®

covers assignment, management, and resolution of these persistent identifiers and are compliant with the IETF's Uniform Resource Name (URN) specification.

ROLE OF THE FACULTY AND REVIEW PROCESS

Faculty will continue to be responsible for upholding the quality of the thesis or dissertation, whether that thesis or dissertation is submitted using electronic formats or through paper. The electronic format can facilitate communication among members of the dissertation committee and the student. Electronic distribution of drafts allows multiple readers to markup and comment within one copy of the work simultaneously, regardless of the readers' physical location, and to see others' comments. It also allows the student to collate the comments of all readers within one document.

For defence, some committees may require that students provide all members of the committee with a paper copy of the ETD before the defence; others may elect to read on-screen or to have committee members take individual responsibility for working from screen or paper they print out themselves. Printed versions of the textual components of an ETD can always be made available to committee members at their request. If non-text elements of the ETD are part of the defence, the committee can consider the most effective way to ensure that all members of the committee have access to non-text elements during the defence. After the committee approves thesis or dissertation, it can be sent to a particular contact person in the library for processing, who will be responsible for processing ETDs by making sure that the file's formatting is correct, the links work, etc. Metadata of ETD can be created and made available for searching and accessing.

ISSUE OF COPYRIGHT

The copyright issue involves two components: Protecting the information/ work produced as part of the research programme; and Granting license to University or to any ETD Programme to make the work available for use. This also includes obtaining permission to use parts of the work that have already been published in other sources. If the material we are quoting or reproducing does not fall under the general guidelines of "fair use" then as suggested, need to get written permission from the copyright owner. Since a dissertation or thesis is published for non-profit educational purposes, the author is permitted limited use of copyrighted material under the guidelines of "fair use." The purpose, amount, nature and effect of the work reproduced determine whether or not one must seek permission from the copyright owner.

INDIAN INITIATIVES

As a bibliographical tool to know about theses of awarded Ph Ds, Association of Indian Universities started publishing of Doctoral Bibliographies in all subjects and Theses of the Month column through its weekly publication *University News*. In 1994, INFLIBNET hosted a regularly updated free online union database of Ph D theses submitted to Indian universities. At present it is freely available for searching at INFLIBNET web site and contains around 1,40,000 of unique bibliographical records covering all subjects and all universities. Being the data supplied by the Universities themselves, it is considered as the only authoritative online-tool available to find-out the research out put of Indian Universities. Recently University of Mysore, in collaboration with NISSAT and Ford Foundation initiated a project called Vidyanithi to host individual full-text thesis from various universities who are willing to become a member of this project. Even though, this project tries to evolve as a national depository for Indian theses, but it is not compulsory for Universities to become a part of this project. All these efforts are, off course, helpful for researchers in locating theses, but in the case of access, still we need remedies.

IN THE END WE CAN SAY

Popularisation of ETDs and its full advantages for faculty, students, and researchers are the foremost attempt to be start of. Brochures, communications, web sites etc conveying this information need to be written, designed, published and disseminated to all affected by this far-reaching change. Workshops and training programmes for both students and faculty need to be developed that cover issues of copyright and choice of access, and that encourage research scholars to carefully consider the ethics of restricting their research from access by the national and international scholarly community. Well-equipped computer labs must be put in place to provide workstations, software, and technical support staff for students writing ETDs. And standards need to be developed for the presentation of dissertation research—standards which facilitate the development of a useful and easily navigable digital collection of works, but which do not unnecessarily constrain the use of software and design considerations graduate students deem essential to their research. Careful consideration of these requirements and their full support will contribute substantially to making this transition smoothly. The potential ETDs have to transform graduate education in ways that benefit both students and the scholarly community depends upon it.

SEARCH TECHNIQUES FOR ACCESSING CD-ROM DATABASES

Due to the development of information technology, information is increasingly recorded in digital format and electronic databases which are continually becoming more complex, information storage and retrieval As the technology obsolete very fast, CD-ROM is also facing problems due to emergence of the DVD. In today's business, education, and government environments the amount of information, data and software being archived and distributed on CD-ROM and DVD-ROM media is overwhelming. For years the medium of choice for storing, archiving and distributing digital content has been the CD-ROM.As capacity requirements of data intensive applications and databases grow, DVD-ROM, with a capacity potential over 13 times that of CD-ROM, is fast becoming the most popular medium. (CD-ROM media can store up to 700 MB of data). Single-sided, single layer DVD-ROM media can store up to 4.7 GB of data. Doublesided, single layer DVD-ROM media store up to 9.4 GB of data). DVD which is used primarily with movie/ video features will not affect the CD-ROM, but DVD-ROMs will be, which can carry information on both sides of the disc. DVD-ROM will replace the CD-ROM, but that it will take a few years.As information is increasingly recorded in digital format and electronic databases are continually becoming more complex, information storage and retrieval processes have profoundly changed. Over the past decades three major migrations have occurred in library academic services: from printed resources to online electronic databases; from online databases to bibliographic and full-text CD-ROM databases; and from CD-ROM databases to online Internet access to bibliographic and full-text/full-image databases.

CD-ROM DATABASES

CD-ROM is abbreviation for 'Compact Disc-Read-Only Memory' a type of optical disk capable of storing large amounts of data up to 1GB, although the most common size is 650 MB (megabytes). The term 'database' has been used in the literature in two different connotations. In Computer Science this is referred to as a database management system. In this sense a database has a logically consistent structure in which records are actually linked. In library and Information science, these are referred to as bibliographic or inventory in nature and comprise a collection of related logical records here a database is defined as an organised and generally unlinked set of machine, or it can be said, these databases are the electronic version of published literature traditionally appearing in printed form in various field. Databases are produced by different agencies in a computer readable form, the contents of which are accessible in various ways according to requirements with the help of suitable software. Various agencies (governmental and non-governmental) are involved in developing databases by collecting information from varieties of sources and packaging the information in the form of databases. Databases can be stored on CD-ROM, on the Internet, or on commercial sites that are accessible only if user's library has a subscription. CD-Rom in the library contains periodical indexes, abstracts, statistics, directories, and other complete texts. Some databases provide information that is primarily numeric, such as data from a recent government census and some contain information that is primarily textual. Database some time also called data bank.

USE CD-ROM DATABASES IN LIBRARIES

Access to Cd-Rom databases is fast, accurate and thorough. A clever search by a users may get them in seconds most of the information they need. In contrast, traditional print services may take months for same task, with still great deal of information left out. As a matter of fact, libraries can not possibly continue with the sluggish manual information service methods and hope to remain in business tomorrow.

Libraries can have economic access to information, space saving and users friendly Libraries and information centers used these databases in providing various library services as mentioned below

- Literature search services, current and retrospective literature searches
- Current awareness services in various forms including SDI
- Full text databases may be utilised for search services
- Document delivery services
- For producing digest trend reports, etc.
- Compilations of bibliographies
- Abstracting and Indexing Services

WHY WE DON'T WANT TO USE CD-ROM DATABASES

It is always beneficial to know about the pros and cons of any information so that one can proceed systematically.

- CD-ROM databases are not updated in time, some web journals or indexing services are available online even before their print editions roll out of the press. For example, Engineering Index on disc is updated quarterly, and Dissertation Abstracts on disc only once in a year.
- Retrieval from CD-ROM databases take seconds, as against online databases, which take only milliseconds, however complex the command search statement may be (of courses with higher bandwidth telecom pipes provided)
- If not acquired from a single producer, CD/DVD Rom databases require skills in using different search engines. Making menu-driven index searching or single keyword searching at command prompt may be easy to use in each system. But, users must make command, or Boolean searches, to get at exacter or less abstract hits. Sometimes users have been found key boarding DIALOG syntax instead of SPIRS one to search into MathSci Disc or PsycLIT from SilverPlatter, and vice versa. Both the search engines are so dissimilar in construct. Again, generally, users keyboard a collection of key words at the command prompt. They are flummoxed to discover that one access engine parses the search statement with "or" operator between words, and the other with 'and' operator. The former results come in too many hits and the latter in too few. Therefore, all new uses require basic education in the techniques of bibliographic database searching.

- If adequate jukeboxes are not provided for permanent mounting of optical databases, it is a great hassle for users to switch from one disc to another for either a different file or part of the same file. By comparison, on online services, like DIALOG's the process is just a click away.

Yet another disadvantage of CD-ROM, they are vulnerable to damage by dust, fingerprints and scratches, etc. Therefore they need very careful handing. Libraries will have to make backup copy of each CDS disc to be kept in safe custody, so fresh copies can be made.

SEARCHING CD-ROM DATABASE

Conducting effective searches requires knowledge of a number of techniques. Users should not only have been an understanding of the nature, content and structure of the database, but also be familiar with the various option available in the search screen, the tools and techniques for searching, and the techniques and formats for display of the search output. The search features commonly available are Keyword Search, Phrase Search, Boolean Search, Truncation, Index and/or Thesaurus Support, Proximity Search, Field-Specific Searches, Free-Text Search, Combing Search Sets and Search Refinement, Limiting or Range Search, Searching through the Retrieved Records and they may vary from one CD-ROM to another.

SELECTION OF DATABASES FOR COMPARISON

Four CD-ROM Databases have been selected for a discussion on the various search and retrieval features available, 'Ulrich's on disc', 'Books in Print' from the category of general or ready reference sources, 'Ei Compendex', 'LISA plus' are Bibliographic databases containing details of documents including abstracts and Emerald full-text database of journal articles.

Ulrich's on Disc

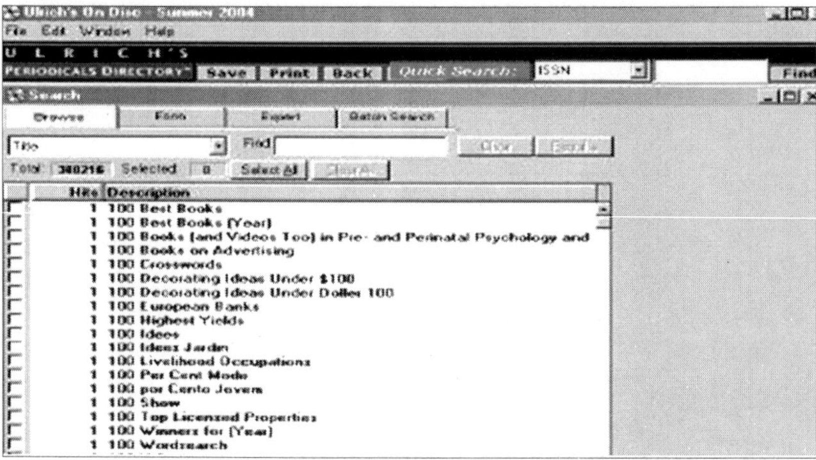

Fig. 'ULRICH'S on Disc' Main Screen.

Ulrich's on Disc from R. R. Bowker provides the ability to search and browse the entire Ulrich's family of databases. They included nearly 250,000 titles from over 200 countries, Information on about 11,000 new titles per year, annotations for almost 90,000 titles, full text reviews from *Magazines for Libraries* and *Library Journal* for over 8,700 publications, indicators for over 21,000 refereed publications and complete names and addresses for 80,000 serials publishers and distributors. The main screen of Ulrich's is shown in figure.

EI COMPENDEX BIBLOGRAPHIC DATABASE

DIALOG OnDisc® Compendex, produced by (Ei) Engineering Information Inc., provides coverage of the world's significant engineering and technical literature. Subject coverage includes but is not limited to the various disciplines of engineering, applied physics, electronics and instrumentation, light and optical technologies, and other areas of significant technology. Compendex contains references to and abstracts from journals, technical reports, books, proceedings and conference papers, and more. Author-prepared abstracts are used when available. Publications from around the world are indexed, including approximately 4,500 journals and 2,000 conference proceedings per year. Approximately 10 percent of the documents indexed are in a language other than English.

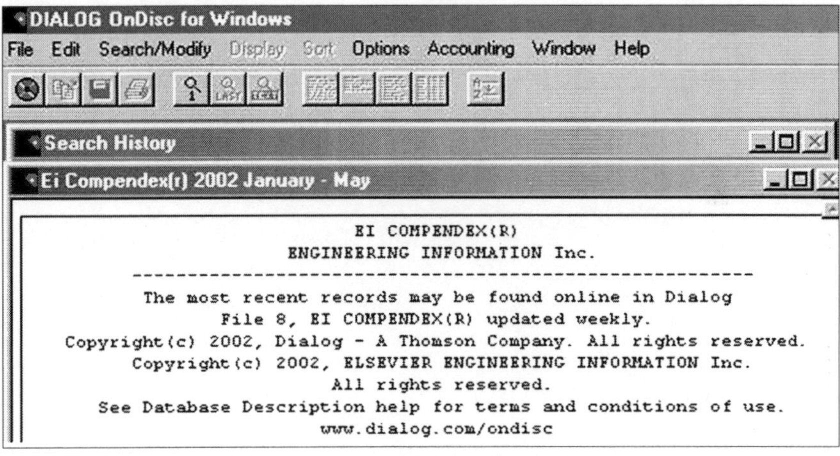

Fig. 'Ei Compendex' Main Screen.

LIBRARY AND INFORMATION SCIENCE ABSTRACTS (LISA PLUS)

LISA plus is the world's best known resource for the coverage of ongoing research in all aspects of library and information studies. Over 245,000 abstracts keep user well informed about such topics as artificial intelligence, information and knowledge management, publishing and copyright, World Wide Web resources and much more since 1969. Lisa plus main screen is as figure.

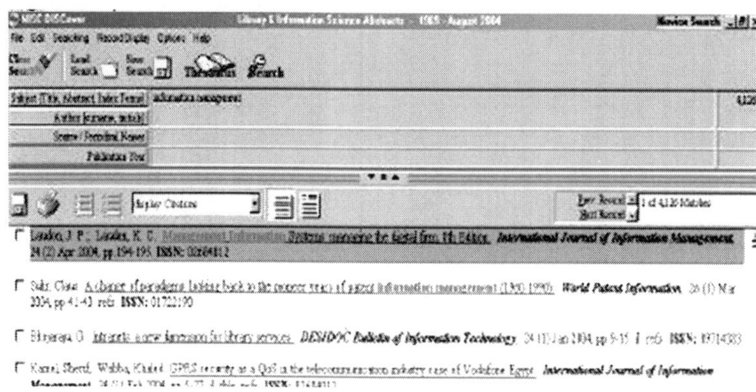

Fig. 'LISA Plus' Main Screen.

EMERALD FULL-TEXT DATABASE OF JOURNAL ARTICLES

Emerald is a full text database from MCB, covers more than 82 top journal across ten broad subject areas. It provides access to the full text of articles in PDF and HTML format published from 1994 to date. The subjects covered include Marketing, Human Resources, Quality Management, Information Management, Library and Information Services, Training and Education, General Management Property, Operations and Production Management, etc. Users can choose any subject and get a list of all the journals covered in that subject. First screen of Emerald is as figure

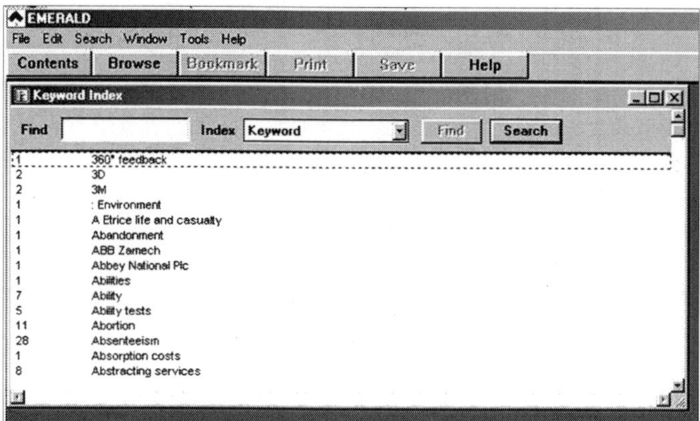

Fig. 'Emerald (Full-Text Database)' First Screen.

ACCESSING DIFFERENT DATABASES

Searching in Specific Field of Selected CD-ROM Databases

There are two forms of searching for information in CD-ROM databases – field-specific and free-text search. A user may know which field to search, or might like to restrict a given search to one or more fields. This is a field specific search. If the user are not sure of the field to be searched, they can conduct a free-text search, which means that the search is not restricted to any particular field. While the free-text search is not universally available, field specific search is the simplest form of search, and CD-ROM databases offer various options to conduct searches on one or more specific fields. The simplest option is the form search, where the user can select a specific box for a particular field and can key in the search term/phrase. Which search field can be searched in a database depends on the content and structure of the database concerned, and there fore they differ from one database to another.

Ulrich's on Disc

Search fields are Abstracting and Indexing Service, Area Code, Circulation, CODEN Number, Country, Dewey Number, Document Availability, Electronic Vendor, ISSN, Keyword, Keyword In Title, LC Class, Media Type, Personnel Name, Price (US Dollar), Publication Code, Publisher, Special Features, Special Index, Status Code, Subjects, Title, US State/Zip, Year First Published. Search screen is shown by figure

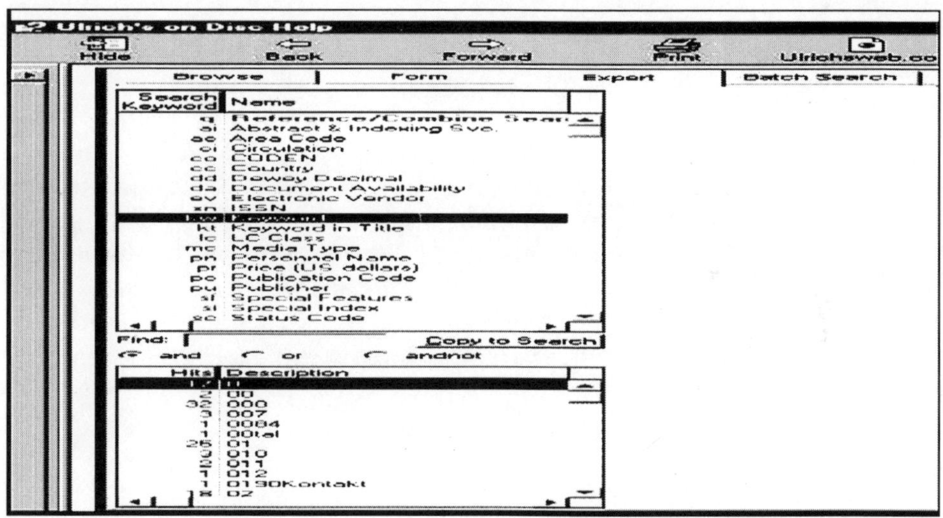

Fig. 'Ulrich's on Disc' Search Fields Screen.

Ei Compendex

Under option 'Search/Modify' search fields are Word/Phrase Index, EI Subject Headings, Author Name, Author Affiliation, Title Words, Journal Name, Conference Search Options (Conference Title, Conference Location, Conference Sponsor, Conference Year), Limit Options 'English…', Additional Search Options (Words/Phrases, EI Classification Codes, Major Subject Headings, Treatment Codes, Year of Publications, Language) different fields and Search results screen shown in figure.

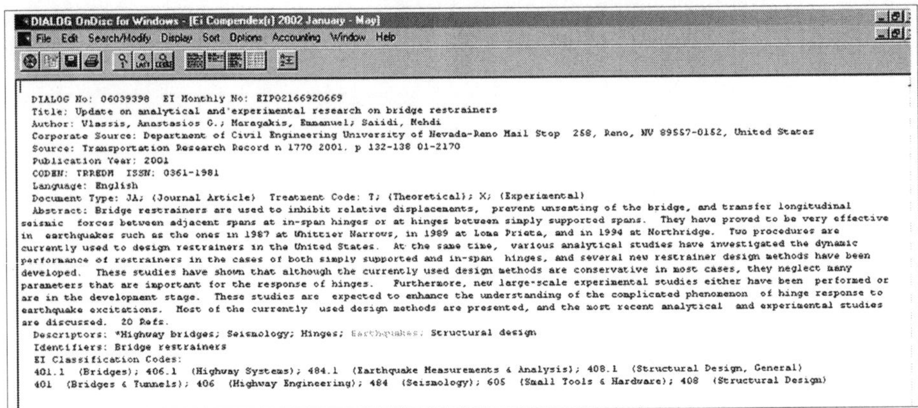

Fig. 'Ei Compendex' Different Fields and Search Results Screen.

LISA Plus

Subject, Title, Abstract, Index Term Or Keyword, Author, Source, Title Database Name,, Keyword, Language, Publication Date, Author Affiliation, Country Of Research, Record Number, CODEN, CATNI name, ISSN, Thesaurus term

Boolen Search

Combine terms to make the search broader or narrower. How broad or narrow the search is depends on the search logic used to combine search terms. Three logical connectors, or Boolean operators, are used to define the relationship between search terms: "and", "or ", and "not". The Boolean operators may be used to join search terms within search fields in all search modes and to join search criteria between search fields in the Advanced and Expert search modes only. (Novice mode always uses a Boolean AND between search fields). Boolean searches can not be conducted in the 'browse index' mode of CD-ROM.-

Ulrich's on Disc

Operators are AND, OR, NOT/AND NOT and Options are, In the Form Search mode user can combine terms/phrases with Boolean operators in a chosen field box, or can type one term/phrase in each box and click on a Boolean operator in the box next to the box next to the term on the right. In the search mode user have to type the Boolean operator to combine terms/ phares from the same or different fields. Ei Compendex: Operators are AND, OR, NOT and Options are: use these operators to combine search terms in the 'Modify Search Option'

LISA Plus

Operators are AND, OR, ANDNOT (not can also be used in free-text search mode) Options: In the Easy Search mode, user can combine terms/ phrases with Boolean operators in a chosen field box, or can type one term/ phrase in each box and click on a Boolean operators in the box next to the term on the right. In the Expert Search Mode, user has to type the Boolean operator to combine terms/phases from the same or different fields. No nesting is possible. Emerald: Operators are And or, not and Options enter theses operators in the search in the search as well as Advanced Search Mode

Truncation Search

Truncation of the three kinds of truncation (left, right and middle truncation), left truncation is not commonly available in CD-ROM databases. The symbols for truncation and their syntax and effect vary, and the user has to learn these to conduct an effective search.

Ulrich's on disc

Ulrich's on disc: * or $ substitute for any number of characters and can be used for right truncation only. '?' Substitutes for one character, can be used anywhere in a word, or user can use multiple '?'Symbols. LISA: Truncation is the substitution of a wildcard symbol for any portion of a word to retrieve a group of words. Most often, truncation is used to abbreviate a word — to trim a term back to its stem, or root word.

Truncating lets user search for word variants thereby broadening the search. The asterisk * is a multicharacter wildcard and the question mark ? is a single character wildcard. Wildcards are typically used at the end of a word but may be embedded within a word as well. Right and middle or internal truncation is allowed. Both the symbols can be used for right as well as middle truncation. User can enter the symbol as appropriate in the Easy Search as well as the Expert Search mode. Multiple ? can be used. Wildcards are typically used at the end of a word but may be embedded within a word as well. Avoid truncating words to less than five characters or user may retrieve unwanted results.

Index Search and Thesaurus Search

The indexes allow users to select the search terms/phrases from the term index, and a thesaurus allows users to consult a map of available terms to widen or narrow down a given search, as required. CD-ROM retrieval software provides index search facilities, ie users can select an index to browse and select from the index for searching. There may be an index file or a separate index for each searchable field so that the user can choose a field and then browse the corresponding index file. Index search facilities are more commonly available than thesaurus facilities. Thesauri are hierarchically structured. This means that they go from broad terms to narrower, more specific, terms.

Ulrich's on disc

User can choose a field from either the search or the From Search mode.

In each case user can display and browse the corresponding index and select a term/phrase from the index.

Ei Compendex

In order to conduct a search, user need to choose an index: author, subject heading, keywords, etc, and then the corresponding index will be open for user to browse and to select the search term

LISA plus

The thesaurus may be accessed via the Browse window by clicking on the Index drop-down list and selecting Thesaurus Term; highlight the required term and click View Titles. In the Expert Search mode enter the thesaurus term in the Search Query Box, click on ok or press Enter. Press the 'View Brief' button to display the results of the search ie the thesaurus block. A thesaurus term can be selected to conduct a search in the database as shown in figure

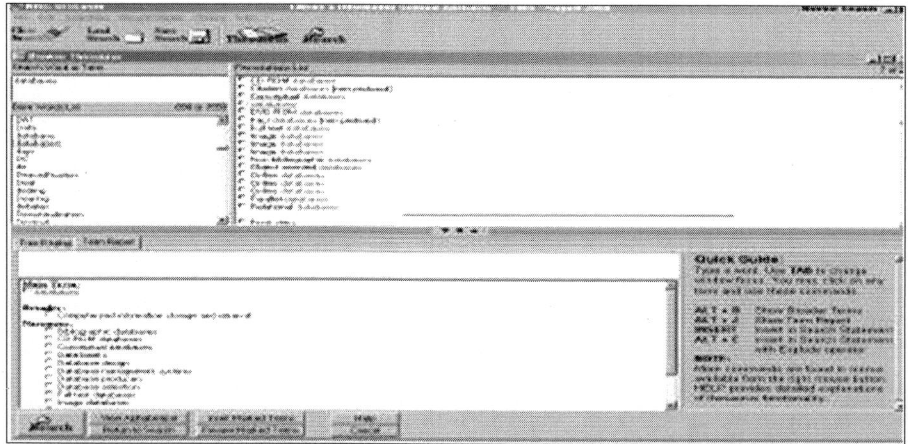

Fig. 'LISA plus' Thesaurus Search

Emerald

In the Advanced Search mode, user can choose one or more fields to search, and once users have entered a search term correspond to a field, they can click on the 'Thesaurus' button to get other words correspond to the search term.

Proximity Search

With a proximity search, user can specify the number of words allowed between the search terms. In a general sense, there is a correlation between the number of intervening words (the words creating the "distance" between search terms) and the topical relevance of users search results.

The closer the distance between users search words, *e.g.*, 5 words, the more relevant but fewer the results may be. Likewise, the wider the distance between the search words, *e.g.*, 20 words, the less relevant but larger the CD-

ROM results may be. The type of proximity search operator to use depends upon whether user need search terms to be found in the same order as listed in the search statement (adjX) or found in the same or reverse order of what user originally specified (nearX).

RESULTS

After the comparison we come to know that all databases have almost same basic accessing techniques as keyword search, Phrase Search, Boolean Search, Truncation, Index and/or Thesaurus Support, Proximity Search, Field-Specific Searches, Free-Text Search, Combing Search Sets and Search Refinement, Limiting or Range Search, Searching through the Retrieved Records and they may vary from one CD-ROM to another with a slight variation as given below

- Boolean searching is possible in all the CD-ROM database, through how it is carried out varies. Boolean searches cannot be conducted in the 'browse index' mode of a CD-ROM database for the obvious reason that only one term/phrase can be keyed in to display the corresponding portion of the index.
- None of the sample databases provides left-truncations facilities. The symbols for truncation vary from one database to another.
- Search refinement of a given search can be refined by adding or dropping one or more search terms or criteria, such as limiting the output to a given language, year of publication, price range, and so on.
- Some CD-ROM products have more than one search interface, for example, Ulrich's on disc, while others have on search interface giving options for both - simple, novice and other advanced/ expert search.
- Some retrieval system such as EI Compendex show the result instantly, while in others the user has to chose the view/display option, as in LISA plus
- Proximity search in CD-ROM databases allows users to conduct proximity searches in order to specify how closely the terms prescribed in a search expression.
- Two types of indexing practice are followed word index and phrase index.in the word index, each individual word in a field is indexed, while in the phrase index, a given phrase that may comprise several keyboard, is indexed. The user may need to check whether a field is a word- or phrase-indexed, by browsing through the index for the particular field, before entering a search term/phrase.
- CD-Rome databases do not usually provide facilities for ranking the search results according to relevance.

CONCLUSION

The standards for organising web-based resources are still in the early stages of development, and librarians are forced to utilise standards for print resources that were not designed for electronic resources. Additionally web-based information resources are volatile in the sense that may be moved from one site to another or may be removed altogether from web. Web-based library services will become more widespread and sophisticated as the web becomes common place throughout the world, and to be successful players in the E-world.

Libraries must continue to address the web design and implementation issues. As we actively transfer library services, our central purpose remain the same, to serve and teach users to find, evaluate, and use information effectively. The librarians should be expert to hold the hands of the users who are moving towards new communication paradigm a shift from face to face human contact to human machine interaction, from paper to electronic delivery, from text centred mode to multimedia and from physical presence to virtual presence. Despite these changes in communication technology, the reference interview will remain at the heart of the reference transaction. To meet these challenges the librarians may play a leadership role in providing better Web Based library Services facilities to their current techno savvy users.

Index